THE MOANING OF LIFE

The Worldly Wisdom of

KARL PILKINGTON

Photography by Freddie Claire
Illustrations by Andy Smith

me&you

CANONGATE
Edinburgh · London

rounded
PRODUCTIONS

THIS PAPERBACK EDITION FIRST PUBLISHED 2014
FIRST PUBLISHED IN GREAT BRITAIN IN 2013
BY CANONGATE BOOKS LTD, 14 HIGH STREET, EDINBURGH EH1 1TE

WWW.CANONGATE.TV

2

PHOTOGRAPHY COPYRIGHT © FREDDIE CLAIRE, 2013
ILLUSTRATIONS COPYRIGHT © ANDY SMITH

BRITISH LIBRARY CATALOGUING-IN DATA
A CATALOGUE RECORD FOR THIS BOOK IS AVAILABLE
ON REQUEST FROM THE BRITISH LIBRARY

ISBN: 978 1 78211 154 2

TYPESET BY CLUNY SHEELER, EDINBURGH

PRINTED AND BOUND IN GREAT BRITAIN BY CLAYS LTD ST IVES PLC

ALSO BY KARL PILKINGTON

THE WORLD OF KARL PILKINGTON
HAPPYSLAPPED BY A JELLYFISH
KARLOLOGY
AN IDIOT ABROAD
THE FURTHER ADVENTURES OF AN IDIOT ABROAD

CONTENTS

INTRODUCTION

I DIDN'T WANT to celebrate my fortieth birthday. Not because I wasn't happy about being forty; I don't mind getting older. I've always been older than my years anyway. My mam said I even acted old and grumpy when I was a baby. Apparently I learned to frown before I could walk and didn't like having a dummy, as it got in the way of me tutting. I suppose losing my hair made me feel older too. I had a head like a wind-beaten dandelion by the time I had reached twenty-two. I don't think stress was to blame for the baldness; it was the extra-strong 'power shower' my dad had bought off a mate and installed himself. It was way too powerful. Taking a shower was like doing a task in an episode of *Total Wipeout*. But being bald didn't bother me, as my hair wasn't that good anyway. Fine, flimsy stuff it was, that my barber described as the 'hair of a Chinaman', so I could never have had a trendy style. Wet-look hair gel was all the rage in England in the early 80s, after Michael Jackson made it popular. It was to help mould your hair, while making it look like you'd just stepped out of the shower. But it was never a big seller in Manchester as everybody had the wet look anyway due to the continuous, pissing-down rain.

'I just want to stay in and have a chilli con carne,' I told Suzanne.

'But it's your fortieth birthday. A few people have asked what we're doing!'

'Well, tell them I'm staying in, having chilli con carne. They can celebrate my birthday without me if they want.'

'That's just stupid,' she said.

'No, it's not. People do it every year with Jesus's birthday.'

The good thing with her asking meant that at least there wasn't going to be a surprise party for me. If there is one thing that I don't like it's a surprise, and she knows it. If you want to know another thing I don't like, it's fuss. I can't be doing with people making a fuss of me. The first time it happened was when I started work. I was on a training scheme at a printing company and the boss bought a cake and called me to the kitchen. As I opened the door, they all sang 'Happy Birthday', which must be one of the most boring songs ever written. It follows you right through your life. Why it hasn't been updated and changed I don't know. They remade the film *Total Recall* recently, and that was totally unnecessary as the original was only made in 1990. Get the bloody birthday song redone.

Anyway, I hated all the bother surrounding my birthday and felt embarrassed. I quickly said 'cheers' and took the cake home. My mam then explained to me that I should have cut the cake there and then and shared it out, but staying in the kitchen handing out cake and talking to people I didn't know was not for me. I think this is why Bob Geldof chucked food parcels out of planes in Africa – it was to avoid the small talk.

'Why should they get my cake?' I remember thinking. I wouldn't mind if I knew all of them, but there were people there from different departments, who I'd never seen in my life, and yet they expected to have some of my cake. My mam made me take what was left into work the next day. After that experience, I always arranged to be away on holiday when it was my birthday. I also preferred to get fired from a job instead of leaving, as people don't tend to get you a card and cake or make a fuss when you've been booted out. In the end Suzanne agreed to make me a chilli and it was well nice, and I didn't have to share it with any strangers.

Like I said, being forty doesn't feel any different to being thirty. Even the aches and pains I have now have always been around. I've had backache since I was about ten, after

I tried to kick my height and ended up landing on my arse. So now I get through as many heat patches in a week as I do teabags. I normally have two or three on at any one time to ease the pain. I give off that much heat I have old people shuffling behind me keeping warm in my jet stream.

For some reason a lot of people think you should be all settled by the time you get to forty and be married with kids, and if you're not they find it odd. That's what triggered the idea of the TV programme and this new book. Why do most people follow the same pattern in life, and is it the same the world over? The number of times I've been asked, 'Why aren't you and Suzanne married? Why no kids?' I say, 'Why does everyone feel that this is what you should do?' They normally follow that up with, 'Well, why are we here?' – a question I've never thought about apart from the time Suzanne took me on a 'surprise' holiday to Lanzarote.

HAPPY BIRTHDAY KARL! 40

Marriage

IT DOESN'T BOTHER me when there are postal strikes, as most of what comes through our front door I'm not in a rush to receive. Gas bills, phone bills, council tax bills, and the thing that fills me with the most dread: wedding invitations. It's like getting summoned for jury service.

You don't want to go, but it's very difficult to get out of, and then it's a long, drawn-out affair that you have to sit through with strangers. You can normally tell it's a wedding invite because the font on the envelope has so many swirls and curls it looks like your address was written out during an earthquake.

I'll check who the invitation is from, and if it's not a relation, I'll try to get it to the shredder before Suzanne gets wind of it. Getting rid of the evidence isn't so easy when the envelope is packed full of bits of glitter and gold hearts that go all over the bloody place when you open it, like a money bag from the bank that's been fitted with an ink bomb.

Then I have to hoover up the evidence. I did this recently, but Suzanne knew what I'd done when she went to

vacuum the stairs and saw the glitter whizzing round inside the Dyson like some kind of Brian Cox CGI universe.

I'm not totally against marriage. If two people want to get married, they should just get on with it. Why all the palaver? I think getting a joint mortgage is a bigger deal, yet you don't have to invite everyone-you-know-plus-one to witness you signing the contract. I might have married Suzanne years ago if we could have done it online.

Just tick a few boxes, agree to the terms and conditions and wait for the automated reply that says it's all gone through and we're now husband and wife. Why has that not been set up? I don't think having a big fancy wedding means you love someone more, it just means you want to show your friends and family how much you love someone.

But I've never been too bothered about what other people think. And there isn't one bit of the traditional wedding that attracts me. I'm a big fan of cake, and yet even wedding cake doesn't tempt me. I don't know anyone who likes it and I don't think I've ever seen anyone eating it either. I've watched people scoffing down kangaroo arse and bulls' bollocks on *I'm a Celebrity*, yet I've never witnessed wedding cake being eaten. In fact, wedding cakes sum up the whole thing for me – over the top, unnecessarily complicated, no one really enjoys it, and it's sickly sweet.

THE WEDDING CAPITAL
OF THE WORLD

People think it's odd that I hate weddings and don't want to get married to Suzanne, even though we've been together so long. They think getting married and having kids is what life's all about. I don't agree, but I was travelling to the wedding capital of the world to see if I might change my mind.

Over 115,000 people travel to Las Vegas every year to tie the knot. My flight was full of single blokes going there to gamble and couples going to get married, which you could say is a different sort of gamble. The couple sitting in front of me were from Newcastle and they were with their friends and family. That's something else that winds me up about weddings: when the happy couple say they're gonna get married abroad and they seem to think it's reasonable to ask you to take time off work, and pay for flights and a hotel just to see them say 'I do'. Well, 'I won't'. The Geordies were drinking champagne, which is always dragged out at weddings too. I've never been a fan, as it gives me heartburn and I don't like the way it doesn't come with a proper lid. Once the cork is out it has to be drunk. Even Pringles supply you with a proper lid.

KARL'S Facts

Statistically, more people are killed around the world each year by champagne corks than by poisonous spiders.

POP!

I went for the healthiest options on the flight to get some roughage in my system. On my last trip to America I travelled down Route 66 and I ended up feeling fat and bloated after just a few days, as I couldn't find many places that served vegetables. The fact that they call fruit machines slot machines in the US just goes to show that fruit and veg aren't that popular.

Twelve hours later (five bottles of champagne for the Geordie couple) we landed in Vegas, which is said to be the brightest place on Earth from space. We got to the hotel, and it was massive. There was a huge casino on the ground floor. I've heard that these places try all sorts of tricks to keep people gambling. They have no clocks or windows so you don't know what time of day it is, and they pump the place with oxygen to keep everyone awake. At the hotel casino all the machines have comfy chairs in front of them to make people stay longer. I'm not sure how successful this is, though, as my dentist's chair is pretty comfy but I don't stay for extra fillings. As we were checking in I watched as old people sat there, feeding their life's savings into the slots. Some of them looked like they could be in their 90s.

The oxygen being pumped into the room was probably the only thing keeping them alive. Maybe they were trying to win enough to pay for a taxi back to their rooms, the place was that big. All the hotels are big here. They boast in Vegas about having seventeen of the world's twenty largest. Even the bellboy who helped carry my luggage to the room seemed a bit lost. The distance he must cover in an evening, he's more of a Sherpa than a bellboy.

After sending him on his way back out into the maze of corridors I made myself a cup of tea. On the tea tray there was a tin labelled 'Intimacy Kit', which contained a condom and some mints. Hardly a 'kit', is it? You get more in a Kinder egg. There was a note in the bathroom asking occupants to re-use towels to help the hotel be more environmentally friendly, which was a bit of a joke considering the amount of energy the bulbs outside were burning up.

The next morning jet lag kicked in and I woke up early. I went down to breakfast and a few people were still trying their luck on the slots. Even though there are no clocks, they must have known it was morning, as the smell of bacon from the restaurant was filling the air. I had the full works – bacon, eggs and a breakfast muffin, which is basically a cake. No wonder obesity is a problem in the US if people are having cake for breakfast.

We drove around Vegas to see what it looks like without all the lights on. It's not half as fancy-looking in the daytime. It's like a Christmas tree – without the lights on, it's just a tree in your lounge during the day. It was pretty quiet too. Vegas is all about the evening; the people are nocturnal. As well as casinos, there are lots of chapels in Vegas. Our first stop was the Little White Wedding Chapel, where they offer a drive-thru wedding service.

The sign boasted that Michael Jordan and Joan Collins were married there. I didn't even know they were an item. We pulled in to take a closer look. You have to drive under a hoarding painted with little naked cherubs. I've always found cherubs a bit sinister. The idea of winged babies flying around with no nappies on seems like an accident waiting to happen. There would be shit everywhere. If I saw a cherub flying about in real life it would terrify me, whereas a Cyclops, which is another mythical being, wouldn't scare me at all, as it's just a bloke with one eye. He'd be registered disabled and get a decent parking space in today's world.

I like the idea of a drive-thru wedding. Minimum fuss. I don't know why this hasn't made it over to the UK when most things from America do. In the main reception area a woman was tidying up a glass display cabinet. It was full of garters. What are garters, anyway? They featured a lot in *Carry On* films, and I know they are supposed to be sexy, but what are they actually for? I've always presumed they're a sort of sweat band for a fat leg.

The woman who owns the place, Charolette, came into reception. She grabbed me, dragged me into the chapel and started walking me down the aisle. I told her that I wasn't married and wasn't planning on getting married, but if I was then the drive-thru option would appeal to me. She explained how it came about.

> CHAROLETTE: I saw so many people coming, and they were handicapped, and they had their little children with them, and the children would be crying, and it was hot, and they just wanted to hurry up and get married.
>
> KARL: Do they use it often?
>
> CHAROLETTE: No, it's for anybody. Now everybody comes and I don't see any handicap people.

I think it's good how something that was designed for the disabled can be used by the able. I got told off by someone in a wheelchair once for using the toilet that was for them. The queue was massive for the loos and my guts were in a bad way, so I didn't see the sense in not using an empty disabled cubicle when all the other toilets were busy. The bloke had a chair to sit in while he waited, so I don't know what his problem was.

> CHAROLETTE: I'm not married.
>
> KARL: Why is that then?
>
> CHAROLETTE: Well, because my husband went to heaven.
>
> KARL: Oh, alright.

CHAROLETTE: He was the only man I wanted. When he left this earth, I wasn't the same. But I knew that I never wanted anybody else and I never went out and looked for another man.

If Suzanne left me I don't think I'd bother looking for someone else either. I would drive them up the wall always talking about Suzanne and how she used to do things a certain way. Charolette said it took around ten minutes to do a drive-thru wedding. You wouldn't even have to turn the engine off. You can wait for a Filet-O-Fish for longer than that at McDonald's. Normal weddings can go on forever, and there's so much talk and planning that go into them too. And I've no idea why people get engaged. Either get married or don't. What's the point of celebrating the idea of possibly getting married? It's just another card you have to buy someone. So many things are dragged out these days, not just weddings. Even though we're living longer I'm convinced we're not actually doing more, we're just waiting longer. It annoys me that when you buy a sofa these days, you have to wait six weeks for it to arrive. Why does it need to be made to order? They should have more than one in stock – make three, sell one, get another in. It's not a kidney I'm looking for, it's a sofa!

Charolette took me through the procedure as we stood by the drive-thru hatch.

CHAROLETTE: We're gathered here today at the Little White Chapel Drive-Thru Wedding of Love. Karl, will you take Suzanne to be your wife, and will you promise to love her, and honour her, and respect her, and keep her all the days of your life?

KARL: Okay.

CHAROLETTE: And, Suzanne, will you take Karl for your husband?

KARL: Yeah.

CHAROLETTE: Will you promise to love him and honour him and respect him and keep him all the days of your life?

KARL: Yeah.

CHAROLETTE: Love is a choice. You have chosen this beautiful lady because you want to be with her. She's on your mind, she's in your ears, she's in your eyes, she's on your lips, and she's in your heart. And she's in your arms. She wants to be loved by you. And you want to be loved by her. It's no accident that you met. It's no accident that you're together. God doesn't make mistakes. God has a purpose for your life to be with her. Not to be angry with her, not to be upset with her, to love her, to understand her, to hold her if she ever has a temper or something . . .

KARL: Is this still the speech?

CHAROLETTE: Yes. Just hold her, and love her, and just tell her you want her. And the wedding ring . . .

KARL: Oh, you still do the ring?

CHAROLETTE: Oh yes. The wedding ring is a symbol

of marriage, it's a circle that is endless, to represent your endless love.

I find it odd that we've named a finger the 'ring finger'. It just goes to show that we have too many fingers. I reckon we'd get by okay if we had lobster hands. People say it's good to wear a wedding ring, as it reminds you of your partner, but you should remember them without that. The rapper Nelly went through a phase of wearing a plaster on his face, and people said it was supposed to be a reminder of his brother who was in prison. He stopped wearing it after a while, so either he invested in some Post-it notes or it fell off in the shower and he forgot all about his brother.

> **KARL'S** *Facts*
>
> The reason we wear wedding rings on the third fingers of our left hands is because the Ancient Greeks believed a vein in this finger ran directly to the heart.

What I like about the drive-thru wedding is it's not about showing off. Take wedding bells: they only exist to show off. People who need to know you're getting married will know about it, so why make a load of noise? It's noise pollution, and there's no need for it. I've never understood why people on *Relocation, Relocation* won't buy a house near a main road cos they don't like the sound of traffic, but think living near a church in a village is idyllic. Virtually every weekend in the summer those bells are gonna be ringing. If it was a car alarm people would complain.

Charolette gave me a quick tour of her selection of wedding dresses before we left. That's another thing that puzzles me – why buy a wedding dress instead of hiring one? You won't need it again, and it'll just end up being shoved in the loft. I'm sure that's why wedding dresses have got ridiculously big over the years – if it's gonna be stuck up in the loft it may as well double up as insulation. I saw a wedding dress in the *Guinness Book of Records* where the train was 1.85 miles long! The bridesmaids could hardly say they were invited, as they were almost two miles away.

When I left I thought back to what Charolette was saying about how she lost the man in her life and hasn't bothered to replace him. If something happened to Suzanne I don't think I would want to go through with finding somebody else either. I'd feel quite lost without her. It would be like separating Siamese twins, as we've been through everything together. Which can also be handy, as my memory isn't what it used to be, so I use hers as my back-up memory drive. I suppose a little bit of it comes down to laziness too. Meeting someone new would be like getting a new phone. You have to start again, input all of your information into them while trying to get to know their functions. But if I did want to try and find somebody new I don't even know how I'd go about it. I've never been one for chatting up women. It's not so complicated for animals. I've heard male pandas attract the female by showing off how high they can piss up a bamboo shoot! It's like some sort of challenge blokes would do on a stag do. The problem is, I'm not the romantic type and I don't agree with trying to charm people. That isn't the real me, so they'll only end up disappointed. I blame romantic films. They set women's expectations too high. In films, when the man puts a coat on a puddle for a woman to walk over – why would you do that? Especially with the way the weather is these days; the rain never bloody stops. Add to that the amount of potholes, I'd be working day and night just to pay my dry-cleaning bills for my wet, muddy coat. And why is the woman walking in puddles all the time anyway? Am I dating a woman or a frog?

THE ART OF PICKING UP WOMEN

I went to meet Vinnie, a professional pick-up artist who was supposed to help me learn how to approach women, should the need ever arise. He runs a boot camp for people who lack confidence to teach them how to do it. The boot camp was in Nipton, a small town in the Mojave Desert about an hour away from Vegas. There's not much to say about Nipton other than it has a population of sixty, one café and a few desert tortoises. Even though tortoises live for a hundred years, I doubt they've seen much change around Nipton.

By the time I got there Vinnie was already in full swing. Vinnie was a forty-five-year-old Italian fella. Not your stereotypical tall and dark Italian, Vinnie was small, dark and pink. If his neon pink hair didn't grab your attention, his earrings, eyebrow ring, chin ring or tattoos might. He explained how his look is carefully put together to attract women and is known as 'peacocking', which is basically making yourself stand out from the crowd like a peacock showing off its feathers. I've always thought of them as earth's natural drag queens. There were five other blokes at the boot camp. I got in line.

VINNIE: In the 50s the rules of dating were well defined. You would go to a dance, approach a woman and dance with her. Then came the 60s, and women realised that they had a form of power. We call it PUSSY POWER. Right, grab yourselves. (*grabs crotch*) This is your social workout. If you don't exercise it now, it's probably not going to happen, because, gentlemen, remember, we are real men here. IT'S NOT GONNA SUCK ITSELF!

BOOT CAMP MEMBERS: It's not gonna suck itself!

VINNIE: Come on, grab it! IT'S NOT GONNA SUCK ITSELF!

BOOT CAMP MEMBERS AND KARL: It's not gonna suck itself!

VINNIE: If you wait for it to happen, it's probably not going to happen. When was the last time you heard a knock at the door, and they say, 'We have girls here, they want to talk to you'? No. If you want it, you got to go get it.

Vinnie could talk. But none of what he was saying was making sense to me. It was like watching a trailer for a film that's exciting, but you haven't got a clue what's going on. I'm the sort of person who needs one-on-one training. This is why school didn't work for me.

Vinnie told us all to grab a piece of wood and then explained that he wanted us to chop it in half using our bare hands. This was to teach us how not to fear tackling the unknown. I wasn't keen. I damaged my right wrist when I was a kid and it's not been right since. It aches when I plunge the toast in the toaster, so smashing it against a bit of wood didn't seem like a good idea. He told me to use my left hand instead.

VINNIE: In life we sometimes have a tendency to make things harder than they are. Each of those boards has a slight natural curve. You want to make sure that you're going to hit that side, because there is no point in making things harder in life.

MALICK (BOOT CAMP MEMBER): Yeah.

VINNIE: Now, there's nothing worse than the sex going down the drain because then it's only logistics, you're just running a household. Nothing will keep a woman more interested than amazing sex, and it'll make you feel good too. Research has demonstrated that men who have great sex do better at all levels. So pick a board and identify the side that should be facing. Does that make sense?

EVERYONE: Yeah, it does.

Don't get me wrong – the sex thing, it's alright. But I'm not a great believer in going at it all night. Get it done, get to sleep; it's not something you should drag out. I've had neighbours who do that, and it drives me up the wall. To me it's like getting a sofa through a doorway: you can waggle it about and try different angles, but you just want to get it into the hole, just get it done. I say be like a pigeon. They don't mess about, they just jump on the back of another pigeon and it's done in about two seconds and then they wander off again to find a bit of KFC chicken.

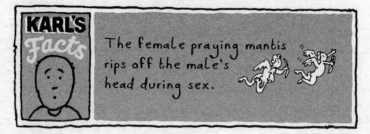

KARL'S Facts

The female praying mantis rips off the male's head during sex.

One by one we took it in turns to smash the wood. I broke it in half with no problem. It made me feel quite good. Left hand as well. I passed the test. Though I didn't need to break any wood when I met Suzanne. I wasn't looking to meet anyone at the time, as I was busy working. She worked in a newsroom at a local radio station in Manchester where I was doing some work in the evenings. I wanted a hot chocolate but had no money, so I asked her if I could borrow 20p. She said yes and then never asked for it back, so I thought 'she's alright' and I've been with her ever since. I know Disney wouldn't buy my story to make into a romantic cartoon, but I think our relationship is built on what's important. Romantic films have got to be responsible for most divorces – people are trying to live in a make-believe world. Suzanne buying me that hot chocolate is certainly a better reason to be with someone than that bloke who went out with Cinderella cos her foot fitted a glass slipper he found on the street. Isn't picking someone based on the size of their feet a bit of a gamble? I mean, a slipper suggests she does very little, anyway. And a glass one at that. The noise alone would do my head in. Then there's the fact she lost it. I don't want to be going out with someone who's constantly losing shoes.

Vinnie went over a few different ways to approach chatting to a woman using Alice, his assistant, in the role-play.

> **VINNIE:** If you don't know what to say, tell her, 'I got no clue what to say, but you're really cute.' When you do that, they've got to at least say hello. *(Alice chuckles)* No, seriously. 'I'm Vince, what's your name?'

> ALICE: Alice.
>
> VINNIE: Alice, you have a strong handshake. Oh, let's play who's got the most bracelets! Let's see, how many bracelets do you have?
>
> ALICE: Seven.
>
> VINNIE: Seven? Ah, too many to count. You're cute. So, anyway, it will come, because when you're closer to her she may talk to you, and you will notice things you can talk about.

I couldn't do this sort of thing. It's just not me at all, and I reckon women would see right through it. I wouldn't approach a woman who is wearing a load of bangles, anyway, as the jangling noise would get on my nerves. It would be like going out with a bloody wind chime. Also, if I was a woman and the only word that could be used to describe me was 'cute' I would not be happy. Things that are 'cute' are usually also useless – they're 'cute' because they've nothing else going for them. I'm sure that's why babies are cute; otherwise most people wouldn't have them, as they don't bring much else to your life for years. I'm sure the only reason we try and save pandas from extinction is because people find them 'cute'. The Cape stag beetle is on its way out, and no one gives a shit, as it's not cute, is it?

Rather than chat-up lines and false charm I would get someone interested by telling them good animals facts like:

- Bats hang upside down even when they're dead, as their claws automatically close.

• Wombat poo comes out in squares.

• A lot of koala bears have bad backs, as they sit up all day even though their spines aren't designed for it.

At least then, if they don't like me, I haven't totally wasted their time. They go away with a little nugget of information that they'll remember, which also means they'll remember me.

Next, Vinnie told us we were going to be walking on fire.

> **VINNIE**: Why would we walk on fire? Well, most men see women who they want have goals and dreams, and they hesitate. So this is symbolic for charging forward. Interacting with women, you see her in the distance – what comes first? Foot first, everybody. What comes first?
>
> **MEN**: Foot first.

It didn't seem like a sensible thing to do, but neither did smashing a piece of wood with my hand. But I'd done that, so I thought I'd give this a go. Plus, I'd had a few verrucas of late from staying in hotels where the bath hadn't been cleaned properly and I thought this might help get rid of them. While we took off our shoes and socks, Vinnie continued talking. It was relentless. He could do his speech in his sleep, that's if he had time to sleep between all the having it away. If he wasn't talking to us he was kissing Valerie, his French girlfriend.

I'm not a fan of people kissing in public either. Fine if it's a quick peck, but when people are all over each other it does my head in. They seem to think it's okay to do what they want because it's 'love'. Again, in the films when some bloke holds a plane up to get on board to propose to some woman and all the passengers cheer – it's ridiculous! I wouldn't feel like cheering. We'd probably have missed our take-off slot and we'd then be waiting on the tarmac for another forty-five minutes. Selfish, that's what it is. It's the same with Romeo and Juliet. She was shouting to him from her balcony, yet no one ever considers the person who lived in the ground-floor flat who might have been trying to sleep. As it happens, on this occasion I didn't mind Vinnie kissing Valerie, as at least it meant he couldn't speak.

Shoes and socks off, I joined the queue to fire walk. I was in agony. Not from walking on fire but from walking over to the fire. The ground was covered in sharp stones and bits of twig that I'm still removing from my feet now. Vinnie got us to chant 'Sex NOW, Sex NOW' as we waited in line. It came to my go. I don't know what the fuss is about, as it actually didn't hurt that much. Nowhere near as bad as walking over the ground to the fire. Once we crossed the coals everybody high-fived each other, and Vinnie told us we were ready to put what we'd learned into practice.

Vinnie had rented an apartment where we all met up at 7 p.m. It was a bit of a bachelor pad. Lots of black and red, dim lights, a round bed that rotated, and a shower that could fit fifteen people with a pole in it. I didn't want to ask why you would want fifteen people in a shower cos I know for a fact that it isn't because Vinnie wanted to be environmentally friendly. I don't think I've ever had fifteen people in my house at the same time, never mind in my shower. And what is it with pole dancing? I don't understand it. It seems like a wasted skill to me. Has anyone ever told one of them women who do it that they could probably make a fortune putting up scaffolding? They'd be able to do it in no time.

We headed to the Strip in a huge pink Hummer limo. It was stupidly long, like an aeroplane with the wings taken off. Inside, music was pumping. As we were driving about, Vinnie showed me some YouTube clips of him doing his thing around the world. Basically, videos of him going up to strangers and kissing them, and I'm not talking just a peck on the cheek either. It was like a front cover of a Mills & Boon paperback.

It was a cold night, and as we wandered about on the busy sidewalks Vinnie kept getting us to chant 'Some will! Some won't! So what!', which must have been taught on another day of boot camp, as it was new to me. It has a bit more substance to it than the classic 'It's not gonna suck itself!' Vinnie was also dishing out advice on how to approach girls.

VINNIE: Look both sides, be strong, you gotta go for it, start sooner and start stronger. What is it? Sooner and . . . ?

MAN: Start stronger.

> **VINNIE**: Sooner and stronger, alright. Walk first, foot first, faster. Okay, now you're ready.
>
> **MAN**: Yeah.

Vinnie kept using the expression 'she's hot', an expression I've never used. Vinnie was in his element, but I couldn't help thinking he could put his skills to better use by becoming a charity collector. A lot of those blokes in bibs collecting for endangered species seem to use it as an excuse to chat up women, anyway.

Alice, Vinnie's assistant, asked me what my 'type' was, but I don't really have one. It's not a battery I'm looking for. I'm sure there are loads of different types of people I could get on with, but I wouldn't go for someone who is knocking around the busy streets of Vegas at this time of night, as I don't live that sort of life. I'd prefer to be at home with a Twix watching the telly. And I don't believe that 'opposites attract'. Whenever I think of that phrase I always think of the film *King Kong*. When the big monkey starts fancying Naomi Watts, people in the cinema were crying and wondering, 'Will they or won't they get it on?' As if it was ever going to work out. He was a bloody hundred-foot gorilla! You know every love story has been done when a gorilla is trying it on with a woman. Anyway, Alice wasn't giving up.

> **KARL**: Have you heard of Kim Wilde? The singer?
>
> **ALICE**: No.
>
> **KARL**: Right, well, in the 80s she was alright. In the 90s it was Patsy Kensit. Have you heard of her?

ALICE: Maybe?

KARL: In the late 80s Kylie Minogue was vaguely popular. She was in *Neighbours*, have you heard of that? Now, I didn't like her in that, but, come 2000, I thought, 'She's alright.' So it just goes to show, your tastes change.

Thinking about it, I reckon haircuts attract me to women. I've had arguments with Suzanne when she lets her hairdresser do what he wants and she comes back with a daft haircut that I then have to put up with until it grows out. Nice hair is important. Look at cats, nice and cuddly. If they were bald they'd have died out by now.

ALICE: Any situation where you're trying to convince someone to do something, whether it's to buy a product or to go out with you, whatever it is, the 10–10–80 rule applies. So 10 per cent of people will say no, no matter what. I mean, you can offer them everything under the sun and they'll say no. Ten per cent will say absolutely yes. You could walk up to a girl with a sign that says 'Will you sleep with me?' and they'll go for it . . . even if you are absolutely disgusting. But the remaining 80 per cent, they're sitting on the fence, and all the techniques that the pick-up artists will teach you, everything applies to that 80 per cent, because it's a matter of how skilled you are as to what level you can pull towards you. Those skills – practice really does make perfect, so when you do find that beautiful woman you're already gonna have that ability.

As much as some of what Alice said made sense, it's just not the way I work, so I left Vinnie and his followers to it. People who I've gone out with have been friends of friends who I've got to know over time, so there was no going up to strangers and trying to chat them up needed. I didn't even like a couple of them that much to start with, but then we ended up getting on over time. It's like my relationship with olives. They were always plonked on a table when I went out for dinner even though they were not requested, and I didn't like them. Couldn't see the attraction. I didn't even look at them. But over time I got used to seeing them, tried them one night, and now I love them. This is the way it works for me. Each to their own, though.

'Nice hair is IMPORTANT. LOOK AT CATS, Nice and Cuddly. IF they were BALD they'd have DIED OUT by now.'

THE SCIENCE OF ATTRACTION

One of the main problems with trying to find a partner is that we leave too much of the decision up to our eyes. Too much is based on looks. So I was curious about where I was going next on my trip. It was a pheromone party at a bar called Los Globos in LA. This is a new way of meeting people using your nose. Rather than the way people look, you go for their smell. There must be something in this concept, as it's going back to basics and using other senses to find the right partner, just like the cavemen and -women must have done.

The smell of someone isn't something you ever think about, is it? On the way out to Vegas I watched the film *Frankie and Johnny* with Al Pacino and Michelle Pfeiffer. I thought she was quite attractive, but she might really stink, for all I know. All these good-looking Hollywood types – Angelina Jolie, Jennifer Aniston and Reese Witherspoon – they could all stink to high heaven. It makes sense now. We see all these showbiz stunners splitting up from each other all the time and we think, 'God, why aren't they happy, she's really nice.' It's probably cos they stink. If someone stinks, how can you live with them? If you've ever had dogshit on your shoe, you'll know you can't think about anything until you get rid of the smell. You can trust your nose more than your eyes too, as eyes don't focus on the right things. The number of times my eyes are busy looking at my phone or the newspaper and forget to check on the toast, it's the nose that says, 'Your toast is burning!' My nose never gets tired either. After fourteen or fifteen hours eyes need to sleep, yet the nose keeps going.

The T-shirt I had been wearing since I left London was placed in a plastic freezer bag with the number fifty written on a Post-it note. Blue Post-it notes for men, pink for women. Everyone there was sniffing bags searching for a pheromone match. If you found a smell you liked, it meant you were attracted to that person's pheromones.

> WOMAN ON FRONT DESK: Pay close attention to the screen, because women who like your scent will take your bag and hold it up, and if you'd like to go and talk to that lady, go and talk to her.

There were plenty of bags on the tables as well as a few cups of coffee beans. These were there to be sniffed between each bag to reset your nose senses. A bit like a palate cleanser, like a sorbet. It wasn't long before I found a smell that I liked, so I went and had my photo taken with it like the woman on the front desk told me to. I went back to the table and found another. Either there were quite a few women who were well suited to me, or I'd just found out that my nose is a bit of a slag.

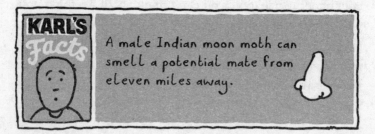

KARL'S Facts

A male Indian moon moth can smell a potential mate from eleven miles away.

It's funny how smells stay with you and bring back memories, even horrible smells. The mustiness of one bag I smelled reminded me of a woman from the estate I grew up on who was known as Scruffy Sandra. She used to get a full seat to herself on the bus cos of her smell. The thing is, though, sometimes women wear so much perfume it makes me wonder what they are trying to hide. It makes me suspicious. My favourite smell is fresh air. When Suzanne has been out and comes in I like that smell. And it's free. Or when she's cooked a Sunday dinner and her hair smells of lamb chops.

MAN: The first one is better than the second one?

KARL: Yeah, because that was forced on me when the woman sort of said you've got to smell this. I was expecting something better.

MAN: Right, right, right, yeah, that kinda turned me off too.

KARL: Oh Jesus, that should be binned.

MAN: Do you go for guys too?

KARL: No. Oh, is that a bloke's?

MAN: Blue Post-it is guys.

KARL: Oh yeah . . . Forgot. Jesus. It wants bloody burning that does.

Getting a whiff of another bloke's T-shirt made me think I was in with a good chance. I don't smell that much, as I don't really sweat, so I've never had to cover myself in aftershaves or spray. I've never bought aftershave in my life; it's always been a gift. Same applies to underpants and tea towels. Suzanne recognises my smell, though, and she says she keeps some of my clothes around when I'm away so it smells like I'm there. It's probably just an excuse not to get the washing done.

I didn't feel any stress at this event. If a girl doesn't like you because you're boring or ugly it could be quite hurtful, but them not liking the smell of me doesn't seem so bad.

I pulled out shirts and blouses and had a good whiff. I found my eyes started to interfere by looking at the size of the garment. I suppose that's where there is a bit of a flaw in this scheme. It's not that I find bigger women unattractive, it's the cost to run them that worries me. Food isn't cheap.

A woman came over after seeing me hold up her number.

KARL: Which one were you?

WOMAN: Twenty-nine. What did you like about it?

KARL: Can I have a smell again, or I could just smell you?

WOMAN: You don't remember?!

KARL: Well, I've had me nose in a lot of stuff.

WOMAN: So you've just been willy-nilly choosing shirts that you smell, just like 1, 2, 3?!

KARL: No, I wasn't! I wasn't picking willy-nilly. I picked three. I smelled it for like twenty seconds. I'm not . . .

WOMAN: You picked three. So how many have you smelled? Three out of how many?

KARL: We're not getting on, this isn't happening.

WOMAN: No, it's not working.

KARL: Listen, you smelled nice. You were me favourite.

WOMAN: I would be complimented if you even remembered which one I was.

KARL: I liked it at the time.

WOMAN: Okay, which one was it then?

KARL: Twenty-something . . . twenty-three?

WOMAN: No, sorry.

KARL: So that's it?

WOMAN: Yeah that's it. *(walks away)*

KARL: Jesus!

She might have smelled okay, but I guess smells don't warn you about mentals. I think she was being a bit unreasonable. I'm human, not a bleeding police dog. A bigger woman came over. She looked like Velma from *Scooby Doo* – all curly hair and glasses. She told me I smelled 'chocolatey'. Which was probably about right as I'd been eating Minstrels for about twenty-four hours.

KARL: Has anything ever come out of these events as a relationship?

WOMAN: Well, yeah. I mean, Judith who created this party tracks what happens to people, and relationships come out of it.

KARL: Well, that's good then, ain't it? Can't knock it.

WOMAN: It's no worse than any other singles party. It's instinct. We're animals.

KARL: Well said. See, I thought just chatting and showing knowledge helped attract people. Do you know what a wombat is? When a wombat has a shit, it's square.

WOMAN: Really?!

KARL: Yeah, is that good?

WOMAN: *(laughs)* I do like that you know that, cos I like animals a lot myself. Did you know that when koalas are born the way they get their gut to digest eucalyptus is by eating their mum's shit?

KARL: I haven't heard that, no . . . I wasn't aware of that.

WOMAN: I like facts very much, but I don't always find that gets me a lot of dates.

KARL: It's a start, though.

WOMAN: I haven't found it to be a start so far. I was raised with the belief that guys don't like smart girls. 'Men don't make passes at girls with glasses' and stuff like that.

KARL: No, that's a myth. Glasses are like a bit sexy in rude films. There's always some sort of secretary with glasses on. It's something to take off, isn't it?

The woman who moaned at me earlier came by again. She told me I had good taste but that my brain was soft. I told her she was doing my head in. And, on that note, I left. I still think there's something in it, though. There's no point just going for looks, as they change as you get older. You lose them, and your body doesn't look good forever either. I'm sure I've heard that we're constantly shedding skin and it is totally replaced every seven years. So every seven years you're a different person. That's why people get the seven-year itch and stop getting on with their partner – it's because they're a different person.

ARRANGED MARRIAGES

I left LA and headed to India, where finding somebody to marry is not so complicated. In a lot of cases the parents take control and help you find the right person for you to spend the rest of your life with. People always seem to be well against this idea, saying it should be up to the person to decide who they want to be with, but do we really know what's best for ourselves? People don't do anything for themselves any more. They need help from Phil and Kirstie on *Relocation, Relocation* just to find a bloody house.

I see this arranged marriage set-up a bit like a set menu in a restaurant – you try something new, as you have no choice, and end up liking it. This was how I ended up trying scallops. We're sometimes not best left to decide everything for ourselves. There's a woman in America called Linda Wolfe who's been married twenty-three times. How mad is that? She could have fed a small village in the Congo if she'd thought to sponsor her walks up the aisle. I can understand making a mistake with one marriage, but twenty-three?! Apparently, two of her husbands were gay and two were homeless. Surely there should be a limit to how many times you're allowed to get married? I mean, I get locked out of my online bank account after three wrong attempts at a password. Britney Spears got married at the Little White Wedding Chapel I visited in Vegas. Her marriage was annulled fifty-five *hours* later. Fifty-five hours! I've had longer relationships with bottles of milk. The problem these days is nobody works at fixing problems. Whether it's a relation-

ship or a toaster that's broken, they just re
bound to fall out and have arguments and you
at getting the relationship back together, but no
to any more.

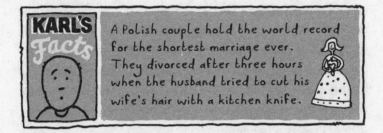

KARL'S Facts

A Polish couple hold the world record for the shortest marriage ever. They divorced after three hours when the husband tried to cut his wife's hair with a kitchen knife.

My first stop in India was at A to Z Matchmaking Management to meet Gopal, a marriage broker. Gopal runs a matchmaking service for parents who want to find someone to marry their son or daughter. Seeing as my mam or dad weren't there, I went to look for myself to see if anything took my fancy.

As soon as I arrived I had to fill out a form with information about me, and then information about what sort of wife I was looking for. They wanted to know my name, email address, height, weight, exam results, how much I earned, was I a meat-eater, what my mam and dad did for a living. They also wanted to know what my blood type was! What difference does that make? I've never heard someone say, 'I've finished with Lesley.' 'That's a shame. Why's that then?' 'Oh, it just wasn't working out. She didn't have the right blood.'

Even though it wasn't asked on the questionnaire I made a note that I was bald, as I think some women wouldn't want a bald man and it's best to be honest from the outset.

Then I filled in the part about the sort of person I was looking for. A woman, aged between thirty-five and forty-five. Not fussed about exam results, I just want someone with common sense. There's no point in her having a degree in South American literature if she's got no common sense. It would be handy if she was good with plumbing or electrics, though, as they're not my strong points. Height at least five feet five but no more than six feet. Skin type? Just . . . nice. Smooth, I suppose. Don't want bruised. Jesus, this is how I select a banana.

I ended up putting 'skin – not too much', as this was a polite way of saying I didn't want a fat lump of flesh. I don't want someone who's been married. Non-smoker. She can drink but not too much. I took the questionnaire in to Gopal to input the information into his system.

GOPAL: So you know the meaning of an arranged marriage?

KARL: Not fully, no.

GOPAL: Actually, we seek here destined soulmates, not partners, so we are going to arrange the thing so we have everything that is important. We have to see social, financial, intellectual compatibility of the person and their families also.

KARL: Do you think education is important?

GOPAL: Education is very, very important. Intellectual compatibility should be there, obviously.

KARL: But it's funny, with my girlfriend, she is quite intelligent, yet I didn't do that well at school. But I learn from her.

GOPAL: Okay.

KARL: If you put two nutters together, it's not good, is it?

GOPAL: It's not good?

KARL: I don't think so. I have changed my ways. I used to be a little bit dodgy when I was younger, but she's keeping an eye on me and telling me not to do things. It's interesting how sometimes education isn't always the key to a relationship.

GOPAL: Yep.

I'm not sure he understood what I was getting at. He had hundreds of profiles on his system, so to speed things up he searched in the age category to narrow it down a bit. He read out details like an estate agent telling you about a property. 'This one just in, fair-skinned, slim, charismatic, fashionable, classy, animated, social, lively, good size. Enjoys reading, current events, world politics, room for improvement.'

GOPAL: Shoma. She's a doctor . . .

KARL: *(reading from screen)* Softly spoken, nice, slim, smart, sharp features, often mistaken for a student rather than a doctor because of her looks . . . Did you write that or did she tell you to write that?

GOPAL: No, she has written herself.

KARL: Umm. Bit big-headed then.

GOPAL: We match horoscope also. Horoscope match-making.

KARL: No, I don't believe in all that. Next.

I wondered if he was trying to palm off some women who had been on his books for ages. Eight or nine profiles later he found Shivani.

GOPAL: Shivani.

KARL: Shivani.

GOPAL: She can marry with British guys. She can go abroad, there is no problem. Everything will suit you, and her parents will permit for you to settle over there . . . Should I show you that profile?

KARL: Yeah, let's have a look. *(reading from screen)* Hmm . . . non-vegetarian, that's alright. She's never married.

GOPAL: Born . . . '78. Her weight is around 47/48 . . .

KARL: How big is that?

GOPAL: She's slim.

KARL: Yeah, er . . . swearing . . . She's not loud and she wouldn't swear?

GOPAL: Swear means?

KARL: Like effing and blinding . . . effing and jeffing . . . erm . . . cursing . . .

GOPAL: No, no. She's not a loud person. She's very calm and sweet. She doesn't speak so much.

KARL: And how much jewellery? Does she wear a lot of jewellery?

GOPAL: No, no. Do you like jewellery?

KARL: No.

GOPAL: Okay, no, she is also not fond of jewellery.

KARL: Okay, let's have a look at her again. Can we just see her head again . . . just a picture?

GOPAL: *(showing photos)* She's slim girl. She's not wearing any jewellery here. She's a very simple person.

KARL: She has a phone there . . . She on her phone a lot? Do you know if she's constantly speaking?

GOPAL: Everyone keeps phone. It's mandatory nowadays.

KARL: I know, but can't she put it down while she has a photo taken . . . *(to director)* Will I see her?

DIRECTOR: She sounds like quite a good match.

KARL: Yeah, alright, let's go and see . . . Let's have a look. And do you know if she's happy being in an arranged marriage?

GOPAL: Yep. She needs this kind of marriage. It is in her blood, it is in her family. In arranged marriage she can get everything. She get happiness, for future. She will be happy because she has taken everyone's view, everyone's permission and everyone is with her for every decision.

KARL: But say I go along and meet her and she gets on with me and we're really happy, but her dad isn't keen on me. Who gets the final say?

GOPAL: If he is not agreeing, we will try to convince him. After all, he has to marry his daughter.

KARL: Alright, let's go see her. Her name again?

GOPAL: Shivani. So we charge something for matchmaking you go through, we take something at once. When the ceremony is arranged we take lots of money.

KARL: Not very good at foreign currency . . . How much is this going to cost me, in pounds?

GOPAL: In pounds? Eighty . . . eighty pounds.

And that was that. After a few calls it was arranged for me to meet Shivani later that evening. I was nervous but looking forward to seeing how much we would get on. We're two total strangers from different parts of the world who would never have met. But then again, this is what that chef Heston Blumenthal does: puts things together that shouldn't work, like a fried egg and Viennetta ice cream as a main course, and people say it's an odd match made in heaven. So who knows? At the end of the day, there are over 1.2 billion people in India, so you can hardly spend time searching for 'the one', can you? It's hard enough finding a parking space in India, never mind 'the one'.

After buying myself a suit for £30 we were on our way round to meet Shivani and her parents. I was knackered, as shopping in India isn't a very pleasurable thing to do. I'm not a fan of shopping at home due to noise and crowds, but it's fifty times worse here. Wherever you walk it seems everybody else is going in the opposite direction and it's one big battle. Every space is taken up. You think you find a quiet alley to just get a moment's peace, but a moped will come hurtling towards you driven by a man holding a pig. The shop I bought the suit from had very little room for customers due to the stock taking up so much space, so there was no changing room, which meant stripping off by the cash till.

We allowed plenty of time to get to Shivani's place, but we were still late. You can never guess how long it's going to take you to get anywhere in India, as the roads are chaos. It looks like when you disturb an ant nest. Two lanes are made into five lanes; one-way roads are definitely not one-way. An Indian sat nav probably just wishes you luck and tells you to go wherever you want. I suppose that's what I find odd about arranged marriages: not that they exist, but the fact that they exist in India, a place where it seems nothing is properly arranged.

Luckily, my being late wasn't too much of a problem, as Shivani's dad, Harash, informed me she wasn't ready yet, as she and her sister were struggling to decide what to wear. I wandered off to find a toilet in a nearby hotel, as even though I'd only been in India for just over twenty-four hours, the dreaded Delhi Belly had already hit me. About forty-five minutes later Harash took me through his rug shop and into his home. I'd decided that I wouldn't tell them about Suzanne, as I wanted to see how far I could get and if I could pass the test.

> HARASH: I'll introduce you to my wife. Her name is Neena. And this is the younger sister of Shivani. Her name is Sakshi. And this is Shivani.
>
> KARL: Shivani. Good to finally see you.
>
> SHIVANI: Hi, how are you?
>
> HARASH: Well, let us see if you are highly qualified and that you've got a good job.

Jesus. I hadn't even sat down and he was already quizzing me. They have more chitchat before the questions start on *Mastermind*. I felt like I had to impress him more than the girl I was there to possibly marry. Shivani looked nice enough, though. Quite a smiley face. I thought it could work. I don't understand when people say, 'Oh, they don't really match'. What are we, a pair of bloody socks? If people had to match, Quasimodo would have been knocking about with a camel and not Esmeralda.

> HARASH: Tell me something about your parents to start with.
>
> KARL: They're just normal, you know, haven't got much money. They've retired now, but me dad's done all sorts of jobs from tiling, gardening, courier work . . . He's been a taxi driver, he had a butty shop, erm, loads of stuff.
>
> HARASH: Tell me something about your childhood and your schooling. What type of school were you in?
>
> KARL: It was what you call a comprehensive, not like a

grammar, just a normal school, erm . . . I wasn't a *bad* bad kid, I tried me best.

HARASH: Can you tell me something about your education, please?

KARL: There's not much to tell, they're called GCSEs, the exams in England. Have you heard of them? Right. Well, I got one of them, in history.

HARASH: Did you pass?

KARL: I got an E, so it's a pass.

HARASH: So what do you do now? For living, for job?

KARL: I write books, I do travel programmes.

HARASH: You write a book? You're getting good amenity from books?

KARL: Yeah, not bad, they do alright. I mean it's not *Harry Potter*, but I earn a wage. I don't owe any money. I think that's important.

HARASH: Tell me, are you living with your mother and father or are you living in apartment alone?

KARL: I've got a house.

HARASH: A complete house?

KARL: Full house, five bedrooms.

SHIVANI: Very big house.

SAKSHI: So he's got space for us.

KARL: Well . . .

SHIVANI: So everyone can fit in then.

KARL: Yes, maybe . . . in time.

SAKSHI: That's good.

KARL: So how old are you?

SHIVANI: I'm exactly thirty-three.

KARL: I'm forty. Isn't forty quite old for you?

NEENA: I think that's the maximum . . .

SHIVANI: Yeah, I would say about thirty-eight, thirty nine. But, obviously, if other qualifications, if other things are there . . . So if smartness is there, or you like working, then I think one could always just . . .

SAKSHI: Age is just a number. I think there are other qualities that matter more . . .

HARASH: Are you looking for a girl who is homely, somebody who is domesticated? Or would you like your would-be wife to work?

KARL: A little bit of both, if possible. Work, and a little bit of home duties sort of thing, but we'll share that. I like cleaning, I'm very good. You're asking about hobbies and things, I quite enjoy cleaning windows. I find it very relaxing.

HARASH: What is your income like? That's very important, for us . . .

KARL: Yeah, but I don't want that to sort of be the decision-maker.

HARASH: Well, I would like to know your income.

KARL: I know, but I don't think that should matter. I've been honest about my age, and my exam results, and I'd like to be picked on whether she thinks I'm the man who could look after her. Money can cause a lot of problems, it doesn't bring you any happiness.

HARASH: It's not a question of happiness, I'd like to know whether you . . .

KARL: Put it this way, I don't owe anyone any money.

SAKSHI: That's good. That's what matters.

KARL: You know, she won't starve. She'll have a roof over her head. At the end of the day, I could say I'm earning thousands, but then I might not tell you I'm a big gambler. There's a lot of nutters out there earning fortunes, but they're idiots.

SAKSHI: Yeah.

KARL: Just common sense, like I say. The exam results, I'm not proud that I've only got an E in history, but it was years ago. I've tried to do the best I can with what I've got. And you'll struggle to find someone who I've really upset in life. I've not annoyed anyone or battered anyone. If we're being really honest, I used to do a little bit of robbing when I was younger . . . nothing big . . . you know, toffees, chocolate.

SAKSHI: That's okay.

SHIVANI: Yeah, that's like when you were a kid, so it's fine.

HARASH: For us, it's important that we should have a meeting with your parents. You think that's possible? Your parents, in the next meeting?

KARL: So would they come here, or would you come to theirs . . . ?

SAKSHI: Either way. Whatever suits you better.

KARL: Right. And it's the same sort of questioning to them?

HARASH: No, no, no questioning . . . Just so we know.

SAKSHI: We like when the family is involved. Since we are also very family-oriented, we would like to meet your extended family.

Extended family?! Even I've never met them. My mam and dad have never met Suzanne's mam and dad either. I don't see the point. I chose her and she chose me, so why drag other people into it? Research shows that arranged marriages last longer, and I wonder if it's down to the fact that it's other people putting you together, like when a family member buys you a gift it's not easy to throw it away, as there's a chance they'll come to visit and ask where it is and get upset when you say you've binned it.

HARASH: How marriage do you want to take? English-style marriage, or church-style marriage?

KARL: Now, this is an important bit cos . . .

SAKSHI: In the Indian culture, you know, you just get married once in a lifetime . . . hopefully. So a lot of people like to go all-out, and they're very extravagant about it, and it's not a one-day affair, it's like a couple of days.

KARL: Well, I've never even had a birthday party. Ever. I don't really go out in big groups. You know how people go out, sort of seven or eight people . . .

HARASH: Then marriage will be like this. You can invite your parents from England, and a few people from our family, ten to fifteen people, then we go to the temple, church, whatever it may be. And let the priest announce, both of you husband and wife and . . .

It had all got a bit out of hand. It was too late now to announce I had Suzanne at home. I'd only spoken to her a few hours ago about a problem with the boiler. I might have a five-bedroomed house, but no matter where I live I always end up with boiler problems. She has no idea that I'm with some woman and we're talking about getting married. It's madness how quick they decide. I've waited at the doctors longer than this. I can't believe how easy it is too. I didn't even have to use any of Vinnie's chat-up lines, not once have I had to chant 'It's not gonna suck itself'. I kind of agree that meeting a potential life partner shouldn't be as difficult as we make it at home, but I really didn't know anything about her. No wonder Bollywood love stories have all the singing and dancing. It's to pad it out, otherwise they'd meet, get married and have kids in twenty minutes flat.

> **HARASH:** So, now, before you leave would you like to fix up a time with her for tomorrow for lunch or dinner, so that you spend a couple of hours together to know each other better?
>
> **KARL:** I'll have a chat with . . . erm . . . because I'm not sure where I'm meant to be tomorrow, so I'll find out . . .

If we did go for a coffee I think I would have taken longer deciding which coffee I wanted than Shivani did to decide what man she wants to spend the rest of her life with. I agree that too much choice can be a bad thing. Coffee, for example, we used to be able to just ask for a coffee and get one, whereas now it's latte, cappuccino, frappuccino, decaf, espresso, mocha, flat white and all that. There's even a coffee now that is fed to some kind of monkey, digested and then pooed out for a richer flavour. What is going on? Honestly, just give me a Nescafé instant. I left and thanked everyone for a nice evening. Shivani said I should text if I wanted that coffee.

Because so many couples get together without really knowing each other in India, detective agencies are a thriving enterprise. It's common practice for the family to pay someone to follow the potential partner to check if everything they said was legit. As mad as it sounds, I guess because marriage is talked about so early, this is a bit of quick research. I'd like the locals to record their version of the Craig David song '7 Days'; they'd be singing about moving the gran-in-law in by Friday.

I met with the boss of one of these agencies and was told I was going to spend the day with a detective following a guy who was supposed to be getting married soon. He gave me a photo of the fella and a profile similar to the one I had filled out the day before. It said that he was on a wage of 35,000 rupees, didn't smoke, didn't drink and was vegetarian. It was my mission to follow him for a while to see if he was true to his word. I was looking forward to my little job, as I like people-watching. I prefer watching people to actually having to deal with them. I've always been like that. I was never one for having loads of mates when I was younger. I think that's why I didn't do that well at school. If I'd had more mates I could have copied their work and got better grades. My teacher always accused me of not thinking before I spoke, but looking back I wonder if I did this cos I spent a lot of time alone and it made my own company more interesting when I didn't know what I was going to say next.

Being a detective reminded me of some school homework I was given to keep me busy over the Christmas break one year. We were asked to observe an activity and then make a pie chart from the information collected. Some kids counted the cars that passed their house between certain hours and then presented the most popular colour of car in a chart. Someone else did something about how many different meals were made from one bag of potatoes. I gave myself a little mission of tracking a neighbour called Mrs Knowles. She was an old woman who lived alone and didn't go out much, so I thought I'd make a pie chart showing how many minutes a week she was away from her home. I also took note of any visitors. She only ever wore two cardigans, pink and blue, and my research showed she wore the blue one more often. On one day when I hadn't seen much movement for a while, I pushed a newspaper through her letterbox but left it hanging out a bit, so if she pulled it through I'd know she was okay. In all my time in school this was one of the only things I ever got a good mark for. After that, my teacher used to ask how Mrs Knowles was keeping and if she was getting out more. I like to think I came up with Neighbourhood Watch well before it had been created.

The boss of the agency said I would be partner to Detective Aakash. He looked like a detective from *Miami Vice*: smart-casual jacket, jeans, shoes and shades. I got some coffee and cake from the café next door to the detective agency to keep our energy up during the case. It's also the sort of thing you see detectives do in films when they're on a mission.

Trying to find a person in such a heavily populated place was not going to be easy. I thought I'd seen the bloke we had to find about seven times just on the walk to Aakash's car. Luckily, one of the other detectives from the agency was already tracking him and said he had been seen at a local shopping mall, so we made our way over there.

KARL: Do you change your look so people don't notice you following them?

AAKASH: Yes, yes. Just yesterday I visited a hair salon, and he just changed the shape, so that I can change my look. I mean, these are very small assignments. We also go on some very, very big assignments, some corporate assignments also. Glasses are the biggest friend of a detective. We can judge anybody by looking into the eyes of someone, but when we are with the glasses – you cannot read the mind of anybody.

This would be a problem for me. I can't change my look. If you're bald you can't change which side your hair is parted. So I popped on some shades to help mask my face. I looked really gormless. Aakash must have looked like he was driving a bluebottle about.

KARL: So is he working today?

AAKASH: He is working, but he's on the field today.

KARL: On the field? What does that mean?

AAKASH: Field, I mean work that's outside the office.

KARL: So that would be a good time to see a woman if he had someone else on the go?

AAKASH: Exactly, exactly, exactly.

We pulled up and waited. You can pull up where you want in India. Maybe this is why the roads are so busy. They're full of detectives following people and blocking up roads. I had the photo of the man and was looking for him. It's a game of patience, which I think I'm pretty good at. When Suzanne goes shopping she dawdles too much and I just wait in the car, so I think I'd quite like this type of job. You're your own boss in a way, and you don't have to be too brainy either. A lot of TV detectives are simple people. Columbo is my favourite detective and he had a glass eye, and the criminals always thought he was slow. Ironside was in a wheelchair. Miss Marple was an old woman. My weakness could be getting one GCSE in history.

After fifteen or twenty minutes, the man we were after turned up. It was quite exciting. The shop he came out of was next to a McDonald's. Was he going to go in? 'He's supposed to be a vegetarian,' I said. Aakash pointed out that they do sell veggie burgers. You could tell he'd been in this game for a while. I suggested that it might be quicker if I get out and walk up to him and ask if I could borrow a cigarette as a test, but he told me that we should stay back in the car for now. I think we could have found out some useful things about the person if we'd got more involved. We could have checked his temper by nicking his parking space before he had a chance to pull in. That always gets a reaction from people. Surely living with someone with a bad temper is more dangerous than someone who eats burgers?

I made notes of what I saw. He had a rucksack, which I thought was an odd bag to take to a work meeting. I suggested he could be having an affair and have a change of clothes in there. He was smiling a lot while talking on his phone. Could be another woman. It didn't look like a business call. But none of this was any use, as we needed evidence. He just kept walking around a car park. I don't know what he was up to. Never mind his future wife, I felt like telling his boss he was wasting time hanging round car parks all bloody day when he should have been seeing a client.

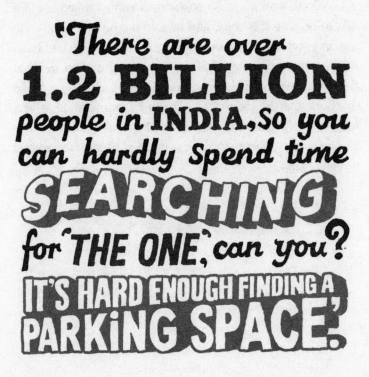

'There are over 1.2 BILLION people in INDIA, so you can hardly spend time SEARCHING for 'THE ONE', can you? IT'S HARD ENOUGH FINDING A PARKING SPACE.'

As he left the car park we slowly kerb-crawled, keeping on his tail. I was just having some of my cake when Aakash jumped out the car and ran across the road, as it looked like we may have lost him in the crowd. I stayed and ate the cake. It was good stuff. Chocolate with an Oreo biscuit crunch. Five minutes later Aakash came running back. He had managed to get a really clear photo on his phone of the bloke buying a drink from a stall while smoking a fag. Caught red-handed.

Aakash's phone was constantly ringing. I asked him if it was to do with this case, and he told me he was also working on another assignment looking for a lady who had been missing since the night before. It seemed odd to me that there was a woman missing and we were chasing a bloke to check that he didn't eat burgers or smoke fags. It was fun for a bit, but it was all quite silly, really. I'm not sure someone lying about smoking is enough of a reason to end a relationship.

THE BIG DAY

The next day I was to witness a wedding in Bangalore to see how it's really done in India. Seeing as I'm not into the kind of weddings people have back home, I wasn't holding out much hope that I'd be keen on one of these big affairs. Weddings here are massive. The two wedding planners, Vithika and Divya, had asked me to help out.

KARL: Stressed?

DIVYA: Yes, it's a big day.

VITHIKA: We've been working a long time for this wedding. I hope you're ready for it.

KARL: How much time have you spent planning this one?

DIVYA: About two months goes into the planning.

KARL: That's normal?

DIVYA: Yeah.

VITHIKA: And also so much changes every day, you know. It's four days of events.

KARL: The wedding goes on for four days? Why's that?

VITHIKA: Well, we have rituals, celebrations. We just finished the dancing and singing, the day before yesterday. Yesterday was painting-your-hands ceremony. Today's the actual wedding.

KARL: That's mental. I mean, four days. That's too much.

VITHIKA: Unless you experience something you don't know what it is like. When you go to the wedding and see the parents and the close family members you see how much they are part of the bride and groom's life. I think the other thing to understand is, in India a wedding is also about social status.

DIVYA: It's a statement of your wealth. It's a statement that you're now married, and it's the beginning of a new life for the whole family.

KARL: And how much are we talking?

DIVYA: I think they start about $200,000.

KARL: How much?! That's mad.

VITHIKA: You have to understand that people here spend more money on just a couple of occasions and they save all their life for them. The parents, when the daughter is born, they start saving for her wedding.

KARL: Hmm. How long's he known the woman?

DIVYA: You know, we really didn't ask him that. Probably a year.

KARL: Is that all?

VITHIKA: That's a long time.

I suppose, considering Shivani was talking about marriage after knowing me for just over an hour, a year is a long time in India. Before setting off for the ceremony I checked my phone and Suzanne had sent me a text saying Happy

Valentine's Day. I'd been too busy to remember. I think it's all a con, anyway. If there's one night that I can guarantee I'll be in, it's February the fourteenth. If you go out, you're getting ripped off paying over the odds for an average meal. It's just another day for card companies to make some money. Did you know the diamond anniversary was invented by a diamond company? It won't be long before we have a Brillo Pad day. I actually blame shelving. If it wasn't for shelving, people wouldn't have cards. In fact, get rid of shelving and we'd get rid of a lot of crap in the world. Ornaments would also go. We don't need them. Shelves just hold shit these days, so get rid.

KARL'S Facts

Valentine's Day is banned in Saudi Arabia, and nothing red can be worn or sold on the day.

DIVYA: We go to the groom's house now. Please help him to get ready and be around him, so if he needs any help he can ask you for it.

KARL: How old is he? Why does he need help getting dressed?

VITHIKA: We don't mean that you're putting his clothes on for him, but there are things he needs to put on his head that you have to make sure are straight, because for every picture he has to make sure that the turban sits properly on his head.

DIVYA: Basically, you are not to leave him unattended at any given point in time. Just be around him.

I was given a traditional-looking suit to wear to the ceremony. Considering I'm not the groom it was pretty fancy. It's the sort of thing my Auntie Nora likes. Even the colour, magnolia, is right for her. She loves magnolia. Everything in her house is magnolia. I reckon if she went to play paintball she'd only play if she could shoot magnolia. It was the sort of suit Elvis wore on stage in Vegas, yet all I'd be doing was making sure some bloke's hat is on straight. It was covered in beads and little plastic pearls. Washing machines up and down India must get jammed all the time with people washing these things. We went round to the apartment where the family were getting ready. I knew it was going to be a long day . . .

9.30 a.m.
I met Vik the groom. He was having his turban fitted. Vithika explained again that it was my responsibility to make sure the turban wasn't covering his eyes. I told her Vik would know himself if it was covering his eyes, as he wouldn't be able to see.

9.40 a.m.
I was asked to move all the guests upstairs to the roof terrace where the puja was going to take place. This would

involve close friends and family blessing Vik before leaving for the temple. I asked them about three times to move, but people were ignoring me. I asked louder and then got told off for shouting. I got confused as I thought I saw the same girl twice and it turned out they were twins. They were the spitting image of each other. It would be odd to go out with a twin, as when the other one gets married you would know that their husband also fancies your wife. That's why I can't believe it when people say they've found 'the one'. If it's a twin you're going out with, how do you know it's 'the right one'?

9.50 a.m.

Everyone was finally upstairs, candles were lit and rice was sprinkled over Vik for good luck. Guests dipped their wedding finger into some red powder and then touched Vik's forehead to leave a mark. This is considered important, as it represents the third eye. They believe the usual two eyes see the outside world and the third sees inside and helps you trust your intuition. I suppose this is similar to how we have a 'gut' feeling. I go with my gut rather than my head to make decisions. Maybe they use the third eye in India as they can't trust their guts as much due to all the spicy food. Mine had been playing up since I had arrived in India – I had a red eye, but it wasn't on my face.

10 a.m.

I tried to get everyone downstairs to the cars to head out to the temple. I'd have had more luck herding ants. No one seemed to be listening. Some woman was helping herself to some cornflakes in the kitchen. I don't even know if she was part of the family or someone who had wandered in off the street.

KARL: Let's go, everybody!

VITHIKA: Karl, just say, 'One last call, we're leaving.'

KARL: Okay. *(to guests)* This is it now, we're not messing about. We're leaving now. If you don't come . . . I've told you.

DIVYA: Be polite.

KARL: It's hard to be polite when they're not listening.

VITHIKA: Guests in India are like gods, so you do not . . . It's okay if they don't come, you carry on to the next thing. But, please, you cannot get angry.

There was a kerfuffle in the hallway as people tried to find their shoes. I stayed in the apartment until they had cleared. I prefer to wait than be in a crowd. I do the same when boarding a plane. I waited for five minutes, and two pairs of shoes were left – mine and the pair that must have belonged to the woman who was busy eating cornflakes. It was like an advert for Crunchy Nut. If she wanted breakfast she should have got up earlier.

11.15 a.m.
We arrived at the temple and waited for the bride to turn up.

I had to stand by Vik's car like a spare part to be ready to open the door when it was time for him to get out, but after twenty minutes of standing in the heat I decided to get in the back. Vinnie, Vik's brother, was in the driver's seat.

> **VINNIE**: It's a lot more complicated than a Christian or Catholic wedding, hey?
>
> **KARL**: Dead right. I was in Vegas a couple of days ago. They do drive-thru weddings, all done in ten minutes.
>
> **VINNIE**: Seriously? Drive-thru wedding?
>
> **KARL**: Telling ya, drive-thru wedding.
>
> **VINNIE**: The whole custom? In the car?
>
> **KARL**: Yep.

Mind you, with the traffic in India being so mental, a drive-thru wouldn't be as straightforward here. Nothing is straightforward in India. I noticed Vithika was watching me, so I checked Vik's hat and gave her the thumbs up. I heard trumpets being blown and was asked to get out of the car. Deepa, the bride, had arrived. Divya told me to hurry over to the entrance to welcome people in. If the whole point of these massive weddings is to impress, I reckon having me, a bald white man in a magnolia beaded suit, at every corner, the guests are just going to think it's been done on a shoestring. The trumpets were making a horrible sound. It was similar to that sound you hear when you trap a wasp behind a curtain and its wings go mental.

11.30 a.m.
Managed to get a good seat at the front inside. Vik and his family were on one side and Deepa's on the other. The twins from earlier were stood with her as photographs were being taken. Having the twins there made it look tidy. Like bookends. I played spot the difference to keep myself entertained.

11.45 a.m.
Around five hundred people were crammed into the temple. I honestly don't know that many people. I've only got fifty-seven contacts in my mobile, and that includes the local chip shop, the old chip shop and a bloke I met once who can replace car windows. I was just hoping people wouldn't start doing speeches, otherwise this could be a long day. Maybe that's why the celebration goes on for four days. Divya gave me a big plate of rice to hand out to the guests. This is thrown over the couple once they're married. It's better than confetti in a way, as it's easier to vac up and it can be re-used, whereas paper confetti sticks to the carpet. I've never been a fan of confetti, anyway, as the amount of fun it gives versus the time spent cleaning it up isn't worth it. Same with party poppers.

Noon
The ceremony started, and there was a lot of noise. People were chatting, and I couldn't hear what was going on at the front. As I sat and watched I wondered if Indian weddings are massive because of the amount of people in the country.

Watch a Bollywood movie and it has a cast of thousands. Nothing is ever a small, private affair. If you're a bloke and you go to the doctors to let a nurse check your bollocks for lumps she probably does two fellas at once. I doubt there's such a thing as a one-on-one here.

12.05 p.m.

I got dragged into the canteen area to help prepare the food. There were twenty-five items of food to be handed out to each guest. I was put in charge of salt. Again, more evidence that there are too many people in the country – where else would someone be given the job of handing out salt? I know I haven't got many skills, but I didn't feel like I was being used to my full potential. I'd spent the morning making sure a hat was on straight, and now salt.

12.30 p.m.

Promoted to serve poppadoms.

1 p.m.

I gave a helping hand to the naan bread man but got told off for giving three naans to a few people. The man in charge of the kitchen said I mustn't waste food or there wouldn't be enough for everyone. Waste food?! He's having a laugh. There's about a hundredweight of rice chucked all over the temple next door, and all I've done is give away six naan breads.

1.30 p.m.

I got a glimpse of Vik and Deepa on stage while people got up to have photos taken with them. They were starting to look weary. I served fruit salad and ice cream to five hundred people before leaving.

6.30 p.m.

Divya and Vithika showed me round the grounds of the party venue. It was about the size of Old Trafford. There was a drinking area with around fifty tables, four hundred seats were in lines in front of a stage where Vik and Deepa would come and receive blessings from the guests, and a food area where there were too many stalls to count serving every type of food you could wish for. My jobs for the evening included making sure candles on the tables were always lit, that everyone had peanuts and clearing away any rubbish. Jesus. I doubt someone had the job of taking care of peanuts at William and Kate's wedding.

7 p.m.

Some cameramen were setting up to record the blessings. A huge pole with a camera on the end, it was the sort of thing you see at the Baftas or the *TV Quick* awards. I don't know why things like this get recorded, as I doubt anyone ever gets round to watching it back. They can't even say they're recording it for people who can't make it, as Divya said they were expecting around five thousand people, so surely that's got to be everyone they know.

8 p.m.

Vik and Deepa stood on stage with their family as guests queued to shake their hands. No wonder the divorce rate in India is a lot lower than in other parts of the world. I can't imagine that many people would want to go through with all this fannying about a second time. Just because you have a big celebration it doesn't mean the relationship is any stronger, does it? Look at swans. They don't have a big party, but they're known to stick with their partners for life. Saying that, I've always wondered if that's because they all look the same, so there's no point in them running off with another swan.

9 p.m.

I had a break from candles and peanuts round the back of the venue near the car park, and had a knockabout with a football with some taxi drivers. This is where the toilets were. They only had two portable cubicles. Five thousand people, $200,000 and yet there's only two toilets. With the amount of nuts that had been consumed this was definitely going to cause problems later.

10.30 p.m.

Vik and Deepa were still on stage shaking hands. Most people say your wedding day is the best day of your life, but I just can't see this being the case for them. Vik and Deepa didn't seem like show-offs, so I doubt they were enjoying all the fuss. After so many days of it, surely everyone has had enough. You can have too much of a good thing. It's like when I bought the box set of *The Sopranos*. I loved the first few, and even though it was still good, after that I just couldn't take any more.

11 p.m.

The food area opened, but people were still requesting nuts. Two men in fancy outfits and headgear welcomed people – imagine a type of over-the-top, drag queen Ronald McDonald with a Freddie Mercury moustache. I didn't see the point in this. Stuff like this is just to give people something to talk about. It's like ice sculptures. No one really needs a six-foot ice sculpture of an owl at a party. They don't come cheap either, and these days with global warming they don't even last as long as they used to.

1 a.m.

I finally got to use some of my skills and DJ for twenty minutes. I used to do this at social clubs when I was younger with my mate Makin. We called ourselves Pilkies Makin Music. We had business cards made up on shiny blue card with a gold font, but we never gave them out as they were too expensive. We'd hand them over to people wanting to book us and then get them to write down the phone number so we could have the card back. I didn't have any Indian tracks on my iPod, but I dug out a few songs I thought any culture could dance to.

1.30 a.m.

Had a bit of a dance. Suzanne always says I'm not that good at dancing, as I don't know what moves are gonna come. I suppose I dance in the same way that plankton swim. They just go where they're taken. That's how I do most things in life. Unlike this whole celebration.

GETTING MARRIED THE PILKINGTON WAY

After everything I had seen during this trip, it made me think about how I would do things if one day me and Suzanne decided to get married. I know for sure that I wouldn't be up for a massive wedding like Vik and Deepa's in India. It seemed like they hadn't had any control over their day. As soon as there are wedding planners involved, it's no longer a personal or unique experience. You're getting the same package they sell to everyone else, and then it just becomes about spending money on things that really aren't important. The fact that I'd spent the whole evening wandering round their reception checking that everyone had enough peanuts proves my point. Did giving people peanuts mean it was a better night for everyone? Has anybody ever come back from a wedding and said, 'Yeah, had a lovely time, the bride looked nice – no bloody nuts, though!'

The thing that did strike me as interesting on this trip was the pheromone party I attended in LA. Since I've been back home and looked into it, I've found out that bees, lizards, beetles and loads of other creatures meet their partners through this method, so there has to be something in it. I've never liked women who smell like they've had a bath in perfume. It's too much. Maybe it's because I can't smell the 'real them', which makes me suspicious and wonder what they're trying to hide. It's no coincidence that the women who spray perfume all over themselves are always the ones with an orange tan too. I put it down to the fact that all the

CFC gases they pump out burn up the ozone above their heads, so the sun tans them the most. Obvious, innit.

I know I didn't find anyone who could've been a potential partner at the pheromone party, but that's because they weren't there that night. If it was that easy I probably wouldn't believe in it so much, but I'm sure if I attended a few of those events I would find a match. And to be fair, the women my nose picked were pretty good. If anything, the problem was they were too good. My nose has high standards. I don't think it realises what sort of face it's attached to. But I do think smell is one of our strongest senses and is there to help with the big decisions in life. It's not just for smelling the boiled ham in the fridge to check it's not off. Eyes can't be left to do all the work when choosing a partner cos they change their mind far too often. I remember my eyes liked the first iPhone. They thought it looked futuristic and had nice curves, then a new one came out a year later and they went right off the old one. Yet I've always liked the smell of Apple products and that hasn't changed. It's pretty rare to go off the smell of something. It made me wonder if the reason why marriages are arranged in India is because people can't really trust their noses to pick a partner. They never get to know the real smell of a person due to all the spicy food they eat.

When it came to planning a wedding, the way I'd want to do it, it seemed important that smell would play a part. I also liked the simplicity of the drive-thru wedding with no frills, fuss or guests. So what better place to have a low-key, cheap wedding than a launderette? A couple called Angie and Jon were happy to give my unique style of wedding a go. Charolette from the Little White Wedding Chapel was going to do the service to make it all legit. I popped on the suit I'd bought in India and headed down to the Laundromat.

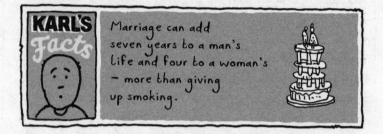

KARL'S Facts

Marriage can add seven years to a man's life and four to a woman's — more than giving up smoking.

The way it was going to work was that the happy couple, Angie and Jon, would each turn up with a basket full of their dirty laundry. Charolette would then do an introduction about the importance of marriage before they swapped baskets and had a big whiff of each other's dirty garments. This would be their last chance to decide whether or not this was the smell they wanted to spend the rest of their lives with.

CHAROLETTE: We are gathered here today at the Laundromat in Las Vegas, Nevada, to join you together in the most beautiful moment of your lives. So, will you please exchange your dirty baskets. I ask you first, Jon, will you take this beautiful lady to be your wife?

JON: I will.

CHAROLETTE: Will you promise her that you will do the laundry and help with the household chores and kiss her beautiful face every day?

JON: I do.

CHAROLETTE: Angie, will you take this wonderful man to be your husband and will you promise to wash his dirty laundry?

ANGIE: I will.

CHAROLETTE: I would now like for you to sniff each other's dirty laundry, please.

KARL: Alright, you've both had a whiff, so are you sure you're happy with each other's smell? Because if you don't like it you'd best say now, and we can knock this on the head and go home. So you've had a smell and you're definitely happy?

JON: Definitely.

KARL: Angie?

ANGIE: Definitely, yes.

KARL: That's going to be the smell for the rest of your life. Day in, day out, when you wake up in the morning that's the smell that's going to greet you.

It was going well. They seemed calm and relaxed, which I put down to them not having all their friends and family gawping at them. Plus, I didn't get the impression they were religious, so these surroundings were probably more relaxing than being in a church. And the good thing about getting married this way is that every time one of them puts a wash on at home they'll get a flashback of their special day and the memory will stay fresh.

At this point they both put their dirty laundry into one machine, joining their smells together to become one. They then helped each other to add the cleaning detergent and fabric conditioner. Never mind a white wedding, this was a whiter than white wedding. Then together they inserted the dollar token to start the wash. I told them to select the ten-minute wash cycle in order to air their dirty linen and get everything off their chests about each other that annoys them.

KARL: It's not all going to be rosy. You're going to have arguments and that's a fact. So, Angie, is there anything Jon does that annoys you and you'd like him to stop?

ANGIE: I would like him to stop leaving his dirty clothes everywhere. I can't tell if they're clean or dirty, so if you could just put them in the laundry basket when they're dirty and put them away when they're clean, please.

KARL: Alright, fair enough. Jon, anything that does your head in?

JON: Ummm . . . I would like you, whenever you get mad at me, to just relax a little bit. I'm going to mess up once in a while, you know.

KARL: Is that it?! She doesn't do anything else? Be honest, I don't believe there's nothing else that Angie does that drives you up the wall.

JON: I don't think so, not really.

KARL: What?! She doesn't ask for too much? She doesn't want you to go away on holiday all the time? She doesn't ask for a new car or new carpet?

JON: Nope.

KARL: Okay, what about the telly? Does she watch reality shows or . . .

JON: She does watch reality shows, yeah. I hate her judge shows, like *Judge Judy*. Judge Alex . . . Judge whoever else on TV, all those guys.

ANGIE: Well, he's always on Reddit. I don't like him being on Reddit all the time.

KARL: Reddit? I don't know what that is, but it's all coming out now, you see. Anything else? Are you sure she doesn't waste any money? She never comes home and says, 'I've bought this,' and you go, 'You've already got one of them, why do you want another one?'

JON: Every now and then.

KARL: Right, so there's something else she does.

ANGIE: I don't bargain shop. I go and get what I need no matter how much it is.

JON: And she spends way too much money on it.

KARL: So there's something else you've got to watch because money does cause arguments. See, he's looking a bit doubtful now, isn't he? Look at his face.

CHAROLETTE: Well, I'm looking at her face and I'm seeing her smiling. She loves him in spite of it all. No matter what, she wants him and needs him and loves him and can't live without him.

KARL: But is she thinking that because he's a bit of a walk-over? Seems like he's getting shat on from a great height all the time.

CHAROLETTE: Well, I think two different personalities are good.

Even though they had their differences they were happy to accept them and carry on with the wedding, so after taking the clothes from the washer we headed over to the tumble dryer where, for another dollar, they popped their clothes in to dry. Charolette then went through the vows.

CHAROLETTE: I would like you to hold hands. Jonathan, repeat after me: 'I, Jonathan, take thee, Angela, for my wife, today and forever. I give you all of my heart, all of my love and all of my happiness. I promise you I will never leave you, I will love you and trust in you, I will be honest and faithful to you all the days of my life. You're my best friend, you're my wife, you're my everything. I love you.' Jonathan and Angela, by the power vested in me by the state of Nevada I now pronounce you husband and wife. You may now sniff your bride.

And that was it. Just under an hour and they were married. It cost around $200,000 and took five days for the Indian wedding; this one lasted an hour, cost a couple of dollars and the end result was the same. Except Jon and Angie also got their washing done.

Kids

IT ALL STARTED in a hotel room in Tokyo. There was a knock at the door, and I didn't want to answer it in case it was one of the hotel staff. I didn't want them to see what I had in my room, as I knew it was against their rules. The problem was, if it was one of the staff and I didn't answer the door, they would let themselves in anyway, as I hadn't put the 'Do Not Disturb' sign up. I had no choice but to answer it. Luckily it was just Richard, the director.

'How are you feeling?'

'I'm knackered, as I've not slept much,' I said. Then I showed him my problem.

'What the . . . Why have you got a turtle in your bath!?'

I never thought anyone would have cause to say those words to me. And all because I went out to get a bite to eat. The plan was to get some food close to the hotel and then come straight back and get to bed to try and fight the jet lag. But that's not what happened. I headed off down one of the narrow side streets looking for somewhere that did takeaway noodles, and that's when I made eye contact with the Chinese softshell turtle. It was sitting on its own in a glass box, using all the energy it had trying to get out.

And this wasn't a pet shop, it was a restaurant where the turtle was waiting to be sacrificed for the next customer who had a taste for turtle hot pot. I felt bad for it, so I ended up going into TokyuHands (a homeware shop) to buy a cool box and then bought the turtle. I took it back to my hotel room, noodle free. I suppose if it had been a member of the hotel staff at my door I could have just told them it was a snack I had bought to munch on while I had a bath. Thinking about it now, I could probably have ordered another one of them on room service so it had a mate to play with. It's odd how the hotel rule book says you're not allowed pets in the room when they don't draw the line between pets and food in this country.

'What are you going to do with it?' asked Richard.

It was a question that had been on my mind all night, and I still had no idea. I'd been googling 'turtle + japan', but I couldn't find any kind of animal home or RSPCA kind of charity online. I just found instructions for how to cook them. Japan isn't a great place for any sort of animal to live, as they seem to eat everything here. I'm sure when they read the story of Noah and him getting the animals on the boat two by two they just think he's doing a weekly food shop. I know that dinosaurs were meant to have been wiped out by some giant meteorite, but there's a bit of me that wonders if it was the Japanese that ate them all.

'Have you got a name for it?' Richard asked.

'Tony.'

'How did you come up with that?'

'Tony the turtle. It just seems to roll off the tongue. Just like it'd be rolling off someone else's for tea if I hadn't saved it.'

I felt sick with tiredness, as I had been up and down all night worrying about the turtle. I kept hearing it paddling about in the bath and was worried that it was going to strangle itself on the chain that was attached to the plug. Then there were moments when it wasn't making any sound at all and that worried me even more. I was up and down checking that it was still breathing, which isn't easy when the creature in question is encased in a shell and you can't see its belly moving. It's funny, as for this part of my trip I was supposed to be thinking about kids and why I've never felt I wanted them. One of the main reasons I don't want kids is the fact that they take over your life. Tony was proof of this. I'd missed my tea the night before, hadn't slept properly all night and still hadn't had breakfast, all due to me worrying about him. This is how it would be if I had a kid. I've seen it with mates who have them who say, 'Oh, you should have kids, it's a life-changing experience.' But what does that mean? Losing a leg is a life-changing experience, but that doesn't mean you'd actually want to lose one. 'Oh, but you're missing out,' they say, as if they know what I want more than I do. Would they say to a gay bloke: 'Oh, you should get your hands on a nice pair of tits, you'd love it, mate'?

Having kids is the biggest decision you have to make in life, cos once you've had one, you can't send it back. And you don't get a chance to try it out first. It's a bit like Marmite – you might love it or you might hate it, but either way you can't just go and pop the lid back on if you don't like it. You can't read reviews before you commit to it like you can before you buy something on Amazon. In fact it's more like buying something off eBay where you don't know what you're going to get until it turns up. Everyone always says having kids is amazing, but people said that about the pyramids in Egypt and I didn't feel the same when I saw them. When people find out I'm not keen on having kids they ask me how Suzanne feels and whether she wants them. Once she mentioned that she would like to hear the patter of tiny feet around the flat, so I told her to get a dwarf cleaner. The problem is, she has these ideas one day and then gets bored of them the next. She hassled me for an ice-cream maker once, so we bought one and she only used it twice before it ended up in the cupboard under the sink. She couldn't do that with a baby, especially not now that the ice-cream maker is taking up all the space.

LIFE WITHOUT KIDS

We were in Tokyo to go to a fertility festival, and Richard said we had to get a move on. So I had to leave Tony the turtle in the bath for a few more hours and deal with him when we got back. We put the 'Do Not Disturb' sign on the door and headed off.

The Kanamara Matsuri festival happens once a year at the Kanayama shrine in Kawasaki. It's an event couples go to together to receive a kind of fertility blessing if they want to have kids. It was set up back in the Edo period in Japan (1600–1868), which made me think it was going to be a really traditional kind of affair, so I was surprised to be greeted by a man wearing a nob on his head. It didn't look like part of any kind of ancient tradition to me, he just looked like a dodgy low-rent *Doctor Who* character with a pink centre parting. He was waving a plastic penis about in his hand too. I wasn't sure if he was some kind of official at the festival or just a local nutter. There used to be a man on our estate called Mad John who did this sort of thing on the back of the 261 bus into Manchester, and he got put away for it.

There were loads of stalls selling all sorts of merchandise, all with the same theme – everything featured a nob on it in some way. Pens with nobs on the end, nob-shaped ice lollies, nob balloons and nob ornaments. It was great for the guy selling hot dogs, as he didn't have to make any extra effort. I bought a pack of Kama Sutra playing cards. Each card featured one of the Kama Sutra positions so they were ideal for playing 'poke her' with (good pun that).

You'd think we were at some kind of bachelor party, but this festival was supposed to be a celebration of fertility and procreation. I don't believe in things like this. I think staying at home eating asparagus would improve your chances of having a kid more than buying a novelty tea towel with a nob drawn on it. The reason they have all these nobs on things is down to a local legend. An old story goes that there was a sharp-toothed demon who fell in love with a beautiful young woman. She wasn't interested in him, and when she married another man the demon became so jealous he decided to move into her vagina (squatters' rights and all that). The night before her wedding, the demon got his revenge by biting off the penis of her husband when they were having sex. Everybody in the village was upset, so the story goes, and the local blacksmith decided to forge a steel phallus that they could trick the demon with. The demon bit into the steel phallus, broke his teeth and moved out of the girl's vagina for good. You could say she had an STD – a Sharp-Toothed Demon.

KARL'S Facts

An elephant's penis can grow up to five feet long, and they use it as an extra leg to swat away flies and to scratch their stomachs.

I met a local woman called Ai, who was hoping to have a kid soon and was at the festival to get a blessing. She told me she wanted a child as she didn't want to be alone in the future and was worried she was running out of time. Everyone always says you'll regret it if you don't have children, but what about regretting it if you do have them? If you decide to have kids, there is no guarantee that they will be there for you when you get older, especially since people don't tend to stay in the same city as their family any more. Another reason people give for wanting kids is to carry on the family name, but that doesn't interest me at all. I'm not bothered about it because no one seems to be able to get my name right anyway. My post is always wrongly addressed to Mr Pillington, Mr Dilkington, Mr Pillinglington or Mr Tilkinson. The only good thing about it is that it makes it harder for someone to steal my identity, as they couldn't be sure which name goes with the address. Anyway, there are loads of Karl Pilkingtons out there in the world. I know this, as when I tried signing up to Skype recently I couldn't use my own name as it was already taken.

Ai told me that I would be getting involved in the festival by helping to carry one of the giant nobs in the phallic procession. The nob I was to help carry was a black one made of steel that was about four foot tall. It sat in a wooden shrine, which I had to carry on my shoulder through the town with the help of about twenty other men. The streets were crowded with the thousands of people who had turned up to the event, and Ai was pushed up so close against me there was a chance she'd end up carrying my child if we weren't careful. The crowd whooped as the shrine was lifted and we headed out onto the road. As the men chanted, the shiny phallus bobbed up and down, and thousands of onlookers took photos. I don't know who was guiding us but they weren't doing a very good job of it, and we must have looked like the Chuckle Brothers carrying a ladder, as we were moving around all over the place. It was like we were trying to do the hokey-cokey (more like the hokey-cocky) as we kept taking three steps forward and then two back. I got stubble burn on my face from the shaved head of the bloke in front of me who kept stumbling back. I was not enjoying the experience at all. I didn't see why I was carrying the bloody thing when it was Ai who wanted a kid, not me. Seeing as I don't want kids, carrying my bollocks around with me all the time seems a bit like unnecessary luggage, never mind the four-foot steel nob I had on my back.

As we walked I took it upon myself to try and explain to Ai how much her life would change if she had a kid. The cost of it all, the fact that she'd have no more free time and wouldn't be able to get a good night's sleep. Having kids is just like having some kind of disability, in a way, as things you could do before are suddenly no longer possible without a lot more messing around. In fact supermarket car parks are evidence that having kids is a disability, as they always have special parking spaces allocated for shoppers with kids. It's hard to find a parking space anywhere these days unless your legs are knackered or you have kids. You could say having a disability isn't really a disability at all any more, as it can also be an advantage. I wish they'd go one step further and allocate space for parents and their kids everywhere. On trains they could have their own carriage, so all the screaming and kicking of chairs could be contained within one area.

Ai agreed with me that having kids was a bit of a gamble and that it wasn't an easy decision for her to make.

We eventually got the shrine back to where we started. People were queuing to get a blessing and were ringing a bell and then writing a wish on a wooden plaque that was hanging inside a small shelter. Most of the wishes were for healthy babies and happy lives. As we walked over to the shelter I told Ai that I didn't think having a kid should be a difficult decision if you knew you wanted one. She took out her Sharpie pen, drew a question mark on her wooden plaque and hung it up alongside the hundred or so other wishes. I hope I didn't put her off ever having kids. I just wanted her to know for sure that she really wanted them and how it would change everything.

When we got to the hotel my back was really aching. I could have killed for a nice relaxing soak in a hot bath, but that wasn't possible due to the turtle crawling around in the tub. It was time to let Tony back into the wild. We popped him into the cool box and set off on a hunt for a lake or a stream where we could set him free. We did find a small lake, but when we took a closer look we noticed there were already turtles in it. They didn't look like Tony, so I didn't think it was a good idea to mix breeds. We drove for another hour before the sat nav showed up what looked like a large pond, but once we got closer it turned out to be in a privately owned park that was fenced off. By this point everyone was a bit pissed off with me. I'm pretty sure Michael the cameraman would have eaten the thing if he'd had a tin opener to get into it. It was 8 p.m. and we were almost three hours away from Tokyo by the time we spotted that there was water running underneath the motorway we were on. But it wasn't easy getting down to it, and we ended up parking the car and walking down a muddy hill towards the river, which was made all the more difficult because we were carrying the cool box containing Tony. When eventually we got there, I tipped him out of the box into the water and he scrambled away downstream. He looked happier than I'd seen him in all the time he'd been with me. He was suddenly full of energy and was swimming around all over the place. He even swam back to where we were standing and stuck his head out of the water as if to give me the nod and thank me for my trouble before shooting off. Even though I was totally wet through I felt quite happy. It felt like a huge weight had been lifted off my shoulders for the second time that day, after the four-foot steel nob – further evidence that I'm not the sort of person who could put up with the stresses of looking after a kid.

KARL'S Facts

The world's oldest turtle lived to be 255 years old. Adwaita died in an Indian zoo in 2006.

We got back to the hotel really late, but before I went to bed I cleaned Tony's food out of the bath and squeezed out the hotel towels that I had used to make little islands for him to climb up onto. I'd not even had him twenty-four hours, but now the place seemed a bit empty without him around. I suppose this is what happens when you have kids. After stressing you out for years and years they suddenly leave, and all you're left with is silence and the mess they made. I guess I would have kids if they came and went as quickly as that. That's how it works in the animal kingdom, and it's much better, as the parents aren't stuck with their young for years and years. Plus animals are usually running within minutes of being born, whereas human babies can't do anything. It makes me laugh when I hear about a baby being born premature – all babies are born premature, as they can't do anything for ages.

In Japan, people like me who aren't keen on the idea of having kids but would like to fill a hole in their life can buy a special doll that's designed for adults. The Primopuel is a sort of replacement child in the form of a doll that talks, laughs, asks for hugs, and cries if it doesn't get any. When I stopped off for some dinner in a local restaurant a small group of people had four of the dolls sat on their table. They're odd-looking things, sort of like furry Teletubbies with a hint of Wayne Rooney about them. I went over to

VINNIE

WHAT A LOAD OF PLANKS.

LAST PERSON TO FIND
AN ANT IS A NOB 'ED.

:NIPTON:

MARRIAGE

GETTING THE NOVELTY LAMP I'D BOUGHT IN THE CHRISTMAS SALE HOME WASN'T EASY.

NO, I SAID ALL HANDS ON DECK!

the table to get a closer look. One woman who was sat with her boyfriend told me that the doll was part of their family and she takes it everywhere she goes. As she was talking to me she kept patting the doll on the back and tickling it to get a reaction while her boyfriend just sat there, quietly looking on.

KARL: Do many men get involved with these, or is it more for women?

WOMAN: When he comes home at the end of the day, he says hello to me and then rushes to it, so I think he also enjoys it.

The boyfriend was saying nothing.

To be fair, she would probably make a good mother. She certainly seemed to pay more care and attention to the toy than some of the women on the estate I grew up around did with their real kids. I wonder if it's seeing kids grow up on my estate that has put me off having them. Seeing the struggles people had taking care of them. If someone announced they were pregnant, 'Congratulations' wasn't the first thing people said. 'Whose is it?' was the most common response. But the woman in the restaurant wasn't using it as a trial run for the real thing. They had no plans to actually have a baby. As far as they were concerned, this was their baby, and had been for eight years.

The dolls are fitted with a clock, a calendar and a thermometer and can make around 300 remarks like 'Good morning', 'Cold morning, isn't it?' and 'Happy Christmas'.

They are clever gadgets, but they were starting to do my head in, as they kept interrupting when I was talking to the 'parents', going off like a faulty alarm clock. One of them kept saying 'Let's play' and then started laughing to itself. Another woman's doll started to cry, so she had to pick it up and hug it to make it stop. It's bad enough when real kids start screaming their tripe out in Starbucks cos they can't have a 'babyccino', but it would be even more annoying if the racket you could hear was coming from a toy. But just like a real mum with a real kid, the noise coming from the toy didn't seem to bother her. Kids are like farts in that way. They never seem to bother the owner as much as they bother everyone else.

I found it odd how something that isn't real got so much attention, but then again I suppose you could say the same thing about me, as I pay too much attention to my phone. I check it as soon as I wake up then throughout the day I'm always looking for messages, making sure it has enough power, checking for updates and browsing for the latest apps. The only difference is that I don't have to hug it to stop it ringing. But at least my phone serves a purpose and I can use it to get hold of people. Where's the payback from the doll? With a real kid you might get some joy from it when it smiles or when it's learned a new word, but this woman had had the same doll for eight years and the only changes she has seen have been the batteries. One good reason I can see for having a kid is that you would always have someone to send on errands or to help clean the car, but these dolls do nothing but distract you from what you're trying to do. I would not be happy if Suzanne had one of these dolls and I came in from work to find there was no food in the fridge for tea and the house was a mess because the doll had been having a bad day. I'm telling you, it would be straight in the bin. And surely you can't keep on loving something when it isn't giving you any real love back? You may as well carry a brick around with you. When I was growing up there was a woman on my estate who used to push a pram around that held a bucket with a face drawn on it. It was a bit mad, but at least a bucket might come in useful now and again.

KARL'S *Facts* Most pregnancies last for about nine months but it is possible to be pregnant for a whole year. The world's longest pregnancy lasted 375 days.

The next day I was going to have a check-up at a local clinic to see if my sperm were even capable of making kids. Who knows? All this talk of me not wanting any and I might not even be able to, anyway. I was sure that if the test results said I couldn't have kids that I wouldn't be too bothered, but then sometimes when you find out you can't do something you suddenly want that thing more. Like the athletes in the Paralympics. I often wonder how many of those people with disabilities would have devoted their life to pushing their bodies so hard if they didn't have a disability in the first place.

I got to the clinic, where I met the doctor. He led me down a corridor and into a little cubicle, where he gave me a plastic cup and showed me a selection of rude magazines and DVDs to help me on my way. He apologised that they were all in Japanese. I thought it was an odd thing to say, cos I wasn't planning on reading them or trying to follow a storyline, but then I realised it was probably because they weren't that rude, as anything slightly dodgy had been pixellated out. What's the point in having a rude magazine if the rude bits can't be seen? I ended up opting for a DVD. The batteries in the remote were knackered, so with my trousers round my ankles I took a battery out of the clock on the wall and put it into the remote so that I could get past the main screen on the DVD. Which was a slight mood-killer. The DVDs weren't that good either, as they were also pixellated. It was like watching an episode of bloody *Crimewatch*! I may as well have been staring at some mosaic bathroom tiles. And it was stressful enough knowing the doctor was waiting outside for my specimen, never mind the film crew, who were also waiting for me to perform. I normally get stressed out when the doctor asks me for a urine sample in case I'm not able to deliver the goods, but this was a whole new level. I can't even do a burp on demand. I wonder if this is why pandas struggle to procreate, with people constantly watching them. As soon as one fancies a bit, the *News at Ten* team turn up with cameras to report on a possible new arrival among the endangered species.

KARL'S *Facts*

Before the boys of the Etoro tribe of Papua New Guinea can be called adults, they must consume the semen of their elders.

After some time I eventually managed to do the business. I don't know how long I was in the cubicle, as I'd taken the battery out of the clock for the remote. I came out with the goods in a bag held high, looking like one of those pictures you see of proud fishermen holding up a big shark they've caught. The doctor took the cup off me and set to inspecting the contents under a powerful microscope. It was weird seeing it on a computer screen. Sperm the size of tadpoles, all whizzing about like moths around a light-bulb. They looked like they were having a great time, but seeing them didn't make me feel broody at all. I just found it odd to think I was one of them once. I suppose life was more simple back then, living inside a bollock, just zooming around with all your nameless relatives with no arguing, no stress, no complications. No matter who you are or where you're from, we're all the same at that point. People always say schooldays are the happiest days of your life, but I disagree. I think my happiest period was when I was a sperm. I still can't believe I was the one that won the race to get to the egg. Out of millions of sperm how the hell did I win?! I won the toughest race going, where you get nothing for coming second, and yet I've never won a race since. I'm just not the sort who rushes about anywhere. I never rush to the buffet when I'm at a hotel on holiday, I've never rushed onto a plane or to get my luggage off the carousel, I don't think I've ever even run for a bus. I must have won the race as a sperm because I got pushed to the front by all the other millions of sperm who didn't want to leave the comfort of the bollock. Either that or I came last in the previous race and just stayed near the exit of my dad's nob until the next one began. The doctor talked me through what he was seeing under the microscope. It was quite complicated.

> DOCTOR: The normal range in terms of semen volume is over 1.5 millilitres. Your semen volume is 4.6 millilitres. Sperm density is measured in the number of sperm per millilitre and normal density is over 15 million. You have 42 million, so this is a very excellent result. Your sperm motility rate was 42.2 per cent, so a little lower than the normal rate.

I was quite happy with that. I'd released 193 million sperm. How mad is that? That's like the whole population of Brazil in my balls, and the way they were dancing about on the screen I'd say it was carnival season. The only thing that wasn't great was the motility rate. The doctor explained that meant my sperm weren't always travelling in a straight line; they were going all over the place instead and were a bit erratic. Which proved to me that it definitely was my sperm we were looking at, as I tend to be the same when it comes to most things in life. If I go to the shops I never take the direct route. I like to potter about a bit and try new routes. I never can focus on one thought; I have loads going on in my head at once. They were only sperm, but I was proud they took after me.

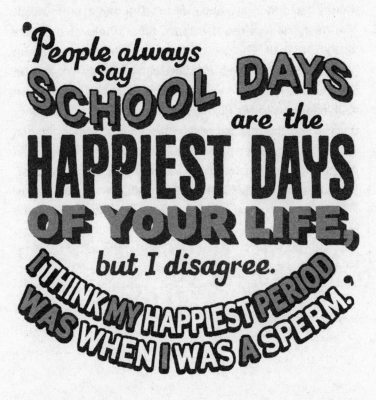

'People always say SCHOOL DAYS are the HAPPIEST DAYS OF YOUR LIFE, but I disagree. I THINK MY HAPPIEST PERIOD WAS WHEN I WAS A SPERM.'

Even though I got good results it didn't make me want to suddenly dash home to knock a load of little Pilkingtons out. At the end of the day, just because I can have kids, it doesn't mean I'd be a good dad. Plenty of people who have driving licences are shit at driving. This was probably as close as I wanted to get to seeing one of my kids, so I asked for a photo of my sperm that I could pop in my wallet like other blokes do with photos of their kids. Wallets are more use as photo albums these days, as kids cost you so much money you don't have any money left to put in your wallet. You might as well use the space for a photo of the ones who spend it all. The doctor said he couldn't take a closeup photo, but he did give me a card with all my sperm info on it. As usual, my name was spelled wrongly on the front. It was made out to Mr Pilkigton. I wasn't sure then whether it was a spelling mistake or whether I'd just been looking at someone else's sperm. Before leaving I asked what would happen to the sperm and he said it would be disposed of. It worries me a little bit that I just walked away and left it. If I get a visit from a Kasumi Pilkigton in twenty years I'll be livid.

THE MIRACLE OF BIRTH

Richard wanted me to experience the miracle of birth, as he thought it might make me realise what I was missing. For this we had to head to Bali to go to a special clinic called Bumi Sehat. It's a non-profit organisation, a sort of village where women go to have a natural birth without drugs or medical intervention. When we got there I met a woman called Ibu Robin Lim, who had set up the clinic. She explained the services they provide, which include general health check-ups, emergency care, antenatal classes, midwifery and breastfeeding support.

> IBU ROBIN: Our focus here is on natural childbirth. We don't use epidurals or anaesthesia and we don't do Caesareans. If there is a need for that, we transport. We do water births and we try to put flowers in the room and float flowers in the water when the baby is being born. We sing to the babies as they are coming into the world because we acknowledge that it's not just a medical experience, it's also a miracle. We like to greet the babies as souls.

I wouldn't be happy with that. Petals floating about in the bath blocking up the plughole. It does me head in having to unblock the shower from Suzanne's moulting head. And what's it all for? They'll be chucking a few frogs and a couple of ducks in there next. Saying that, I had a turtle in my bath in Japan so I can hardly talk.

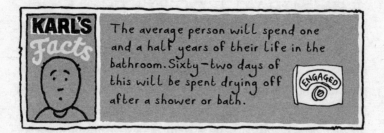

KARL'S Facts

The average person will spend one and a half years of their life in the bathroom. Sixty-two days of this will be spent drying off after a shower or bath.

ENGAGED

Ibu Robin pointed to the organisation's logo on the wall.

KARL: That's some logo, isn't it?

IBU ROBIN: Yeah, I've been told it's mildly pornographic and that we should change it to something a little more mellow, but all of our patients, of all religions and faiths, love our logo, so we're not going to change it.

It was a good logo. Sometimes logos are like a little puzzle and it takes ages to work out what it's for, but not this one. It was a pregnant woman with her legs akimbo and a baby coming out of her. I could have done with it when I was at the sperm clinic a few days ago. It would have got me going more than the pixellated stuff they had on offer. We were at the clinic so I could get involved and help out in whatever way I could. Ibu Robin told me to be on standby, as you can't always predict when a baby will be coming. As I was going to be spending three days at the clinic I decided to keep a diary to give me something to do while I waited for the babies to arrive.

Day 1

The clinic was quite basic, but it was a friendly, busy place with a never-ending queue of pregnant women arriving for check-ups on high-pitched mopeds that sounded like mosquitoes. I imagine it's going to be a long few days. I'm hoping to see a baby being born, but who knows if that will happen. Ibu Robin said a baby will come when it is ready, which is proof that they take over your life before they're even born. It was like waiting in the house when you're due a delivery. You know it's coming, but nobody seems to be able to tell you when. I had some fence panels delivered a couple of weeks ago and they couldn't give me a rough idea of the time of arrival. They just said sometime between 7 a.m. and 6 p.m. I don't know why it still has to be this way. The flight to Bali from Japan had a predicted arrival time, so why can't a bloke dropping off some fence panels manage it?! I needed the loo all day but had been putting it off. As soon as I couldn't wait any more and sat my arse down on the toilet seat, the bell went. It was the man with the fence panels. His drop-off had to wait while I did mine.

It was hot in the clinic, so I went outside to sit in the shade and play with a local cat until Ibu Robin gave me a job of sweeping up and fluffing the pillows. I didn't mind. I prefer having something to do rather than just sitting around feeling like a spare part and getting in the way. After I'd finished my job, I was asked to go with a midwife who was doing a home visit to check how some young parents and their baby were getting on. When we got there, the midwife weighed the chunky baby, who was called Radha, and chatted to the mother. She told me that it's a custom in Bali never to let a baby's feet touch the ground for the first six months of its life. To be honest I'm all for this. If I had a baby I wouldn't let it on the floor, the sofa or the carpet. I'd be up for keeping it in a box until it was less accident-prone, just so any sick and crap, and spilled food and drink wouldn't stain the furnishings. I'm quite house-proud. I've worked hard over the years to get a house I'm happy with, so the last thing I want is a baby coming along making a shitty mess. There's that saying 'Don't cry over spilled milk' – well, I'm afraid I would, cos it bleeding stinks once it goes off.

The midwife said it would be good if I did a bit of baby-sitting for the couple so they could nip next door to see their friends and have a much-needed break. I thought the mam and dad wouldn't be keen on the idea of their one and only three-month-old baby that can't be put down being left with me, a stranger with no experience, but before I could point this out they were gone. I've never babysat on my own before. I think it's worse than looking after your own kid, as there's the added responsibility. If it's your own kid and you drop it, it's pretty bad, but if you drop someone else's, it's really, really bad. It's like driving a hire car. I'm always more worried driving one, as just a little scratch or dent can end up costing you a fortune when you return it, whereas when it's your own car you have no one to answer to.

I carried Radha around the garden for a while showing it various things to keep its mind busy so it wouldn't start crying. I showed it a few cats, a chicken that was wandering about, some guttering and a breeze block. At the end of the day it doesn't know what anything is, so everything should be of interest. My arms started to ache, so I went inside and popped it on the bed. I noticed a lot of jobs were unfinished around the house. They had obviously built an extension to make room for Radha but clearly hadn't had time to finish it due to the all-consuming thing in their life, a black hole, in a nappy, that sucks up every waking hour. It startled me with the odd scream and crying fit for a few seconds before going quiet again. What was all that about? How can it get so fed up it actually cries and screams but then just totally stops? They're not right in the head, babies. Some people feel joy being around them; I just get a headache. They cry far too much, and the noise stresses me out so I can't think straight, and then I'm in no position to sort out an emergency if one was to happen. This is why I could never be an ambulance driver. The siren would stress me out too much.

Richard said I should talk to her as she needed to be stimulated. I didn't see the point in that, as she didn't understand her own language yet, never mind English. I've heard that pregnant women can wear belts these days that have little speakers placed on the stomach so you can play the baby nursery rhymes and stories! Parents seem to be obsessed with teaching their kids earlier and earlier, but I think it's better to let them learn in their own time. It's like they're brainwashing the kids. There'll come a time when a pregnant woman isn't going to be woken up at night with the baby kicking in her belly, it'll wake her up doing the two times table from inside her. Next they'll be making one of them belts for men to fit on their bollocks to teach their sperm the alphabet.

Richard told me to try singing a nursery rhyme, but I didn't know what to sing. These days a lot of them have been altered to be more politically correct. The lyrics to 'Baa Baa Black Sheep' have been changed to avoid any upset. The latest I'd heard was that the rhyme 'Rain, rain, go away, come again another day' had been dropped, as people don't think it has a good environmental message. Now it's something more along the lines of 'Rain, rain, come again, we need more rain every day'. My brother was all for bringing nursery rhymes up to date. This is one he taught me:

> Mary, Mary, quite contrary,
> How does your garden grow?
> I live in a flat,
> You stupid twat,
> So how the f**k should I know!

Radha started crying and wouldn't stop. I couldn't stand it. I have really sensitive ears and can't cope with loud, sharp noises. My mam says I wasn't much of a crier when I was a baby, and I'm sure it's because my own noise would have annoyed me. I asked Richard to go and get its mam and dad from next door. I couldn't be doing with it. I'd thought Tony the turtle was a handful, but he was an angel compared to this. It was a proper little taste of what it would be like to have a kid of my own.

KARL'S Facts

Newborn babies cry without tears until they are several weeks old.

We went back to the clinic and found Ibu Robin working her way through the backlog of people who had come in for check-ups. She invited me in to see a woman who was at forty weeks and was getting a scan. Ibu Robin let me have a feel of her belly so I could make out different parts of the baby. She asked me to feel around for a foot and then pointed out where the head was so I could have a grab at it. It was like on Christmas Eve when you have a feel of your presents to see if you can work out what they are.

Ibu Robin had to leave again, as someone had called her, but she said it sounded like a false alarm so I shouldn't build my hopes up just yet about seeing a birth. I couldn't be doing with a job when you're on call all the time. How do you ever relax? If I was her I would charge for any false alarms to stop people taking the piss. It won't be long before she'll be getting people calling saying, 'Ibu Robin! Quick! I think my waters are breaking . . . Oh, and if you pass the shops on the way can you get me a Mars Bar, a can of Coke and a packet of crisps.' They'll be using you to do errands. People always take advantage so that eventually services have to be stopped altogether.

Day 2

I didn't sleep very well last night cos my back was aching. I think it was due to carrying big baby Radha yesterday. It was a right dead weight. No wonder they're upholding the tradition of not putting it on the floor; it would probably crack the floor tiles if they let it loose.

I was worried that my back pain could be the return of kidney stones, as that was how it started when I had them back in 2007. I was thinking of asking Ibu Robin to use the scanner to see if she could see anything. Kidney stones gave me the worst pain I've ever experienced. The doctor told me that it was worse than giving birth. As luck would have it, there were a few people in the clinic giving acupuncture to the pregnant women with bad backs, so seeing as not much was going on I gave it a go. The woman who worked on me asked what level of pain my back was giving me from one to ten, ten being extremely painful. I struggled to answer this question. It definitely would have been a ten when I had kidney stones, but I don't remember anyone asking me the question then, as I think the way I was swearing at the top of my voice in A&E gave them a good idea of how I was feeling. But, anyway, why isn't the fact that I've bothered to report the problem enough to show it's bothering me? I shouldn't have to start giving my pain points as if I'm judging it on *Strictly Come Dancing*. I've said it before, but until we can exchange bodies with another person I don't think we can really know how we feel. I might think I feel good, but if I was transported into some healthy bloke I might find I was actually feeling shite. Maybe I'm just used to feeling bad. I gave my pain a seven.

I lay on my front and the woman popped about twelve pins into me, on the back of my legs, my back, my hands and ears. I looked like a hedgehog with alopecia. She then put some herbs on the end of the bed and set fire to them. This made me nervous, as I've got quite a hairy back – one little stray spark and I'd go up like a forest fire.

I lay there for about twenty minutes watching mothers doing baby yoga with their children. This is another strange new trend. I know babies need good strong legs to walk on, but at these classes they had them working on their abs. I don't think babies should have six-packs. I wonder if this is why parents have trouble controlling their kids these days. They can't chastise them any more because they're scared their kid is so strong it'll get them in a headlock. After twenty minutes the needles were removed and I was told I probably wouldn't feel any benefit until the next session.

Ibu Robin took me to see a couple who had had a lotus birth. On the way she explained that this is when the umbilical cord is left attached after birth so it can drop off naturally. Ibu Robin said this is better for the baby, as it can lessen the chance of infection and it allows a complete transfer of blood into the baby at a time when it needs it the most. We got to the house where they were staying. Pan-pipe music was playing on the stereo. There was a young couple from Russia who had come to Bali especially to have a natural birth. The mother was sat on the bed with the baby and the placenta was in a little box. She took the lid off so I could see it. It looked like a little garlic naan bread. She had spices in the box to stop the rotting placenta stinking the place out.

Ibu Robin told me some people eat it once it's detached! For me, this is when it starts getting silly. 'Some make pâté from it,' she told me. What is going on?! There's a Tesco Express on every street corner these days, so if you need something to pop on some crackers you should have somewhere to go. The way I see it is if you can't afford normal pâté and need to start eating placenta, you shouldn't have had a kid in the first place! It's mental. People treating it like some sort of 'meal deal' that comes with a brand-new baby. There's loads of decent food not getting eaten cos of 'use by' and 'sell by' dates yet people are eating pâté made from placenta.

'Some take it home and plant it in the garden,' Ibu Robin said. 'Are you allowed to take it through the airport?' I asked. Ibu Robin didn't answer me, as she was too busy checking on the baby, but I'm pretty sure placenta isn't on the list of things you're allowed in your hand luggage. I had a banana taken off me on my last flight, so surely a placenta must be a no-no. Why on earth do people want to bury it anyway? I have enough problems with foxes without burying bits of old placenta for them to dig up. Surely all your attention and time should be spent on looking after the new baby?!

It's funny that all this natural birth and lotus business is about giving the baby a stress-free welcome into the world, but then the baby will have to fly back to Russia, which is about an eleven-hour flight. That ain't gonna be stress-free, is it? I just think it's an excuse to have a nice holiday in Bali. If I did have a kid I can imagine Suzanne pulling this trick, saying, 'I want what's best for the baby,' while stashing a bottle of Ambre Solaire in her bag. If the best thing was to go to Alaska and give birth in an igloo, would they be as keen?

Day 3

The midwife who got me to babysit the other day was on duty. She informed me that a woman who was in labour had just come in. She asked me to help keep the woman calm. She suggested I use this thing that looked like a sort of hot cigar to warm the soles of her feet and help the contractions. It all seemed pretty basic to me. I watch *Casualty*, *Holby City* and *House*, and they have all the top-notch machinery and devices even though it's not real, while this is real life and I'm using a bloody cigar to help deliver a baby! The woman started to make quite a bit of noise. I didn't know what to do with myself. I really felt like I shouldn't be there. I actually got up and left at one point, as I didn't like it. People talk about 'fight or flight' and I'm definitely a 'flight', but Richard said I had to stay, as this was what we had come all this way for me to witness.

The woman's name was Ni Nyoman, and her boyfriend, Gede, was by her side. I think I was more stressed than him. I stopped using the cigar on Ni Nyoman's feet and used it on myself instead to try and calm my nerves. It was around 9.30 p.m. and with all the noise she was making I was sure the baby was going to be out soon. I found myself doing heavy breathing. Another midwife noticed I was a bit stressed, so she gave me some essence under my tongue to help calm me down.

KARL: I don't know how women can be bothered going through all this.

MIDWIFE: (*laughs*) But it's a little different when you're the one having the hormonal rush. You don't get the adrenalin and the endorphins that she gets. You guys get the nervousness, and that's harder to channel and deal with. She's getting a surge of endorphins that allows her to kind of be more spacey and cope with the pain, and the adrenalin is giving her the energy to do it, so she's in a completely altered state.

KARL: I had kidney stones and I can remember the actual pain.

MIDWIFE: Right, because you weren't having oxytocin released through your uterus. I have heard from women who have had both a natural childbirth and kidney stones that they would give birth a hundred times again before they would have kidney stones because it was so horrible. Labour contractions are like a wave, they come and they go, but kidney stones, it's not a wave, it's sharp and it's constant.

KARL: Yep. Constant.

MIDWIFE: So it's very different here. It's like a wave of contractions that last about a minute and then it calms and she has something positive to look forward to. She has a baby at the end of it. I don't think it's so positive to pass kidney stones.

KARL: No, you're right. I didn't even get to hold my stones once they were removed.

Knowing all this put me at ease, plus the herbal essence she had given to me had kicked in, so I went to sleep for a couple of hours on one of the empty hard beds. I nodded off to Ni Nyoman's groans. Next thing I knew, Richard was waking me up to say the baby might be out soon. It was after 1 a.m. and Ni Nyoman was still screaming. They should rename this place Bawli, with all the noise.

After close to eight hours, Ni Nyoman was making different breathing noises, a more frustrated kind of huffing, and she had a screwed-up face that was a bit like the face I make when I'm trying to separate shopping trolleys in Sainsbury's. I think she had had enough by now and just wanted it out, and to be fair so did I.

She started to push. More family members had appeared around the bed now, so it was a struggle to see what was happening. It was like being in the scrum in a rugby game and trying to keep an eye on the ball. I kept getting a glimpse of the head popping out. I'd seen it time and time again on nature programmes, but here it was happening right in front of my eyes. She gave one final push and the whole thing flopped out into the hands of the midwife. And that was that.

KARL'S *Facts*

In ancient Greece, children of wealthy families were dipped in olive oil at birth to keep them hairless throughout their lives.

I didn't know what to make of it. I'd been asleep just minutes before and I think the baby was probably more alert
than I was. All that messing around was over with. It's like
a Sunday lunch, where hours of preparation and sweating
and waiting lead up to just a few minutes of eating. Richard
wanted me to explain what it was like watching the birth
and what I was feeling, but I've never been good at that sort
of thing. All I remember thinking as the baby fell out was,
'Jesus, what the fuck is going on!' I suppose swearing was
invented for moments like this, as well as for when you're in
pain with kidney stones.

They named the baby Fidelia. I wanted to suggest they
call it Fidelia2013 instead so that it has a better chance of
getting its own name on Skype.

RAISING KIDS A DIFFERENT WAY

I don't think kids really need to be as much work as some parents seem to make them. I've been to a lot of places around the world, and whenever I visit a tribe or a community in the middle of nowhere I always notice how the kids never seem to be half as much trouble for them as they are in our part of the world. The mums and dads in the tribes aren't constantly rushing about taking little Emburkoo to violin lessons, chess class or ballet, as he's probably too busy helping out catching food and building the village with his dad. I've also never come across a kid in a tribe who has a wheat allergy or is allergic to nuts. I've always wondered whether if I had grown up in a place like that, I'd have had kids myself. I probably would have.

On this next part of the trip we were going to find out if that was the case. We headed off to Wakitobi, which is just a few hours from Bali, to meet with a community of sea gypsies who have roamed the waters for at least 400 years. They all live in wooden huts on stilts out in the sea, around a kilometre from land. It was a right mad sight. From our boat we got a view of a massive sprawling wooden platform of homes like in that film *Waterworld* with Kevin Costner. If the tribe had any money, they'd be the ideal target market for Ronseal wood preserver. Before our boat had even reached the stilted pier I could see kids everywhere running around on the decks and bridges that connected all the huts together, diving off the edge into the sea like lemmings to come to greet us. I'm guessing these kids learn to swim before they can walk. As we got closer, they could obviously hear the boat engine, because more and more kids appeared from nowhere to see who the visitors were. Young faces peered around every corner and every crack in the wooden huts. It was like a scene from *Annie*. There wasn't an adult in sight.

As I climbed up from the boat they didn't seem to be worried about a stranger entering their area. They were all smiles and they looked healthy enough. Not a fat kid among them due to all the playing outdoors and a diet of nothing but fish.

One of the kids grabbed me by the hand and led me through the maze of huts, where we passed more kids playing with old tyres, seashells and pet crabs. Another reason I would be worried about having a kid is the cost, but here that's not such a problem, as another mouth just means an extra fish to catch. No call for Xboxes or DVD players. Living in an area surrounded by water means they don't need expensive trainers or even socks, as they're not worth the trouble of taking them off and putting them back on all the time.

The young lad led me into one of the many small homes. There was just one room, but it was like *Where's Wally?* trying to find the parent in the mass of kids' faces. The families must be quite close here. They have to be, as they all live together in one small room. I guess they talk to each other more than we do at home too, where kids hide themselves away in their bedrooms surrounded by PlayStations, laptops and DVD box sets. I think this is why prison is no longer that much of a threat to young kids these days, as they don't go out of the house a lot anyway due to their parents being so terrified of letting them play outside. They could probably continue to watch TV and play on their Xboxes just as much in prison.

The kid who had taken me into the hut spread a yellowy-green gunk onto my face to protect me from the sun, as the plan was for me to join them out in their boat while they fished for food. It was refreshing to see kids being useful. I don't see kids doing much to help out back at home any more. I used to run errands and wash my dad's car, but today's kids are straight on the phone to ChildLine if they're asked to put the kettle on.

The sea gypsy kids don't go to school. Instead they learn everything they need to know from their parents, which is pretty much the way I learned most things. I did quite well at infant school, when my brain was still new and worked faster and had a fresh memory like a new laptop, but unfortunately the teachers wasted that decent stage of my brain teaching me about 'Humpty Dumpty' and 'Tubby the Tuba'. By the time I went to secondary school the best years of my brain were over. To be fair, all the kids seem to struggle, as they try to teach you too much. The fact that you no longer have just one teacher like you do in infant school proves to me that they teach you too much in secondary school. If one teacher couldn't remember it all what hope did I have!

The kid's dad joined us to go fishing and he was wearing a pair of sea goggles he had made out of some driftwood. It took about ten minutes to get into the kayak without it capsizing before we headed off to the fishing location. Rather than using rods, they had made a type of spear gun from wood with an elastic band to fire the arrow. They were underwater for ages, to the point that it made me wonder if these people were born with gills. Richard told me the sea gypsies have managed to learn to slow down their heart rate and stay underwater for up to five minutes. How amazing is that? I'm useless in water. I wake up at night drowning in my own saliva.

KARL'S Facts

A German free diver broke the world record for the longest time underwater with no air. He lasted twenty minutes and twenty-two seconds.

I'm sure some people would say that it's wrong that the sea gypsy kids are not getting a chance to live out their full potential, but there are loads of kids at home who don't get to do that either for one reason or another. Parents work really hard caring for their kids, but they still get measles, chickenpox, broken bones, the upsets of relationships, schooling, college and university, and then they eventually leave home to get a job for the local council operating a leaf blower. So are the sea gypsies really worse off?

After catching a few fish, we headed back, and the young lad went back to playing with his mates while his mother set about cooking the fish. That's another thing that's different about this place: the kids don't get a choice of meal, they get whatever they managed to catch. The amount of times I've heard kids having fits about what they will and won't eat, the judges on *MasterChef* are easier to please. On my flight back from my last trip away I was sat next to an old woman who was well into her 90s. When the stewards came round serving different types of juices, she picked the guava juice, as she said she'd never tried it before, yet these days kids have had everything by the time they're ten. I don't know why this is happening when we're living longer than ever. Wouldn't it be better to spread all the fun stuff out so you can have things to look forward to? I hadn't had pasta until I was in my 20s and it was all the better for it. And it's getting to a point now where kids get more choices than adults do. I went to a restaurant last year that had fish fingers on the menu. I thought, 'Oh, I just fancy that,' but when I tried to order them I was told I couldn't have them. 'Why not?' I said. 'It's on the menu.' Turns out I couldn't have them as they were for kids only. Why?! It's adults that are paying for them. If I'm willing to pay I should be able to have fish fingers and Arctic roll if I want! Why are kids getting special treatment? It's not like I asked for some blended pumpkin baby food with a rusk; fish fingers are eaten by grown-ups too. When I was a kid I wouldn't even be allowed in a restaurant, and yet now they're getting their own menu. I suppose that's a reason for having a kid. I could get some bloody fish fingers and pretend they were for the kid. It's happening more and more. Most pubs these days are aimed more at kids than adults, with their booster seats, slides and swings, kiddie menus, crayons and paper. They're basically crèches that serve booze. You can't get away from it. I reckon if I went to a strip bar now the women dancing about on stage with their tits out would offer a breastfeeding service.

RECREATING THE EXPERIENCE

Of all my experiences on this trip, the thing that stayed with me the most was the feeling I had when I had to babysit big Radha in Bali. That really did make me realise that having a baby was not for me. I only looked after it for an hour, I didn't even have to worry about feeding or clothing it, but it was the way it took up all my time and gave me no chance to think about other things that convinced me. I really think it would be a good idea if people were given the chance to get a taste of what parenthood is actually like before going through with it: a kind of try-before-you-buy experience. Everyone always wonders if they'd make good parents, but they never question whether they really want to be parents. Yes, I'm sure there can be plenty of nice moments when you have a child, but there's another side to everything. Hearing a baby laugh might be a lovely thing, but if I was woken up in the middle of the night by my baby laughing to itself, it would bloody terrify me.

I wanted to test out my try-before-you-buy concept for real, so we headed to LA to see if we could find a young couple who were thinking about having kids any time soon and were willing to give my idea a run. I met with two actors called Joe and Dave, who would be playing the roles of tod-dlers. I wanted them to be toddlers, as I think that's the age when kids really start giving you the runaround. It would be Joe and Dave's job to act like children for around twenty-four hours. To help make the experience feel even more real, I went for Joe and Dave because they were dwarves, which meant they could hide in lots of the places kids could get to, and would feel more like the real thing when the parents were having to bend down to give them food or dress them. But it was a safe option too, as Joe and Dave are adults and if the couple forgot to close a door or left some matches or alcohol within reach by accident, they wouldn't be in any danger. Joe and Dave were both dads, so they were well aware of the sorts of things kids get up to.

It wasn't cheap hiring two dwarves in LA due to the amount of Hollywood movies that require them. There's non-stop movie work for dwarves these days if they want it. I think it's because a lot of people are watching movies on iPads – they fit on the screen better. Still, paying the fee for this experience would be a lot cheaper than adding a new member to your family. The latest research shows it costs around £200,000 to clothe, feed and educate one child in a lifetime, so a couple of grand paying for the trial was pennies.

The couple who were willing to give my idea a go were called Sam and Megan. They lived in a two-bedroomed apartment on the third floor, which isn't what some would call a child-friendly scenario. But saying that, people are so over-cautious these days around their kids that I think it'll only be a matter of time before parents are choosing to live in a bouncy castle just so there are no rough edges for Tarquin to bang his precious little head on. I couldn't see much outside space where they could let their kids play if they were to have any. Their kids wouldn't have anything like the freedom of the sea gypsies, who can run and swim about where they want. In LA they would need a safe fenced-off garden with enough room for swings, slides and a trampoline that could be monitored from a kitchen window. Pretty much every garden on my street has a trampoline. No wonder crime rates are up. Trampolines make it too easy for burglars to bounce from garden to garden like Zebedee from *The Magic Roundabout*.

We got up to the third floor and knocked on the door.

KARL: Megan?

MEGAN: Hello.

KARL: Is it shoes off?

MEGAN: No.

KARL: Even for the kids it's alright?

MEGAN: Kids are okay.

I remember thinking they seemed pretty relaxed. I always ask people to remove their shoes before coming into my house. The gas man who comes to read the meter always pulls a face when I ask him to take his shoes off, as he has lace-up shoes, but that isn't my fault. He should wear some Velcro-strapped trainers that would be quick and easy to remove. I can't be the only person who asks him to take his shoes off. It's not like I've asked him to come round to read my meter. He's invited himself, so he should go by my rules. He always asks to use our toilet too. He must be visiting so many houses, yet it's always in our place that he needs to empty his bowels. I blame Suzanne for buying extra-soft toilet paper. If we replaced it with the cheap scratchy stuff I'm sure he'd go somewhere else. I never went to the loo at school for that reason: they used to have hard tracing-paper-type stuff that was like wiping your arse with a crisp packet. The head teacher using his cane on your arse was less painful than wiping it with that stuff. No one I know ever used the toilet because of that paper. It was only ever used by the music teacher, not to wipe their arse but to make kazoos with.

It's not just the gas meter man either. Builders always ask to use our toilet too. I think it must just be for a pee, and then I see them going upstairs with a newspaper under their arm. They're up there for a good twenty-five minutes. It's not right, especially when you're paying them by the hour.

As I entered the front room I noticed straight away that all the windows were open. I pointed out that this would not be safe if they had real kids. I wanted them to take this seriously and treat Joe and Dave as if they really were their kids.

KARL: This is Joe, he's six.

MEGAN: Hi, nice to meet you.

KARL: That's Dave, he's five. I want it to be like a proper experiment for you, so no messing about, treat them as if they were your own. Deal with them if they're naughty and treat them like, you know, you're in charge here. As soon as I walked in I saw a window was open, but you know you've got to remember, these kids are five and six.

> SAM: Okay.
>
> KARL: So just look after them and see how you get on.

On the way out I saw that there were loads of photos of Sam and Megan looking happy together on holidays, and photos with friends, which will be handy for when they have kids, as they probably won't see much of their friends any more.

Something that made me think they might actually be ready for parenthood was their fridge. They had loads of things stuck to the front of it – family photos and memos of future dates for family occasions. This would probably increase once they had kids, as people tend to stick their kids' doodles on their fridge doors too. We're always being told to eat less, but fridges are getting bigger and bigger. And it's probably just so parents can keep every bloody doodle and scrawl that their kid has ever done on display. When I was a kid my drawings used to get put straight in the bin as soon as I was finished with them. To be honest they belonged in the bin, as they weren't very good, but these days everything is kept. I've been into homes where the parents have run out of room on the fridge and so the drawings are all over the dishwasher too. They've spent fifty thousand pounds on a kitchen you can't see, as it's been wallpapered with shite drawings of purple dinosaurs with one leg.

As I was closing the door to leave, I heard Joe and Dave arguing over which bed they wanted. I was pleased, as this would really show Megan and Sam the reality of what they would be letting themselves in for if they had kids. People think it's all roses before they take the plunge and do it for themselves. I blame TV shows like *The Waltons* that show these happy loving families, when really life isn't like that. I think *Terminator* or even *Avatar* is probably more true to life than *The Waltons*.

Since I've been back home, I've watched the footage of Joe and Dave giving Megan and Sam the runaround, locking themselves in bathrooms and finding bleach under the kitchen sink. This is something that wasn't a problem when I visited the sea gypsies because: a) the whole family are in one room so the kids can't get up to no good without mam and dad knowing, and b) cos they didn't have a kitchen sink. Or any Domestos.

Dave wandered round the house playing his recorder, annoying everyone. It must be the worst-sounding musical instrument of all time. When I lived in a flat, a kid upstairs played it all evening and it would drive me mad. I say played, but he just blew into it. I think it was 'Three Blind Mice' he was attempting. If any mice could have heard the racket they'd have wished they were Three Deaf Mice. I bumped into the kid's mum in the hall once and told her in as polite a way as possible that the noise of the recorder was horrible. But just when I thought it couldn't get any worse, his mam replaced the recorder with a vuvuzela. Now, that really isn't an instrument. Jesus. He left it in the lobby of our building one morning and I took the opportunity to steal it. Two years on and it's still in the boot of my car. I use it as a funnel when I'm topping up the oil.

I wasn't encouraged to play any instrument when I was a kid, as my dad worked nights, so the only hobby I could have at home was pretending to be a mime artist. I learned to read cos of my dad working nights, as we always had to have the subtitles on the telly.

KARL'S Facts

On average, a four-year-old child asks 437 questions a day.

I went back to my hotel and left Sam and Megan to have a night in with the kids. When I went round the next morning to see how they were getting on, they had already been up a while and they looked very different to the happy smiling photographs around their apartment. And that's just after one night! They sounded tired too. Joe and Dave were sat at the table drawing.

KARL: So, how was it?

MEGAN: Tiring.

SAM: Yes, it was tiring. I'm beat today.

MEGAN: It is just an extra set of hands that you have to watch out for. They get into everything. I usually do the grocery shopping by myself and I take time choosing between brands and checking prices, but there's no time when you have them around. I was exhausted. And that's just going in the grocery store by myself.

SAM: Having to say 'don't do this', 'do that', 'grab onto the basket', 'put that back', 'where are you going?', it's exhausting.

MEGAN: I mean, it was annoying hearing my voice all the time.

KARL: And in terms of your apartment, it's nice and tidy, you know, but now you've got pens left out, drawings, mess . . . Are you happy with that?

MEGAN: No.

KARL: I just wonder if you get to the point where you go, 'What's the point in trying?' You've got a really pale sofa there.

MEGAN: Yeah, I know.

KARL: That's gonna get all sorts of mess on it, innit, and once that's a mess, it doesn't matter any more. The walls will start getting dirty handprints on them. I can't stand handprints on glass and on windows.

MEGAN: I'm with you. That is the first thing the kids did when they got in the car. They like to touch the windows.

KARL: Yeah, so the big question is: you've had a bit of an experience, so has it changed your mind in any way? Has it made you think, 'We were gonna have kids, but now we know we're not ready'?

SAM: Maybe last night around 2.30 a.m. it did.

MEGAN: Yeah, one of them had a bad dream.

KARL: So you both got up?

MEGAN: Yeah.

SAM: I said, 'No, you go ahead,' when she said, 'Sam, they're up.' I said, 'I'm not getting up,' but I got up anyway. And I had only just fallen asleep forty-five minutes before. I always wondered about the work situation. You know, you get woken up, you don't sleep and then you're tired at work, and you might miss a deadline or something. Do people understand when you say you have a two-year-old at home or are they just like, 'I don't care what you have at home'?

KARL: If I was a boss I wouldn't care. I would say that was your choice.

SAM: Yeah, I guess I'm the same way.

KARL: That's what I mean. If you aren't sleeping well and you start getting ratty and then that affects your work, and your appearance isn't the same because you've got sick on your shirt, you know, and then you start bickering because you didn't get your shirt cleaned properly because the mam was too busy looking after the kids . . .

MEGAN: And I'm stuck home all day alone.

KARL: Yeah, so when he comes home you're bored and you want to talk about stuff, but he's too knackered because he's been working and he wants a proper meal. But then you'll be saying you haven't had time to cook. You see what I mean? It affects everything.

MEGAN: Yeah, there is no easy way.

KARL: People always say having kids will bring you closer together, but in a way I wonder if it pushes you apart?

MEGAN: I think so.

KARL: How long have you been together?

MEGAN: Together for seven years, married for one.

SAM: And there's also the financial aspect. I don't really want to have kids until I can afford a nanny or a babysitter. That way, if we have to go shopping or something, then it's just like, 'Hey, come and watch the kids, we've got to go do whatever we need to do.'

MEGAN: We don't live near our parents, and most people who have kids can just drop their kids off at their parents' house, but ours live five hours away.

KARL: But then again, would you be able to still live where you're living? Because this place is okay for two, they're alright while they're this size, but give it another three or four years and, you know, how much does a house round here that can fit you all in cost? So then your lifestyle has to start going down just because of these people you've brought into the world.

SAM: Well . . . assuming the financial situation stays the same . . .

MEGAN: But we'll need more money. We'll have more responsibilities. Doctors, food, diapers . . .

SAM: Clothes . . .

MEGAN: I think we still want to have kids, but we're happy just the two of us for now.

SAM: Do they make sleep aids for babies?

KARL: I'm not sure.

SAM: They should.

"We find delight in the beauty and happiness of children that makes the heart too big for the body."
~ RALPH WALDO EMERSON

'THEY SAY HAVING KIDS WHHAAAA is A LIFE CHANGING EXPERIENCE. But so is LOSING A LEG' ~ KARL PILKINGTON

VOCATION & MONEY

I REALLY WISH I'd trained to be a boiler technician. Virtually every place I've lived over the past twenty years has had issues with the boiler, and I've spent hundreds on services and repairs. As I'm sat writing this now, my boiler is flashing the S.07 code at me, which according to the manual means there's a problem with the pump, so yet again I have no heating. The last time I had someone out (two months ago) it was the same problem, and on top of that the engineer said unless I had some plastic ring fitted onto the flue he would have to declare the boiler condemned, as it wasn't safe to use.

'Well, what's happened to the plastic ring that was on it?' I asked.

'What?'

'The plastic ring it requires. What's happened to it? Why isn't it there now?'

'Oh, this system has never had one fitted. It's a new health and safety regulation that came into effect recently,' he said.

This is what does my head in. There are jobs now where people sit in offices coming up with new rules, making problems of things that weren't a problem before. When this boiler was installed someone somewhere signed it off as safe, yet now, due to it not having a plastic ring, it is deemed deadly. If it was that unsafe shouldn't the people who fitted the boiler have come round with sirens blaring demanding I leave the house immediately, so they could get in and fit the little life-saving plastic ring? I must be so lucky, as I'd been using the boiler without the plastic ring for ages and me and Suzanne are still alive (I wish there was a sarcasm font).

'I can fit the plastic ring now, but it'll be fifty quid.'

'That's good, innit. Why do I have to pay just because the person who designed it forgot to add the plastic ring?'

'You don't have to have the ring, but I won't be able to do any further work on it.'

'Fine. Fit the ring,' I said.

He fitted the life-saver in minutes, and then checked the problem that I had actually called him out for. 'It's the pump. It needs replacing, but I don't have any in the van, so you'll have to call the office and make another appointment.' Brilliant. (Sarcasm font needed again). For a call-out and a plastic ring: £140. Still, I could relax knowing I had the safest gas boiler in the world, as it had the plastic ring fitted, plus it didn't work.

When I was a kid I didn't know how useful it would be to become a gas engineer. I just knew I had to get a job to pay my way and not be a burden on someone else. Work wasn't something that I thought you were meant to enjoy. It was a way to make money, which you could then use to enjoy your life when you weren't working.

I left school with no qualifications worth speaking of, and the only work experience I'd had was playing a shepherd in the Christmas nativity play, which wasn't something I wanted to take any further. My teachers asked me what I was planning on doing when I left, but I've never been one for planning. For me, planning is making sure we have enough milk in the fridge for a cup of tea in the morning. I never like to look too far ahead. That's why I didn't fancy seeing that Hollywood disaster film *The Day After Tomorrow*.

I remember scanning the cards in the Job Centre, but nothing really leaped out at me. I watched nature programmes, and I was jealous of insects, as they know their purpose in life from the moment they're born. Dung beetles don't have career advisors, they just get on with shifting balls of shit. They know that's what they're here for and were born to do – easy. But we humans don't know why we're here. It annoys me when contestants on *Britain's Got Talent* say, 'I was born to do this,' then start juggling chainsaws that

are on fire. Really?! That's what they were born to do, is it? What winds me up the most is the fact that I've got a tree outside my house that's blocking light from the front room, the council said they won't be able to get round to sorting it for three months and yet here's a bloke who has the equipment but is too busy juggling it.

We can't all be geniuses, otherwise there'd be no one to do the jobs the geniuses don't want to do. We give plaudits to people who can remove tumours from brains and cancers from lungs, but we still need people to get rid of the knackered organs from the hospital bins. I think there are loads of unpleasant jobs that need doing in the world that we're going to struggle to get people to do in the future, as when people fail at school exams they're encouraged to do further education. My question is this: who are going to be the dung beetles?

LIVING WITH THE SUPER RICH

When I became an adult, work was about earning money any way I could, as money sorts a lot of your problems out. If you have money it helps you live the life you want to live, doesn't it? Well, that's what I wanted to look at during this trip.

My journey started in South Africa – a place where there are very wealthy people and people who are very poor. Not poor like in the UK, where people feel hard done by if they haven't got the latest iPhone, but properly poor, when they don't even have a pot to piss in. I went to meet a man called Kenny who grew up in a township in South Africa – a poor area on the edge of a town where people live in huts that are often made of scrap metal and sometimes have no running water or power. After five years in prison for fraud, Kenny had managed to turn his life around. He now makes his money from TV programmes and nightclubs. I was interested to see how he treats money after coming from nothing.

Kenny lives in Sandton now, which is quite a posh area with treelined roads and big houses behind high walls topped with barbed wire. Not what you imagine when you think of Africa. When I've seen adverts on the telly saying 'Africa needs water' I didn't think they meant for bloody private swimming pools. Before entering Kenny's house, three of his staff checked me and my hire car out for weapons. I suppose the more you have, the more there is to lose and the more paranoid you get. I used to think money gave you freedom and power, but in an odd sort of way it takes a bit of it away. I always think about this when I see David Cameron, the most powerful man in the country and yet he's not allowed to pick the colour of his front door at Downing Street. It's always got to be black.

I drove in through the big gates, parked my little car close to Kenny's Porsche and Rolls-Royce and was greeted by a gang of women at his front door wearing nothing but bikinis and high heels. It's a daft combination. They're neither ready for work, nor a swim. If I answered the door wearing only a pair of shoes and swimming trunks, the council would put my name on a list. They led me through to Kenny, who was sitting on a big gold throne wearing a red velvet gown like a James Bond villain and watching more women frolic about in his pool necking champagne.

KENNY: Hey, Karl, come check out my chair. Do you know why I wear this robe? It's the Hefner look.

KARL: It's nice, but you don't need it today. It's roasting.

KENNY: Yes, but I wanted to wear it to welcome you.

KARL: You didn't have to go to any trouble, honestly.

KENNY: It's not an effort, it's my life. This is how I live.

KARL: So if I wasn't visiting you, would you still be sat here just doing this?

136

KENNY: I would still be doing this. I'd be next to the pool with my girls. Aren't they beautiful?

KARL: Yeah, not bad. When you say 'your girls', are these your girlfriends then?

KENNY: Yes, these are girlfriends.

KARL: Same ones every day?

KENNY: Different, sometimes . . . Money gives you options.

He offered me his robe and asked me to try out his throne.

KENNY: You feel like a king now?

KARL: Nah, this isn't me if I'm being honest. If I was at home now I would be doing little jobs around the house.

KENNY: That's the problem, you see. Sometimes in life you have to do things around the house, but you also have to enjoy your blessings.

KARL: Yeah, but I enjoy that. At no point do I go, 'I don't mind doing this tiling, but I could do with six women in bikinis dancing around the kitchen.'

Kenny asked me to get in the pool with him and all the women, but I didn't like the idea of that. There wasn't really enough room to have a proper swim, as there was a woman in every space. If I had tried to do the breaststroke in the pool, that's exactly what I would have got. I'm not a big fan of swimming anyway. I'm not so much a fish in water but a duck – I'm happy just getting my legs wet.

137

KARL'S *Facts*

In Australia, Speedos are called 'budgie-smugglers' because the figure-hugging swimming trunks make it look as if the wearer is attempting to conceal a budgie.

I sat on the edge of the pool instead, and when I looked down I noticed there were bottles of champagne at the bottom being chilled. I wasn't sure if this lifestyle Kenny had was what he really wanted or if it was what he thought you were supposed to have when you have money. It was like watching a Puff Daddy video on MTV. I prefer peace and quiet. I wouldn't want women helping themselves to everything as they please. I have to make sure I hide my Twix in the fridge at home so Suzanne doesn't eat it, but it would definitely get eaten at Kenny's gaff. I'd have to bury it like a squirrel does with its nuts. I think the only good thing about having all these people about is that someone is always around to sign for deliveries if you're not in.

KARL: I don't need all this. I'm quite happy. I think you should get one woman, take care of her. She takes care of you. This would annoy me – what are they doing, why are they here?

KENNY: Let me tell you something, Karl. When you are blessed – and I would use the word 'blessed' because that's how I see myself – money gives you options. It is fine if you

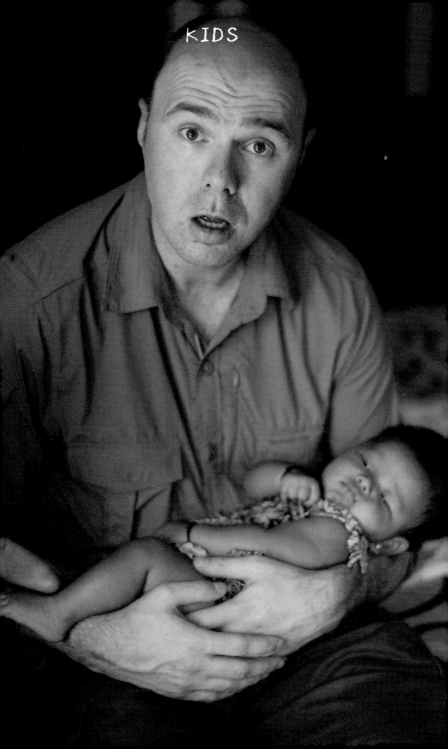
KIDS

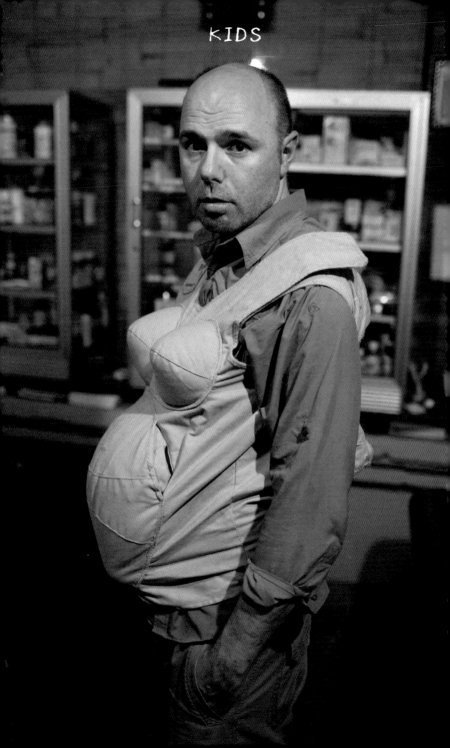

KIDS

KIDS

VOCATION & MONEY

VOCATION & MONEY

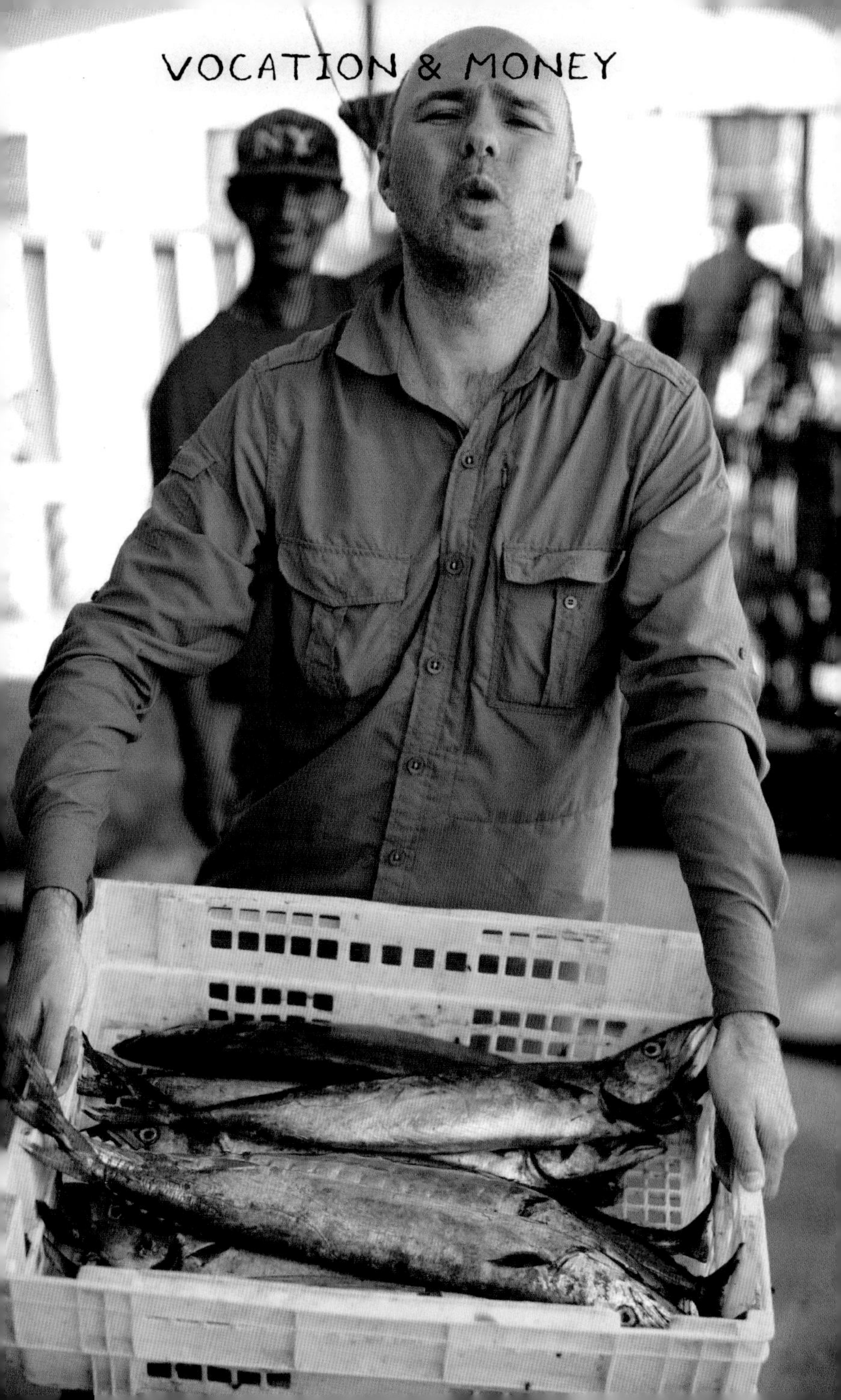

want to take care of one woman, but there are many women out there who don't have a man. They are charity cases, so you have to help them.

KARL: But these aren't charity cases, are they? You don't see her in a 'Help Africa' advert, do you?

KENNY: Not now, but they were charity cases when they met me. I sorted out their problems, and now they are my friends. We enjoy life, we party together. I live with them, travel with them and I bring happiness to their lives. You must not be selfish and think of your happiness alone.

KARL: What do they give you in return?

KENNY: They give me happiness. If I want to kiss them, they will kiss me. If I want sex, they will give me sex. They are not obliged, but we are all happy at the end of the day.

Kenny then took me to see a few of his cars. On the way out he showed me a bottle of whisky he had bought that cost 150,000 rand, which is about £10,000. £10,000! I asked him how he could tell the difference between that and the cheap stuff, and he told me it was because he'd got used to the finer things in life. Thing is, I wouldn't want my taste buds getting too fussy, as there is more shitty food around than nice stuff and it would just make my life more complicated. I feel sorry for the judges on *MasterChef*, as they never seem happy with what's put in front of them, and they haven't even had to pay for it. They probably have to carry some red wine *jus* in a flask just to keep their taste buds happy.

Kenny didn't offer me a sip of the whisky, but maybe it isn't for drinking. It's a talking point, a status symbol. Like those Fabergé eggs that rich people buy. Multi-million-pound egg-shaped ornaments covered in jewels that are so over the top they look like a child has designed them. People with too much money normally end up with ridiculous-sized homes and have to buy things like pianos and harps, even though they can't play them, just to fill up the space. But a Fabergé egg?! The other problem with having something like that is it's easy for a burglar to grab. Owning expensive things is just a hassle. Our flat was robbed years ago and they left pretty much empty-handed. They nicked my Blockbuster card and rented out DVDs and games with it.

We got to Kenny's cars. He had four of them dotted about on his drive – two Porsches, an Aston Martin and a Rolls-Royce. My car is about six years old and has a few bumps and scratches, but it's never let me down. I don't have to worry about it, as it isn't worth a fortune, which is just as well, as I have to park it a few streets away from my house sometimes. If I had more than one car like Kenny I'd probably end up forgetting where I had parked them. As Kenny was walking me over to see his Rolls-Royce his phone went. It was a car dealership calling to say they had a new McLaren racing car in for him to try out. He asked them to bring it round. It was like he was ordering a pizza. I got in the back of his diamond-white Rolls-Royce Phantom. It was fancy. Too fancy, I'd say. I like to be able to chuck things in the back of my car to take down to the tip, but I couldn't do that in this. Kenny was keen to show me the flipdown TV screens, which were very clever, but I've never once wished I could watch a movie on the move. I have problems keeping up with the storyline when I'm watching a film at home, so I'd have no chance if I was trying to follow a diversion at the same time. Though Kenny can probably never be in charge of the remote at home with all those women around wanting to watch the soaps, so maybe the car is the only place he gets peace and quiet. He showed me the champagne cooler in the back. Next time I see a Rolls-Royce on the road I'm going to stay well clear of it, as they might be watching a film and getting pissed up on champagne. What else does he do while driving, have a game of Pin the Tail on the Donkey?!

To me, all these extra gadgets are just a pain. I took my car for a service recently and they wanted £90 just to look at the air conditioning. 'Forget it,' I said. 'I'll open the window.' But then the electric window broke. I never had a problem with cars that just had a handle. I'm sure more things break these days due to them being made more complicated. The amount of times I've been paying for something and the person on the till asks me if I want to extend the warranty for a small fee. It's brand new and they're already talking to me about when the thing breaks. I say keep things simple. I saw an advert on the TV for a bed with a plasma screen that comes out the end of it, which is all very nice, but if it breaks you'd have to send the whole bloody thing back, which would mean hiring a removal man to get your telly fixed. Madness.

> **KENNY:** Now, Karl, if you are blessed with a few million why not have a car like this? You are with your wife, you want to give her attention, why do you want to give your focus to the road when you can have somebody else worrying about it?
>
> **KARL:** Get a taxi then. It's exactly the same. You're sat in the back, driver's getting on with it, and you don't even have to worry about parking.

Kenny's argument didn't really stand up, anyway, as to take his ladies out he'd need a London bus. We heard a really loud engine. It was the McLaren he had ordered pulling up outside. A £600,000 car, yet only room for two. It came with the classic bucket seats that seem to mould around you. Kenny loved the doors opening upwards instead of outwards. These wouldn't work for me, though, as I tend to shove a lot of change and rubbish into the door wells. I'd be chasing spare change every time I opened the door.

He took me for a ride down the road, and it was terrifying. I don't think Kenny could hear me yell over the noise of the engine. It was handy that it came with bucket seats, as I was pretty close to shitting myself. Kenny loved it and said he'd probably buy it.

Later that afternoon Kenny took me for a trip in a helicopter over the area he grew up in to show me how much his life had changed. It was very different to the life he was living now. Tiny tin huts as far as the eye could see. It summed Kenny up, really. Most people would just get a laptop out and show me using Street View on Google Maps, but not Kenny. He had to take me out in a bloody helicopter. He is the ultimate showman.

We headed to Cape Town, where Kenny and his business partner own a club. They had sorted me out with a penthouse apartment to give me a taste of the high life. It was well smart and cost £5,000 a night. It was massive, with huge windows, a roof terrace and a private pool. This to me is what having money is all about. In an overpopulated world, money can buy you space and quiet. The only bad thing about it was the bathroom having one of those trendy sinks you can't get much water in, the ones that are so small you smack your head on the taps when you're trying to wash your face.

The apartment also came with a butler called Lewis. I was cooling down my feet in the pool and enjoying the views of the city, the sea and Table Mountain when he brought me out some fancy drink in a glass made of chocolate. 'You can drink it, and then eat it,' he said. It was nice, but I wondered if this was just Lewis being lazy and not wanting to do the washing-up.

A woman called Maggie turned up to give me a pampering session. She was just putting a face pack on me when Lewis said I had a visitor. It was a couple from a local wristwatch firm in Cape Town. The woman was called Giovanna and wanted to show me what people with money like to treat themselves to. I told her I don't wear a watch – no point when

I can just look at my phone if I need to know the time. The last time I had a watch I was about seven years old. It was digital and played the theme tune to *Star Wars*. The watch Giovanna showed me cost around £8,000 and came in a big wooden box with a pen and cufflinks. £8,000! They'd need to throw in more than a pen and cufflinks to make me pay that for a watch. It doesn't even play the theme tune from *Star Wars*. I don't understand people who buy shirts that need cufflinks either. How are shirt companies getting away with selling shirts with buttons missing? They're basically unfinished shirts and they should be classed as seconds. If they're going to start going down that road they may as well sell the collars separately, sell the whole shirt in bits. And as for fancy pens, what's the point? I tend to nab them from Argos. A pen is a pen. As long as it works, nobody's bothered.

Giovanna got out another watch.

GIOVANNA: This is very special. It's solid rose gold and it's got an open back case, so you can appreciate the movement. You have to understand that each piece is assembled by hand by one person.

KARL: You want to knock his rates down. How much is this one, did you say?

GIOVANNA: It's around £9,000.

KARL: Disgusting, isn't it? I mean, when you opened it I liked the look of it . . . but come on!

GIOVANNA: Watchmaking is an art, a fine art.

KARL: It used to be, but it's not hard now, is it? We've put men on the moon! Honestly, it's a watch. It sort of annoys me a little bit. Who's paying that for a watch?

GIOVANNA: Well, you'd be surprised.

I thanked her for coming but said I wouldn't be buying anything.

Maggie was just about to get back to my face pack when a woman called Fabricia turned up to try and sell me some fashionable footwear. I don't worry about fashion. I'm at the age now where I buy clothing based on comfort, so I asked Fabricia to get the shoes out of the box so I could put them on my feet without seeing them. I wanted to give them the blind-man test. Blind people would only ever buy things based on comfort, which is the way it should be. I walked up and down, and they felt okay, but then I opened my eyes. They were barmy: a pair of Adidas trainers, which I have nothing against, but these were camouflage and had bear heads on the front of them! If I went out in these I'd want my whole outfit to be camouflaged so no one could see me, as they were bloody stupid. Fabricia kept telling me they were designed by Jeremy Scott, but I had no idea who he was, so it didn't mean anything to me.

'They're limited edition,' she said.

'Listen,' I said 'they're not limited enough. These shouldn't have been made at all.'

Just when you think you've seen it all, fashion comes up with something more ridiculous. I went Christmas shopping with Ricky once, and he went into a posh clothes shop to get his girlfriend a handbag. One of the bags on the shelf was made of ostrich skin! How is that a selling point? Who looked at an ostrich and thought, 'I could make a nice bag out of that'? Fair enough if they thought about making leather leggings using its neck, but a handbag! Honestly, all the trouble Noah went to saving the animals two by two and now we're making handbags out of them. I sent Fabricia on her way.

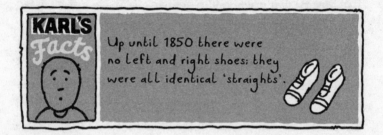

KARL'S Facts

Up until 1850 there were no left and right shoes; they were all identical 'straights'.

Lewis asked if there was anything he could do for me, but there really wasn't. I thought about sending him out for a Twix, but I'd already had my chocolate fix for the day with that chocolate cup. If I had a lot of money a butler isn't something I would have about the house. The only person I could think of who actually needed a butler was Batman. When you're running about saving Gotham City from nutters you haven't got time to be nipping out for a pint of milk.

While Maggie continued to sort my face out more people came to try and sell me expensive pushbikes and jewellery. I was having none of it. Maggie finished by sorting my toes out. She trimmed the nails and popped some stuff on them to make them shiny. I noticed how bent a few of my toes were, but this is what happens if you have too much money. You start worrying about daft things like bent toes and baldness and spend money trying to make yourself 'perfect'. And toes are more trouble than they're worth. Especially that little toe. It only seems to be there for something to bang on the corner of the bed. I'm sure they'll disappear in time. I read a news story recently where a man lost his thumb on a saw at work, so they replaced it with his big toe. I think that's all the toes on our feet are for now. They're like the subs' bench in football. You bring them to the hand if you lose a finger.

I did really like the penthouse and its views, and it was quite nice having Maggie rub my face, but all the watches, jewellery and daft trainers were only things to buy to show off with. They were things for other people to look at, more than for yourself.

'WHO LOOKED at an OSTRICH and THOUGHT, "I could make a NICE BAG out of that"? ALL THE TROUBLE NOAH WENT TO SAVING THE ANIMALS TWO BY TWO AND NOW WE'RE MAKING HANDBAGS OUT OF THEM.'

THE HUSTLER'S LIFE

The next day I was due to meet up with Gayton, Kenny's business partner. They met in prison and decided to work together on the outside. I went to a local market to meet Gayton, and he told me he was going to show me where it had all started for him and Kenny. Before all the nice cars and stuff, they had made money buying and selling fish, and that's what I was going to do today.

I had little business ventures when I was a kid to make pocket money, so I was looking forward to this challenge. I sold fizzy drinks at school that I'd made using the Soda-Stream machine we had at home. I used to collect empty bottles out of bins, clean them and then fill them with Irn-Bru, Coke and fizzy orange and sell them for 25p with a 5p return if they brought the bottle back. I sold computer games that I used to copy onto cassettes. I washed cars for money and sold plants door to door. Gayton called this hustling.

KARL: What is hustling?

GAYTON: I think it's surviving. You know, we can't all go to university, we don't all have rich parents and we don't all get the same opportunities in life. Hustling is basically working with what you've got.

KARL: Why hustle? Why not just rob?

GAYTON: You must understand, most of these guys, they live amongst criminals, and crime is a career choice for them. But what they say is, 'You know what, I can suffer, but I'm going to do it the honourable way.' For me, hustling is one of the most honourable things, because you're not gonna expect handouts.

KARL: It's a tough decision, though, ain't it? Cos if I was here, I reckon I'd think a couple of robberies is a lot easier and could sort my life out more than many years of selling fish.

GAYTON: You're speaking to a guy who took that decision. I succeeded in my first four, five, six, seven robberies until the law caught up with me and sentenced me to seven years in jail. Now, you don't want to be in a South African prison, or any prison. I lost my whole youth, and I look back today and I should have started with hustling. What I want to show you today is: start small. The way I see it, it's faster to take the lift, but there are no lessons in the lift, only trouble. But, if you take the stairs, there are lessons in the stairs.

KARL: Do you get more enjoyment from the money selling fish than you did with the money you got from the bank?

GAYTON: Absolutely. There's a huge difference, because this money of the banks is not safe money. I hear an alarm, I hear somebody's looking for me, I hear my name, I always think it's cops. You're never at peace. The fish money? That's peace money.

I liked the way Gayton was honest about the fact he tried to take the easy option. These days people like to blame their brain. Kids get away with murder cos they make excuses. 'It's not my fault, I've got ADHD.' No, you're just a cheeky little shit. Gayton could have pleaded RBS (Robbing Bastard Syndrome), but he didn't. The funny thing is, I think we need criminals, as they create lots of work. Police, detectives, lawyers, judges, prison wardens, security men, insurance companies – imagine how many people would be out of work if everyone was an angel and never committed a crime. I've said it before but I'll say it again, you sort one problem out and it just creates another.

We got to the market stall where we were to buy some fish known as snoek. The problem was, I'd never heard of it and didn't know the going rate. After a long negotiation and help from Gayton I paid 420 rand (about £27) for ten snoek, which meant for this exercise to be a success I had to sell the snoek at around 50 rand a fish. We set off for a local township, and I asked Gayton if he thought I'd be able to get the price I needed.

GAYTON: You can sell dope to the Pope, depending on how convincing you are. It's never the price, it's how you present it. You know, when we sell fish we say to the lady, 'Oh my, such a beautiful smile,' as women love compliments. Then she'll buy the fish.

KARL: What happens if it's a man who answers the door?

GAYTON: Well, compliment them too, like, 'You're very masculine.' You know, 'You're wearing such a nice shirt, man, where did you get it? I want to buy a shirt like yours.'

I was sure I was going to do okay, as I used to sell mackerel when I was a kid. My dad's mate used to fish, and he'd give us a load to sell at a holiday camp. I sold each one for 25p. We made a fortune. I doubt I would do as well these days at home, as everyone has food delivered to them from supermarkets, plus they ask too many questions about food. They'd want to know where the fish is from, how fresh is it, is it organic, does it contain nuts?

It's good that Kenny and Gayton could do what they did with the fish, as I imagine it would be pretty tough to get a job when you've just come out of prison. If I'd ended up doing a prison sentence and come out flogging fish, I reckon there would be a bloke with a clipboard on to me in no time asking me what I was doing. Even though I'm bald they'd want me to wear a bloody hairnet. I can understand why some people give up trying when people are always coming along to make the job more difficult than it needs to be. I saw a bloke on the telly a few weeks ago on one of those property programmes who had bought an old house for about half a million pounds. Then a woman turned up with a clipboard telling him he couldn't put a door out to his garden as it was a Grade 2 listed building, but if it wasn't for people buying these buildings and doing them up they'd just be Grade 2 listed piles of rubble. Unbelievable. We had the Stone Age and the Bronze Age, now we're living in the Interfering Age.

KARL'S Facts

It is illegal to get a fish drunk in Ohio. It is also illegal to hunt whales on a Sunday there.

HIC!

We got to the township where I was to sell the fish. At the first home I tried starting high – 85 rand a fish. But after a long chat with the lady of the house and me giving her lots of compliments about her clothes and kids, she knocked me down to 100 rand for two, which was a big drop but still okay for me to make a small profit. Little did I know it was going to be my best sale of the afternoon. Ten or eleven homes later I still hadn't sold another snoek. I ended up asking a local woman to give me a hand, as she knew the area and might be able to convince people to buy a few fish from me. Plus she could give me a hand carrying them, as they weren't light and the afternoon sun was baking.

A young kid who looked about six years old showed some interest, but she was difficult. I reckon I stood more chance of getting money off Duncan Bannatyne on *Dragons' Den*.

KARL: Would you like some snoek? Fresh snoek, 70 rand.

KID: If it's cheaper people will want it.

KARL: I can't make it cheaper. I paid 50 for a fish. I can't sell it cheaper than that. You might get it cheaper in the shopping centre, but you'd have to get on a bus to get there.

How much is that going to cost? It won't be cheaper. You'd have to get a bus there and a bus back.

KID: It has to be cheaper.

KARL: Stop following me around. You think I'm suddenly going to sell it for next to nothing? The lowest I can do is 50. So if you buy for 50, we can talk, but I won't drop it below 50.

KID: No.

They were a tough crowd. People who don't have much money are looking at saving every penny they can, yet just the day before I'd seen how people with tons of money chuck thousands away on materialistic things. I think some people with money are embarrassed to ask for the price to be knocked down and prefer to show off how much they can waste.

KARL: Do you want some snoek? 70 per fish.

MAN: 70 rand!

KARL: Caught fresh today. I've got some uncaught if you want to catch it yourself.

MAN: I just want one.

KARL: Just one . . . no problem.

MAN: That's a tiny snoek! That's too small to be sold.

KARL: Well, it's dead now. No point me chucking it back. Have you a small child who could have it?

> **MAN**: A fish that small is supposed to be in the water. It's undersized.
>
> **KARL**: I didn't catch it. I'm just selling it!

Jesus. It was too hot for this hassle. I just wanted to sell them to prove to Gayton I could do it, and now I had the Esther Rantzen of Cape Town on my case. The problem was, there was a regular snoek seller who came to this area, so any possible customers already had some. Also, it was the wrong time of the month, as the people who did work didn't get paid until the end of the month, so it didn't matter how good my selling technique was.

> **DIRECTOR**: Karl, what's happening?
>
> **KARL**: Everyone's got snoek. They can't move for snoek. I didn't even want to buy snoek. It was Gayton's idea. I saw potatoes at the market, said, 'Let's buy some potatoes,' but he said everyone grows their own potatoes. (*to woman*) Do you grow potatoes?
>
> **WOMAN**: No.
>
> **KARL**: Right, so there you go then, straight away. Would you have bought potatoes?
>
> **WOMAN**: Yes.
>
> **KARL**: Sir, would you like cheap snoek?

MAN: It's small. Look at the head.

KARL: Stop looking at the head! I've never bought a fish on the size of its head.

MAN: That's so small, you can't even . . .

KARL: I've had enough of this.

Looking back, I reckon I'd been hustled from the outset. I think I'd been overcharged at the market. And sold small fish. Gayton came over, and I asked him if I could sell the fish back to the woman at the market.

GAYTON: That's the most ridiculous thing I've ever heard. That will never happen! Listen, let me teach you. We're going to go to the next house and I'm going to sell.

KARL: I bet you don't.

GAYTON: You bet me that I can't sell a fish?!

KARL: I bet you 10 rand. If you can sell one for 70 I'll give you 10.

GAYTON: Come on, we're going to the next house that we can find.

KARL: Random house. This one on the corner.

GAYTON: Don't say anything.

KARL: No, listen . . . listen, just before we go in . . .

GAYTON: Don't say anything, don't say anything, don't say anything.

KARL: I won't say anything then.

GAYTON: *(to woman)* Hello, hello, hello, how are you? I came here with a basket of fish, you got the time? I can see the time, and it's time to cook, and now you must get something to cook. Look at this! It's fresh from the sea. This one I call Nemo's cousin, so I will give you discount at 75 rand, no negotiations. Where's the pot? Shall I put it in the pot?

LADY: Let me get a clean one.

GAYTON: Yes. The gut is out, the gut is out. Where's the pot, where's the pot?

LADY: Just leave it in the sink.

KARL: Do you want another one?

GAYTON: *(to Karl)* You say nothing. *(to woman)* Yes, yes, yes, there's no pot, so it's in the sink. 75 rand, cash, cash, cash, thank you so much. I'm going to give you 5 rand back, because it's your lucky day, thank you so much. *(they leave the house)*

GAYTON: You said I would not be able to sell it, but what you didn't understand about the hustling, it's not the hope that they will buy. Selling is not only with your mouth, it is with your body, it is with your attitude, it is how you move. You can't just hope that they are going to buy. You don't give them a chance to talk. I saw the lady and said, 'Yes, you want it,' and she was already in the kitchen. The problem is that when you talk you scare people.

KARL: *I* scare 'em?! That old woman, she was terrified. She shot off to the kitchen not to cook a fish. She was shitting herself when you barged in. She was trying to get out the back door!

GAYTON: I just think you're lazy.

KARL: I'm not lazy! I'm definitely not lazy . . .

GAYTON: Lazy.

KARL: Listen, they're shit fish. Everyone can see that they're too small.

GAYTON: I managed to sell, so what did I do? Feed them before I sold them?

I just had to take it on the chin. It was a bad day at the office. I don't know if Gayton got lucky or if his selling technique was better than mine.

Later that evening I was invited to have a drink with Gayton at his and Kenny's bar. Ben, the director, said I should dress up and make more of an effort with my appearance, but I didn't bother. Clubs tend to be dark places anyway, and knowing Kenny's lady friends they wouldn't bother getting dressed at all. They make Adam and Eve look overdressed.

It was a fancy bar, but it was busy and pretty crammed. Gayton was arranging a few drinks for us when I noticed there was a bit of fuss at the entrance. It was Kenny arriving, wearing shades, a bright suit and smoking a big cigar. The commotion was caused by him chucking money into the air as he entered. The way people scrambled about for it was like he was feeding ducks at the park. He noticed me in the crowd and asked me to join him in the VIP area, where a woman lay across a table with pieces of fish placed on various parts of her body. It reminded me of those displays you see in old pubs where a photo of a half-nude woman is covered with bags of KP nuts. When a customer buys a bag, it reveals a bit of flesh on the photo. Kenny gave me a glass of champagne and asked me to join him in eating some sushi off the sushi girl. I've never heard of the term 'sushi girl'. This one was called Pam.

KARL: No. I'm not a fish fan, Kenny.

KENNY: Listen, you have to eat like me. You are in my club, you are in my town, you are in my country, so you have to eat with me, or this lady will be highly offended. I asked you to join me in the pool at my home and you never did, but this is something you have to do.

KARL: This is what I was saying to you the other day. No matter how much money you have you can always be in control of your own life. You've got to do what you think is right, and right now I don't want to take part in this.

KENNY: No, no, no. Sometimes you have to do things because people are hosting you, and you have to respect whatever culture or tradition they have. You have to taste a few things money can do. A poor man can't pay a woman to lie down as a plate and eat from them. *(Kenny sucks up a piece of fish)*

It's amazing the lengths you have to go to to sell fish round here. Maybe I would have flogged more snoek earlier that day if I'd displayed it like this. It didn't matter what Kenny said, I wasn't going to eat fish off a woman. Not because I don't think it's right or anything. If the woman wants to do it and Kenny wants to pay for the service, fine, let them get on with it. It's just not for me. Though I have to say, it's not that bad an idea, as sometimes at buffets there's stuff you don't recognise, but if it's balanced on a person's tummy you could just ask them. They could even recommend certain things. I just don't know why it all had to be fish she was displaying. There was plenty of room for a pork pie, nuts and some Pringles.

KARL'S *Facts*

In Japan the best sushi chefs prepare octopus by giving it a lengthy full-body massage – while the creature is still moving.

KARL: Is it snoek?

KENNY: No, it's not snoek. This is raw fish, with rice. One bite?

KARL: No, you do one for me.

KENNY: You have to.

KARL: It's getting embarrassing now.

KENNY: Just kiss it then.

KARL: Kiss the fish?

PAM: Why don't you want to lick the fish?

KARL: That just seems daft. You pass germs around like that. You either eat food, or you let someone else have it. You don't go licking it. No wonder there's loads of illnesses in Africa if everyone's going around licking food.

KENNY: This is the Japanese tradition and culture.

KARL: Very good, but we're not in Japan, so . . .

KENNY: So what the fuck is your problem?

KARL: I just don't like it. I'm happy that you enjoy it. And I'm happy to be here. Maybe later, maybe later.

KENNY: No, we have to do it now.

KARL: Why? What's the rush?

KENNY: It's getting hot in here.

KARL: Well, that's why it should be in a fridge and not on her then, innit.

Kenny was a bit annoyed and left me with Pam while he went to have a dance. The problem I have with eating out these days is the way restaurants cram in as many people as they can. There are lots of places where you have to sit next to strangers and can't really have a private chat with the person you're with. Same problem with having a sushi girl there. She's listening in, as she has nothing else to do. So Pam had heard my discussion with Kenny.

KARL: Is it a good earner?

PAM: Yeah, it is.

KARL: And what are the hours like? You've got to stay until what time?

PAM: I've been here long time because you're refusing to kiss it and lick it.

KARL: Not really. Let someone else have it.

PAM: No, someone else can't. I'm not paid for someone else to come lick it or eat it.

KARL: Well, that's just a waste of food, isn't it? We were in a township today where they were starving. They'd love that. And, honestly, they wouldn't stop at that. You'd be a bag of bones. It's a lovely little spread. I'm just not hungry. So what do you do then, when you're lying there? What are you thinking?

PAM: I think of a lot of things. Right now, I think why you don't want to eat it.

KARL: Because I had a club sandwich earlier. So is this what you wanted to do for a living? Is this the dream job you wanted?

> PAM: Well, I just do it part-time.
>
> KARL: Part-time. And do you get to take home what hasn't been eaten, or . . .
>
> PAM: *(laughs)*
>
> KARL: Don't laugh. Your belly is moving, you're going to lose a bit. So no perks?
>
> PAM: No, no. Not at all.

I can think of worse jobs. I can't imagine there's much stress involved, and you don't have to take your work home with you (apart from maybe the smell of fish). The fact is, there are not as many jobs now. I've said before, I put it down to the fact that a lot of animals seem to be on the payroll these days. There's a programme on the telly called *Dogs with Jobs*. It wasn't a one-off either; it was a six-part series about different jobs covered by dogs. They're working in hotels sniffing out bed bugs, sniffing out drugs and money in airports. Bees are also working in airports looking for bombs. Can you believe it?! They're bored of making honey and are now getting positions in the bomb squad. People always say it's immigrants stealing the jobs. It's not, it's dogs and bees.

Pam could have taken the easy option and sat on her arse at home doing nothing, but instead she's sitting on her arse here, with a few fish on her, earning money. I say good on her.

HELPING OTHERS

Ben wanted me to get away from the money side of vocation and look at the idea of helping others rather than just helping myself. I told Ben I think I do help others. When I work I make money to pay my way in life so I'm not a burden on someone else, and I pay taxes to help the country run. I don't claim any benefit, which means it's there for someone else who may need it, and I pay council tax to keep the streets clean, which helps everyone in the area. Yes, I could give up work and spend all day holding a banner in Parliament Square asking people to save the planet, but I have a feeling the way I live is more useful for helping the country right now. To be honest, I don't see the point in protesting in London. It's too crowded and the people doing the march just get lost in the mob. I'm surprised some of the protesters don't end up joining the big queues at the Topshop sale by mistake.

We went to meet a woman called Melissa at her home in Platbos, an ancient indigenous forest outside Cape Town that she now dedicates her life to saving. Ben asked if I did anything for the environment like Melissa does. I told him I do bits and bobs, but if I'm being honest it's for selfish reasons. I don't waste gas and electricity, but that's because I want to keep my bills low. I recycle, cos it's easy, but I don't really know if it's helping the planet out. The main problem with the world is overpopulation. Forests are being chopped down to build houses, too many people create more pollution, and there's a massive strain on the soil from growing food to feed the masses who are living longer and longer. Back in the day, people died in their 20s of toothache, but now we've got old women in their 80s doing star jumps at the gym, and we're making it worse as we're saving everyone and everything. We even attempt to bring stuff back from the dead. Scientists were trying to bring the mammoth back from extinction! Where's that going to live and what's it going to eat?! I can't see things getting better, so I don't worry about saving the planet. I don't think we need to, as the planet will always be here. It's us who will be wiped out, which, if you really care about Planet Earth, is probably the best thing that could happen to it.

Melissa was a nice, softly spoken woman who told me about her concerns for the planet.

MELISSA: How we're living is not sustainable, and I don't think it brings any deep meaning or happiness at the end of the day. I would like to know that I've done everything I can to protect this forest. Its value is far more than you can put into money terms. I hate to see the planet being damaged and destroyed by thoughtless actions.

I agree with Melissa, but I really don't know what can be done. If I was her and lived in the forest I would want to save it too – not for the planet but for me. I think a lot of these planet-saving ventures aren't really selfless acts but money-making schemes. We keep being told carrier bags are polluting the seas, but if they're wrecking the planet why not stop making them altogether? Charging customers 5p for them isn't sorting the problem out, it's just making someone somewhere some money. I tried some of that 'Earth Friendly' toilet cleaner that's supposed to be better for dolphins, but it couldn't remove fly shit from a window, never mind a stubborn stain from my U-bend. And anyway, I live in London, so where's the bloody dolphin I'm saving?!

Melissa asked if it was important to me to save the forests for the sake of my grandchildren. I explained I won't be having any, as I don't have any kids and I'm not planning on having any either, as the world doesn't need me to produce more people. Some would say I'm being selfish not giving new life a chance, but you could say people who have kids are more selfish for adding to the problem of overpopulation. Again, I might be being selfish here, but the idea of no human life in the future doesn't bother me. The way I see it, as humans we've had our go and we've made a right mess. We'll disappear like the dinosaurs did and something else will get a go. That's the cycle of life.

I told Melissa about my journey so far and how I didn't know if I had a proper vocation in life. She said the exercise we were going to be doing might help me figure some stuff out. We were going to meditate with a 1,000-year-old milkwood tree. She called it a tree attunement. I met the other people who were joining us and they all seemed friendly enough. Some wore hippie-style tie-dyed clothing and had dreadlocks. Others wore feathers in their hair. Not the type I would normally hang about with, but if it meant I was going to find out what I should be doing with my life, then so be it. We headed deep into the woods, which couldn't be further away from the money-fuelled city life I'd witnessed with Kenny. We got to the old milkwood, and Melissa asked us to sit down on the ground wherever we felt comfortable.

MELISSA: Close your eyes. And then take a few deep breaths. Just allow the sounds of the forest, the sound of the wind, of the trees, to relax you. And then when you're ready imagine yourself actually being a tree. Imagine yourself with your roots stretching deep into the earth and your branches stretching out into the heavens. Enjoy your first breath out through the roots. Imagine drawing out through the earth. And then exhale that out through the heart. And then take your next breath through the heart. And exhale out through the crown. And then draw in through the crown. And exhale out through the heart. Inhale in through the heart. And exhale down through the roots. And just follow this process, with your own rhythm. The idea is to feel well rooted to the earth.

I've never been very good at understanding breathing exercises. I don't know how to breathe through the heart and out through the crown. I wish I could cos I'm forever choking on food, so it would come in handy, but I didn't question it, as I didn't want to ruin it for the others. I've been breathing the way I breathe for far too long to start changing now. It'd be like asking me to write left-handed. I was aware that I was making quite a lot of noise due to my sinuses. They're always blocked, and I think being in the woods was making them worse. I sounded like a coffee machine trying to brew a cappuccino.

> MELISSA: You might find when you connect with the tree that you get a particular feeling. Or even just a single word will come to you. Often there can also be humour involved. There might be a funny song that comes to mind. Within that there is often a little bit of a negative truth that you can work with.
>
> MAYA: I had this intense feeling and the word 'womb'. And this image of a womb. And this mother that held, like, an entire universe. Imagine all the people. Living a life. In peace. It's insane . . . like . . . incredible.
>
> KARL: When you said think of a word – I'm not messing around – I got 'crisps'. I'm not messing. I've had loads of Pringles the last few days, so maybe that's why.
>
> MELISSA: Well, maybe it's something that gives you pleasure?
>
> KARL: It is, yeah.

God knows if I got the word 'crisps' from the tree or not, but I did find those few moments quite relaxing. I'm not very good at switching off and I get distracted quite easily. I can never focus on one thing normally, but I was properly relaxed around the tree. I know this, as I was aware of a few itches and when I'm busy I never itch. It's the same with whistling. I never do it when I'm pissed off. Though looking back I suppose the itching could have been caused by gnats.

KARL'S *Facts*

Some Buddhist monks can raise their skin temperature through meditation. Sometimes they can even start steaming.

Melissa then asked us to walk around, find a tree that attracted us and sit by it to see if we could get some answers in life. I walked for around five minutes before a tree grabbed my attention, not by sight but by a spiky bit attaching itself to my shirt. Melissa told me it was an ironwood tree. I decided I didn't want to sit by this one as it had grabbed me rather than me picking it. I carried on walking and one did catch my eye. It was a dead tree. Melissa told me it was a wild peach tree.

KARL: It's quite interesting that I picked a dead one. I wonder if, you know, it's me looking on the downside again. What's the point in having a go at finding a vocation? Just get on with life, enjoy it while you can, cos at the end of the day we're all gonna turn to mush and sort of go back into the ground like this tree.

MELISSA: It's an important part of the forest, because as it decomposes it becomes part of the soil.

KARL: It's doing its bit even while it's dead. So maybe I'm not here to find my vocation while I'm alive. Maybe these programmes and books I've written are gonna do better when I'm dead, like Picasso? Nobody rated him when he was knocking about. Van Gogh, was he another one?

MELISSA: Yeah.

KARL: It's not what I do while I'm alive, it's what I leave behind, and I've always really wanted that, cos you're dead longer than you're alive.

MELISSA: Well, what I hear you saying is you'd like to leave something behind, some kind of legacy, yeah?

KARL: Yeah.

MELISSA: You've got your books . . .

KARL: Yeah, and DVDs. In fact, thinking about it, they probably will do better when I'm gone, cos a lot of what I've seen won't be around any more. I've seen all the wonders of the world, and they're not gonna be here forever; they're falling to bits. The pyramids in Egypt are in such a state they'll probably collapse before I'm dead.

We spent the evening sat around the campfire. It was relaxing. So relaxing I don't even remember what we did, as I ended up eating a load of hash cake (without realising) that one of the hippies had made. I could have eaten it off her belly for all I remember.

The next morning, after a good night's sleep in my tent, I went off with Melissa and planted a baby wild peach tree on her land, so even if my work isn't useful after I'm gone, the tree will be around for hundreds of years. Before we left, Melissa gave me some wild peach spray, which is made from the flowers from her forest and can be bought through her website for rand. As I've been saying all along, having a vocation is important, but you need to make money to survive.

Since being back home Melissa has emailed me:

> *I think that your 'crisps' message from the tree had a deeper meaning to it. When we planted your wild peach tree I told you that in the past, extensive parts of the forest there had been felled to farm . . . potatoes! And, of course, crisps (or chips as we call them in South Africa) are made from potatoes! Aha! So that was not such a random message after all.*

LIVING TO WORK

Next we were heading to Tokyo, as Japan is a place where people live to work rather than work to live. The country has one of the highest suicide rates in the world. Thousands of people every year head out into one of the many forests, often after losing their job, to take their life. Which goes to show saving forests isn't always such a great thing to do. Remember, you solve one problem, it creates another. People in Japan are treated like machines in the workplace. It's not unusual for staff to work an extra twenty hours a week, as well as working Saturdays without any extra pay, and they just do it to show how much they appreciate having a job. If workers are sick, there's a kind of unwritten rule that you use your holidays up before your sick days. So in a place like this, is having a vocation so important?

I stayed in a hotel in the red-light district, though it was more like the red, blue, orange, green, pink and purple light district. The amount of lights in Tokyo is mental. If someone does lose their job here, rather than contemplating suicide they should just open a bulb shop.

KARL'S Facts

Sleeping on the job is acceptable in Japan. It is viewed as exhaustion from working hard. Some people fake it to look committed to their job.

My first stop in Japan was at Kidzania. It's a theme park, but rather than rollercoasters and stalls selling candyfloss, Kidzania gives kids a chance to have a go at doing grown-up jobs in a realistic environment. Kids aged from about three to eleven were packed inside this warehouse that was built to look like a city and were trying their hand at working in banks, hospitals, vets and locksmiths. I passed a vets where kids were learning to operate on a cat. There was an office block with three-year-olds dressed in full firemen uniforms aiming hoses at fake flames flickering in the window. They were paid money, which they could then spend in Kidzania on snacks. What I liked about it the most was the way they promoted normal jobs as well as fancy occupations. Kids could try their hand at being a dentist, but they could also be a security man. For those who weren't keen on being a doctor they could have a bash at being a postman.

In Japan it's more important to show yourself as being willing to work and having a purpose than it is to have a high-flying job, which I think is a good thing. In Britain it's getting harder to get people to do the boring jobs and they're trying to tempt them with better job titles. Gastronomical Hygiene Technician – do you know what that is? A pot washer in a pub. Transparency Enhancement Facilitator? Window cleaner! These were the sort of jobs I was looking for when I was younger, but if I was looking now I wouldn't have applied, as I wouldn't know what the description meant. I suppose you might feel better about yourself when you tell someone you're an Education Centre Nourishment Consultant, but when they ask what that means and you still have to say, 'Oh, I'm a dinner lady,' what's the point? And just because you don't have a fancy job doesn't mean you can't take pride in it. One of my favourite jobs was my paper round (Media Distribution Officer). I reckon I was the best paperboy ever. I didn't take one day off in three years and I was up at 4.30 a.m. every day of the week, no matter what the weather. It does my head in these days when I see people using the weather as an excuse not to go into work. Year after year you see it on the news, one little bit of snow and the country comes to a standstill. What annoys me is the way people get snowed in at home, but never at work. It's bollocks.

I suppose being a doctor or a surgeon is a job you'd feel good about, but, like being a dinner lady, you wouldn't want to tell too many people what you did for a living, as they'd start telling you all about a rash they have or a boil they can't get rid of. Which makes me think, is it really such a good job? You can't take a proper day off. My mate's dad was a doctor and he was always being hassled at home. I've said it before, but even when doctors are on holiday they don't get left alone. I've been on flights where the pilot asked if there was a doctor on board because someone in aisle fourteen was choking on a pack of nuts. If I was the doctor I'd want to say, 'I'm on my bleeding holiday! The toilet on the plane is blocked, but I don't hear you calling for a bloody plumber!'

Anyway, I think it's a good idea to give kids a taste of working life and I liked Kidzania. But it made me think – rather than just playing, why not let kids work properly earlier? Obviously not as young as some of the kids here, but I would have loved to leave school when I was about thirteen or fourteen and earn some money. I'm sure it would have been better for both me and the brainier kids in the class, who I probably slowed down, if I'd been sent on my way. No matter how long I stayed at school, my brain was never going to take it all in. It just wasn't interested. It didn't make any difference how much my ears listened or my eyes read, my brain didn't want to know. I wonder what I'd be doing now if I'd had a good brain and whether I'd have been any happier. I might have ended up doing a job I didn't enjoy. People are always saying they were born to do a certain job, but what if you were born to do a job you didn't like? Brainy kids at school were encouraged by their mams and dads to do all sorts of after-school activities they didn't really want to do, but no one bothered with me, so I was free to decide for myself. And there are a lot of people out there like me – there are more daft people in the world than brainy ones. For every one human being who makes an amazing discovery there are a hundred loons. I remember hearing a story on the radio about a surgeon who had taken a hand off a dead man and attached it to a man who had lost his hand in an accident. They said it was a huge step for medical science and isn't it amazing what humans can now achieve, but then the news came on and they reported a house fire that had started after someone had tried to dry their washing with a disposable BBQ! Bloody barmy.

Our next stop in Japan was to meet an old man called Dr NakaMats, who was still putting in the work hours at the ripe old age of eighty-five. He's a bit of a local celebrity and known for his inventions, his most famous probably being the floppy disc, which he invented in 1947. He lives on Dr NakaMats Street, just off Dr NakaMats Avenue and close to Dr NakaMats Square, which is probably quite good for both his ego and the postman, but would be a pain in the arse for everyone else on the street if he ever moves.

Dr NakaMats was a smart-looking man. He looked really well for eighty-five. When I arrived at his house he was sat at his desk behind piles of paperwork. He handed me his business card and asked for mine in return, but I told him I don't have a card, as I don't like giving people my phone number. Apparently it's customary in Japan to exchange cards at the beginning of a meeting. They must get lots of spam and junk mail if everyone is handing out their personal information to anyone they speak to. Mind you, I suppose if you live on a street that's named after you there's no point trying to keep your personal details private. There was so much information on his business card, it was double-sided. It stated that Thomas Edison had invented just 1,093 things in his lifetime, while Dr NakaMats had already reached 3,368. I popped it in my shirt pocket. It would give me something to read on the fourteen-hour flight back home.

Next to Dr NakaMats's desk was something called the Cerebrex chair – one of his inventions. It wasn't a stylish-looking chair. It was browny-grey in colour with a footrest, a very high back and flaps of material that covered the sides of the head. Once you were seated a piece of material dropped down in front of you, so your head was totally covered. I liked the chair. It made me feel closed off from everything. I've never been to confession, but I imagine this is how it would feel. It would be good if trains had these fitted as standard, so you could block off all the commotion around you. Dr NakaMats hadn't invented this for trains though. It was designed to stimulate the brain.

DIRECTOR: Do you use this chair every day?

DR NAKAMATS: Yes, using this every day for at least twenty minutes. Very effective and improve memory power, decision power, 130 per cent just after twenty minutes.

He also said it improves your eyesight and lowers blood pressure by cooling the head and heating up the feet. I asked him if it was actually plugged in as I wasn't aware of any cooling of the head or warming of the feet, but he told me to shush and just relax. I was sure it wasn't plugged in. There was no standby light or any kind of electrical noise to let me know it was on. If you're after a comfy chair, I'd say buy one of these, but don't bother taking out the extra warranty on it, as you'll have no idea if the thing is working or not anyway. I can understand how it would help you concentrate, though, because it blocks out all the distractions around you. It was a chair I could imagine nodding off in quite easily, but Dr NakaMats doesn't believe in having too much sleep.

DR NAKAMATS: How many hours are you sleeping per day?

KARL: If possible, eight or nine.

DR NAKAMATS: According to my research if you sleep over six hours, your brain will become bad direction. Sleeping hours should be within six hours. In my case, usually four hours.

KARL: A day? Four hours a day?

DR NAKAMATS: Yes, 4 a.m. to 8 a.m. Because between midnight and 4 a.m. I call golden time. Golden time to create new things.

Surely this can't be good for anyone? If it's true, and Dr NakaMats does only sleep for four hours a night, that would make him older than eighty-five, as I think your age should be calculated by the hours you're awake. Like air miles for a pilot. The more air miles they have, the more experienced they are. You could say it's the same with life. Koala bears are supposed to sleep twenty-two hours a day, so a ten-year-old koala bear is only ten months old. Dr NakaMats only sleeping for four hours means he's getting an extra sixty days a year on me.

Dr NakaMats took me to his invention room. It was like a museum crammed with amazing inventions, like the Ultra Energy Anorax engine that runs on water instead of petrol, a golf putter that makes a sound when you hit the ball to indicate how well you've hit it, PyonPyon jumping shoes, an air pump that moves liquid from one bottle to another, and a pair of remote-controlled shoes fitted with wheels that

Dr NakaMats had predicted were the car of the future. He also showed me another engine that used cosmic energy – rubber tiles that pick up cosmic rays covered one side of his house and transferred power to run it. He hadn't sold this invention to anyone yet. I have no idea if it was legit or not, but I couldn't help but think of the Cerebrex chair, which I was sure wasn't switched on, so maybe this cosmic power generator isn't quite ready yet.

We went outside onto the street so I could try out the jumping shoes and a water-powered bike. The weather was terrible. The way the rain was coming down, I probably had enough water to power the bike back home to the UK.

Dr NakaMats invited me into the part of the building where he lived. It was a nice, light, open area with floor-to-ceiling windows and minimalist modern furniture that you wouldn't think an eighty-five-year-old man would go for. He wanted me to see his thinking room. The doors to his thinking room looked like the sliding doors you get on a lift. He asked me to hit a button on the wall. I hit it and nothing happened. I hit it harder, but still nothing happened. He laughed and pushed against the wall to the side. It was a hidden door into his thinking room. Which was a toilet. Gold tiles covered the walls and a gold toilet glowed like a throne. This is where he came to sit between midnight and 4 a.m. to think up ideas. Having a toilet as a thinking room made perfect sense to me. It's one of the only rooms you can go in without people hassling you. The 'engaged' sign that comes up when you lock the toilet door is one of the few signs that people actually take notice of.

KARL: Yeah, yeah! I can understand this.

DR NAKAMATS: Golden toilet. You want to see?

KARL: Yes.

DR NAKAMATS: I sit midnight to 4 a.m.

KARL: That's not normal. That's not healthy!

DR NAKAMATS: It is golden time.

KARL: That's how you get haemorrhoids. I sit on the toilet for a long, long time, so long my legs go numb sometimes. But I've been told it can cause piles . . .

DR NAKAMATS: You cannot enter here. Nobody can get in. Me only use it, and only me.

KARL: I can't go in there?

DR NAKAMATS: No, no, no. No. But you can see, look at it. This is a thinking room. You see all gold because gold shuts out television waves, no telephone waves so inside is completely calm. I can create many thinkings in this room.

KARL: But can't I just go in?

DR NAKAMATS: You cannot. Even my family cannot. I'm only one.

KARL: But I don't want to use it. I just mean to sit in there and . . .

DR NAKAMATS: No. .

KARL: Definitely not?

DR NAKAMATS: This here is very clean. Nobody.

KARL: No, I'm not going to do anything!

DR NAKAMATS: No, no, no. Stay outside.

KARL: I can't believe you won't let me in. So even your wife has not been in?

DR NAKAMATS: No, of course.

KARL: So who cleans it?

DR NAKAMATS: Automatic cleaning. That's my invention also.

KARL'S Facts

A woman in Singapore sat naked on her toilet for 902 days. She ate, slept and showered on the toilet. To pass the time, her husband moved the TV in view of the bathroom so she could watch it.

Finally we had found something to agree on. I really do like my time in the toilet. If I ever get to a point where I have to have a colostomy bag fitted I think a part of me would die. I've always felt like this. When I was younger and heard my dad talking about how he'd worked extra hours and the company had paid him 'time in lieu' I thought it meant he could spend more time in the loo as a reward.

Dr NakaMats offered me a meal.

> DR NAKAMATS: How many times you have a meal?
>
> KARL: Um . . . three? With a snack, four a day?
>
> DR NAKAMATS: I only have one meal per day. If you eat three times, four times, too much. Bad for brain.
>
> KARL: But what do you enjoy in life then? Cos you're just working all the time, you're not eating, you're not sleeping, so what's it all for?
>
> DR NAKAMATS: I'm concentrating to create.
>
> KARL: Yeah, but are you getting any enjoyment out of life? Are you happy?
>
> DR NAKAMATS: I am very happy.
>
> KARL: But when do you see your wife if you're constantly working?
>
> DR NAKAMATS: Sunday. Saturday also I'm very busy. Saturdays I'm going to muscle training.
>
> KARL: You only see your wife on a Sunday? So where is she the rest of the week? What's she doing?
>
> DR NAKAMATS: Oh, she is now researching recipe of meal.
>
> KARL: But she only has to cook you one meal a day!

We ate one of his brain meals together. Green beans, sea-weed, carrot, bamboo and fish, with some brain tea he

invented that's good for skin and prevents constipation. I
think I have a good diet. I'm not the one who's sat on the
toilet for four hours a day. It's not brain food he wants to
be eating, it's bran food. And, anyway, the way I look at it,
whatever I eat is brain food, as it's my brain deciding what
I eat. It's my brain telling me it wants chops, egg and chips.
If it wanted seaweed and bamboo it would tell me. Dr Naka-
Mats didn't like the food I enjoy. He said it was bad for my
health and would shorten my life.

DR NAKAMATS: I am eighty-five and according to my
research we can live to 144 years old.

KARL: I don't like the idea of that. I always thought I'd
get to about seventy-four, seventy-five, seventy-six, seventy-
seven . . .

DR NAKAMATS: That is average age.

KARL: Yeah, I'm sort of happy with that. And would you
want to keep working till that age?

DR NAKAMATS: Of course, that is my target.

After the meal Dr NakaMats wanted to show me another
method he uses to come up with inventions. We headed to
his local swimming pool, where he explained that some of
his best thoughts come to him when he's underwater and his
brain is almost completely deprived of oxygen. I was to have
a go myself. I was told I mustn't come up for air until I was
half a second away from death and when I returned to the
surface I would have an invention. I was given a pencil and a

plastic board to scrawl on underwater, as Dr NakaMats said that an idea disappears as quickly as it comes. I agree with that. I come up with many solutions to little problems I have around the house when I'm in the shower, and nine times out of ten by the time I'm out and dry I've forgotten them.

I went under and tried really hard to concentrate. I tried to write something on the board but pushed so hard with the pencil the lead broke. I came up for air. 'Pencils that can take more pressure,' I said. That was my first invention. Dr NakaMats gave me his pencil and sent me back down. I managed to stay under longer this time. When I came up I'd written 'electric tin opener'. I don't know why as these were invented years ago. This is the problem with inventing. Virtually everything has been done already. These days most things are just the same things but tweaked. Everything is 'new and improved'. He told me to go under again. I started to write 'crisps'. The same word I got from the tree when I was with Melissa in South Africa! Now wasn't the time to be writing a shopping list. Even under this pressure my brain couldn't be arsed. I went back up for air. The idea of a toast rack big enough to fit crumpets came to mind. I took a big breath and went back under. It's a mad concept. I pictured Dr NakaMats on *Who Wants to Be a Millionaire?* with a big bath full of water. He'd jump in it instead of phoning a friend.

KARL: How long was that?

DIRECTOR: About a minute and a half.

> KARL: I've never done that long.
>
> DIRECTOR: What did you come up with then?
>
> KARL: Nothing. I was just amazed how long I held my breath.
>
> DR NAKAMATS: Again! Again!

I went under one last time and came up with an idea I'd actually had before. A pillowcase that's big enough for two pillows to stop them separating in the night. We called it a day. Dr NakaMats said this method works for him 80 per cent of the time. But, the thing is, if your brain is at its best moments away from death, why do we never hear stories about people who are dying shouting out, 'Solar-powered SodaStream – aaahhhurghhh!'

I liked Dr NakaMats's attitude, and it's amazing how he's still going strong, but to me it seemed it was his vocation that was keeping him going. It's good to enjoy your work, but it shouldn't be everything. He didn't seem to live life for himself; it was all about work. He didn't see his wife much, he ate food that was only good for his brain and slept four hours a day. It's not the life for me.

A HANDYMAN'S LIFE

If I hadn't got into what I do now I think I may have ended up being a handyman. It's what I enjoy doing the most when I'm at home. If I have any time off from work I always find little jobs that need doing and enjoy taking my time over them. If I'd been born in Japan I might have ended up being a benriya, which is an occupation that's been around for years. Benriya means 'convenience doer'. They advertise themselves in a local paper, online or by word of mouth and offer to do all kinds of jobs for people who are too busy to do it themselves: DIY, cleaning cars, queuing up and buying concert tickets. They might get booked by a restaurant to sit outside acting as a customer to make the place look more popular. At funerals where the deceased didn't know many people, the family call in a number of benriya to make up numbers. And no job is too small. I'd like to hire one at the moment to answer all the calls I get from companies asking if I want to make a PPI claim. I'm sick to death of them.

What I liked about the sound of the job was the variation, but it also offered a real sense of purpose. There are so many jobs these days that aren't proper jobs. Especially in TV. It's all nonsense. The man who wears white gloves and hits the button on the lottery machine, does he get job satisfaction? I'm surprised we still have weathermen on the telly too. They turn up for about a minute after the news to second-guess what the weather is going to be doing, using phrases like 'there's a 50 per cent chance of rain'. We could all do that. There are loads of them too. Every region has someone stood there every night having a guess about what the weather is going to do. I don't think it's a job with pressure or mad working hours either, as recently I've noticed a lot of pregnant women taking it on. One woman I saw was so far gone the people of Plymouth couldn't see what was going on in their area, as her belly blocked it out on the weather map. How do they feel when they get up and open the curtains to find they got it wrong again? No one listens to weather forecasters. Even now and again when they do predict it correctly, no one listens cos they get it wrong so often. They may as well not tell us anything. We may as well have a bloke after the news telling us what lottery numbers he thinks we should pick. Maybe the bloke with the white gloves could take that job on.

KARL'S *Facts*

In Australia, hurricanes were originally named after local politicians that the weatherman didn't like.

I went to meet a benriya called Mr Koyma at his office. When I shook his hand he was busy on the phone. Once he'd finished he explained that he had a few jobs on that day that I could help him with, the first being a cleaning job. His phone rang again. It was another job. A customer was calling to say they thought their cat had fallen off the verandah and onto a neighbour's rooftop and they wanted someone to save it. I was just asking him what the going rate is for saving a cat when the phone went again. It was the same customer calling to say they had found the cat. It was just in their living room. I hadn't been there long, but I got a sense of how much people rely on the benriya here. They are the first people to call when there's a problem.

Mr Koyma gave me a pair of overalls to wear and we headed out in his little handyman van. I like a job with overalls, much more than a job where you have to wear a suit and shoes. I like playing snooker, but having to wear a waist-coat and bowtie would put me off wanting to do it profes-sionally. Mr Koyma's phone was ringing with bookings all the way. The translator wasn't in the van with me, though, so I had no idea what the jobs were. I guess you pick up regular customers over the years, and you don't want to let them down, as there will always be someone else who could step in your place. But I think competition is a good thing. Products are improving all the time due to fierce competi-tion. Except Twiglets. No one else seems to want to make them, and they've tasted shite for years.

We got to the customer's home and she told us what needed cleaning. We had to wipe the tatami mats the Japan-ese use to protect their wooden floors, and then we had to polish the floor underneath. I didn't mind doing it, but what did bother me was the way the customer stood over us and inspected everything we did. It was like being on *Master-Chef*. They always stand over the contestants asking what they're doing and why. It would do my head in. I would make more mistakes. The good thing with the Japanese is they don't have much clutter. I don't think I saw a single ornament. Maybe it's because they have thousands of earth-quakes every year. You'd get sick of replacing broken orna-ments. Still, like I say, I'm not complaining, as it made the job a lot easier. If I had to do this at my Auntie Nora's house I'd be moving so many ornaments about, it would be like playing chess.

As I polished the floor Mr Koyma told me how he got into the job.

MR KOYMA: Well, in my former work I was sitting in front of a computer all day. I realised I wanted to change jobs and do something more active and physical, and also I quite like this job because I can see customers being happy right in front of me.

He wasn't wrong about it being active. I was knackered. I asked the customer if there was any chance of a brew, as I was parched, but she just laughed and said no. It must be a cultural thing cos at home the kettle is constantly boiling if I have workmen in. When I put a budget together for a job I want doing I add the cost of teabags to it, they get through that many.

I noticed a pair of funny-looking shoes in the corner. The woman said she had come up with the design herself to help her with her bad back. I have a bad back, so I gave them a go. I could feel the stretch instantly and it felt good. That's another thing about a job like this – you're meeting new people all the time who might be able to help you just as much as you're helping them. It opens you up to new ideas. Maybe Dr NakaMats would find it easier coming up with inventions if he was out and about rather than locking himself in his toilet for four hours every night.

I don't know why the benriya idea hasn't made it to the UK. Maybe it's because people don't like the idea of being a bit of a lackey and would find it a bit demeaning, but I think I would enjoy it. It's the ideal way to find out what your skills are if you're not sure about what you want to do for a living, and I like the way it's up to you to decide how much work you take on. Though I think I'd only use one if they were recommended by someone I trust. I've been caught out too many times with workmen. The worst was a removal man I once hired when we were moving flat. I found a bloke in Loot who charged an hourly rate that seemed more than reasonable. Well, that was until he came round. He buzzed my doorbell and I told him to come up to the third floor. Ten minutes later, still no sign. I went down to see where he was and found a bloke older than Dr NakaMats, breathing like Darth Vader and struggling with the boxes. Empty boxes! I ended up doing all the shifting and just left him to pack, otherwise God knows how many hours it would have taken him and cost me. He'd probably still be at it now.

The last job we had to do for the customer was clean her windows. I'm good at doing windows. If I was a benriya, doing windows would be my speciality. I do a perfect job of them at home, to the point that some might say I'm a bit OCD about it. Once, I got my windows so clean I could see the neighbour's windows were filthy and it really irritated me. Mr Koyma started cleaning the windows with a dry cloth, which got rid of a thin layer of dust and grime but didn't really make the windows sparkle, so I showed him my technique of using a wet cloth then drying off with a crunched-up piece of newspaper. Cleaning windows is the only reason I buy a paper these days. For some reason the newspaper leaves them spotless with no smears. The woman was over the moon with the result, so I tried for a cup of tea again, but she just laughed.

I think the only thing I would be worried about, doing this job, is if I'd start to let my own gaff go to shit. If I'm doing little jobs like this for work all day, would I lose the love I have now of doing it at home? I know builders whose houses are falling to bits. That hairdresser Nicky Clarke, he's won awards for cutting hair, but his own style is rubbish. It's like he can't be bothered doing anything with his own head.

I was happy that the client was pleased with our work. In lots of jobs you don't get any feedback, but today I felt like I had been useful, which I think is important. I don't think I'd get much satisfaction out of a high-powered job where I just delegated all day. So many big companies just have layer after layer of bosses who do very little. I read recently about the mayor of Alaska. You'd think it would be a difficult job, but it can't be that hard, as they've got a cat as mayor. That just sums it up. A bloody cat that licks its bollocks rather than talking them.

Mr Koyma said I was going to do the next job on my own, as my window-cleaning method had taken up time and he had other jobs to do. He dropped me off at a school and told me to ask for a man named Manu who was teaching an art class. He explained that my job today was to be a nude model. There was no way in this world that was going to happen. Surely if you want someone to draw, you would select from a book, not just hire a benriya and see what turns up?! But Manu said that because I was from a different country it was a good thing, because my skin tone and features were different to what they were used to drawing. But I wasn't having that. Maybe cheekbones are different, but not arse cheeks. It doesn't matter where you are from in the world, nob and bollocks are the same. I made my excuses and said it wouldn't be good for anyone to have me sat there nude. It wouldn't push the students forward, and I thought they'd end up taking up science instead when they saw my odd body. This is the strange part of being a benriya. Variation is good, but I'd be on edge every time the phone went if the jobs were this weird. I've never heard someone say, 'Oh, I've had a right busy day. I've waxed floors, cleaned mats, cleaned windows and got me nob out.' I told Manu I'd compromise and go topless.

Once I'd got used to having the students staring at me, I found it quite relaxing. Like the sushi girl job, because I couldn't move for twenty-five minutes it gave me time to think with no distractions. All the best ideas come when you're relaxing. The mathematician Archimedes came up with his Archimedes's principle while he was in the bath, and Sir Isaac Newton was chilling out under a tree when an apple fell on his head and he came up with his stuff on gravity. In a way this was better than Dr NakaMats's thinking room, as I was being paid at the same time.

I saw a few of the drawings and I thought I looked pretty good. Like I said, you can discover new talents in a job like this. I've never thought I could use my body to earn money. The only odd thing was that the men in the art class seemed to draw my body in a more flattering way than the women, which was a bit annoying.

FINDING A VOCATION

Modelling for the art class made me wonder if it could be a vocation for me, but like a proper catwalk model. It can't be that difficult, can it? After all, I've been walking around wearing clothes for forty years, so I think I've got the hang of it. The thing is, I know it's not just about that. You need the looks too. Sometimes there's no point trying hard to do certain jobs, as you're just not cut out for them. Maybe I'm not cut out to be a model because of the state of my head. I know I'm not much to look at. The only compliments I ever get are from people who say I don't look as old as I actually am. But being young can't be everything, as babies are odd-looking things, so I don't see it as a compliment.

Ben, the director, asked me if I was happy in my skin. I think it's an odd question, as I've obviously never experienced being in somebody else's. Mine seems to fit okay. Maybe it could do with being a bit looser round the back of my legs, as I struggle to bend and fasten my laces, but other than that it's pretty snug. I suppose having a face transplant is as close as you can get to being in someone else's skin. It's amazing we can do this now, but I'm not sure I like the idea. A face will never look as good as it did on the original owner. If something happened to Brad Pitt and for some reason they stuck his face on my head I doubt it would look right on my bones. Maybe this is why some celebrities look weird when they get older. Take Sylvester Stallone. Maybe the real Sylvester died and the man we see now is just a bloke who took his face, and that's why he looks odd.

I wanted to find out how far I could get being a model with my body and my face, so we travelled to LA to find out, a place where many people go to follow their dream. When people say they're going to do this, it normally means they want to be in the entertainment business. It would be rare to find someone who was following their dream of being a lollipop man. It's an odd one, though. I don't think I've ever really tried to follow my dream, as I think I'm more intelligent in my dreams than I am when I'm awake, which could be an issue. A few months ago I went to bed with a problem, fell asleep thinking about it and when I woke up I had a solution. I can't remember what the problem was now, but maybe that's why people tell you to sleep on a problem. The difficulty with me being more intelligent when I'm asleep is that if I wanted to be a surgeon I'd probably be brilliant at it in my dreams, but I'd be useless in the hours I'm awake. I'm someone who would give a better performance if I did actually sleep on the job.

We went to a fashion show where I met a man called Joshua Christensen, who designs clothes for men and women. He was going to show some of his latest designs and he was willing to let me help model them. When I arrived he was busy explaining to the other twelve or so models where he wanted them to walk, stop and pose for the journalists later that evening.

I didn't really look like any of the other models. They weren't what I would class as amazing-looking or beautiful, but they did stand out as being different. I suppose that's what being a model is these days. The ones I see on billboards are quite weird-looking with gaunt faces and gaps in their teeth and their eyebrows shaved off. Back in my day famous models were all hair and breasts like Samantha Fox and Linda Lusardi, but that look isn't so popular any more. I reckon the Elephant Man could get a gig advertising jeans these days.

I sat and watched a few of the models. The women had legs like giraffes and wiggled their hips as they walked as if they were chewing a toffee with their arse cheeks. The men walked in a more normal way in comparison, and had very little facial expression.

KARL: So how would you describe that to me – how to do that face? What is it?

JOSHUA: I tell them to think about smiling, without smiling. So, if you think about it, your muscles actually move and they can see it on your face. It is about confidence and being cool.

Okay. I can do that, I thought. Though I didn't get great feedback from Joshua.

Attempt 1: No good. I was frowning. And when I frown the wrinkles on my head look like an elephant's knee.

Attempt 2: No good. My arms were swinging too much.

Attempt 3: 'No. Close your mouth,' Joshua said.

Attempt 4: 'Walking like a caveman.' 'Chest out.'

Attempt 5: 'Walking too fast.'

Attempt 6: 'You're walking like a monkey again.'

What?! What did he mean 'again'! He said 'caveman' earlier. When did I walk like a monkey?! The more I tried, the more frustrating it got. I'd have said walking was one of my strengths, but now that it was being studied, my legs and arms were getting nervous.

JOSHUA: Brow again!

KARL: *(sighs)* I know, I know, I know, but would you give me a gig with this head anyway?!

JOSHUA: Well, probably not. I probably wouldn't book you, but we're doing this because you know what, real people wear these clothes, so it's kinda good that you're here.

Well, this is how real people walk. Asking me to walk with confidence but then telling me I look like a monkey doesn't help. It's barmy. And if the clothes are any good surely they should sell themselves? I had a break and got talking to one of the male models. He told me he got into this line of work after being approached when he was sat in a café, which just goes to show it's all about the looks and not about the walk. He could have been in a bloody wheelchair for all they knew, which is what Joshua could have ended up in if he'd said I walked like a monkey again. Still, being approached is quite a good way of getting a job, as there's no pressure if someone else has picked you. It takes away the hassle of working out what you want to do too. I think having to make fewer decisions in life is less stressful and gives you more time to do things you want to be doing. These days just being at a pick 'n' mix counter gets my blood pressure up – there's too much choice.

One of the girl models asked me why I was there.

KARL: I'm looking at the different jobs and work people take on. Sometimes you don't always have a say in the job that you end up doing.

MODEL: That's true.

KARL: And this is one job that I'm saying I couldn't do. I couldn't be a proper model because of the way I look.

MODEL: That is correct. No, you couldn't be. Age is part of it too. I'm twenty-five and I would say I am getting old for the business.

My age isn't the reason why I couldn't be a model. At the end of the day my head is too fat and I've no idea what I can do about that. There is no DVD workout that helps you lose weight off your fat head. People say wearing black is slimming, but not for a fat head, and the only way to get my cheeks to be active is to eat, so it's a bit of a vicious circle, innit.

Joshua said it was time for me to get into the clothes I was going to model: a dark-red shiny suit, pointy shoes and a black shirt with red feathers on the front. It isn't the sort of thing I would even think about trying on normally. It's because I don't go to places where this sort of look would be appropriate. I only take Suzanne to Nando's, if she's lucky, and I couldn't go in there wearing this. Especially with all these feathers, as there's a chance they'd throw me on the grill and cover me with peri-peri sauce.

The trousers were weird too. The crotch area was so low it offered no support. At the end of the day, the outfit wasn't one I would buy. I always wear the same trousers and shirt if I'm going out for a sit-down dinner, and because they're quite plain no one ever notices it's the same outfit. But I couldn't get away with it if I wore this suit, as it's not a look people would soon forget. 'Karl, isn't that the same red suit with feathers, low crotch and pointy shoes you wore last time to Nando's?' The other male models wore silver suits and bow ties with leather gloves that looked like cycling gloves. It's not the sort of gear you find in Gap. They looked like *Star Trek* characters or game-show presenters. The women looked the best, but I think that was down to the make-up they were wearing. They had dark eyeshadow that gave them that come-to-bed-eyes look, whereas I had the go-to-bed-eyes look from all the travelling.

Joshua came to see what I looked like wearing his work. He was really chuffed. 'Sooo good. It's sharp . . . Gosh,' he kept saying. I think he was surprised that I didn't look totally shite. I asked him again whether he'd think about using me as a proper model, but he didn't really answer and just told me to go and check myself out in the mirror. I did look okay, but maybe that's because I was surrounded by blokes who looked like Captain Kirk on a bike ride.

The room filled with journalists and other people from the fashion world all waiting to see Joshua's new range. The music started, the lights dimmed. I was number six in line. My heart started to flutter a bit, which is odd considering all I had to do was walk. When it was my turn to parade my stuff, off I went. The walk wasn't very relaxing in these pants and I couldn't help but frown this time, as my bollocks were swinging about in the loose trousers. I'm glad the walk wasn't too long, otherwise my testicles would've ended up as red as the suit.

When it was over I asked Joshua how he thought it went. 'I'm sooo proud of you. I saw you walking down and I was like, he did it, he did it! Seriously good job.' Seeing that he was pleased was the best bit of the day really. Thinking about it, all the jobs I've had I've always tried to do my best. I think that's what's important to me, giving something a bit of a go and trying my best. I decided to push myself one step further and have a go at another job I'd encountered on this trip. After seeing Pam be a sushi girl at Kenny's club in Cape Town, I wanted to try my hand at it here, and the after-show party was the perfect place to try out a new concept on these trendy types. I decided to put my own spin on it by serving a range of snacks rather than just sushi. So I removed my clothes apart from underpants and socks, lay on a table and covered my body with a few tasty treats, including Custard Creams, Twiglets, Wotsits and a few Ginger Nuts. Not too many, though, as I was going for a more minimal, classy look.

Ben, the director, wasn't keen on the idea of eating anything off me. I don't know why, as food is always being messed around with by chefs these days. They're constantly touching bits of carrots and parsnip on your plate. I'd had a bath the day before too. Anyway, Wotsits are so light they didn't even touch my skin, they just balanced on top of my chest hair. I also think I look my best when I lie down, as all the fat on my face disappears to the back of my head. I don't know what his problem was.

I lay there quite relaxed as the party went on around me. The only thing that put me a bit on edge was the scab on my knee from when I was cleaning floors in Japan. I was worried someone would pick at it, thinking it was a walnut. But really it was an ideal job for me. I'm not a very sociable person and yet, in a way, I was still on a night out. And I didn't even have to get dressed up. Perfect.

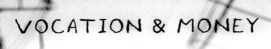

YOU DON'T TAKE THESE
SHOES TO THE COBBLERS,
YOU TAKE THEM TO KWIK FIT.

VOCATION & MONEY

HAPPINESS

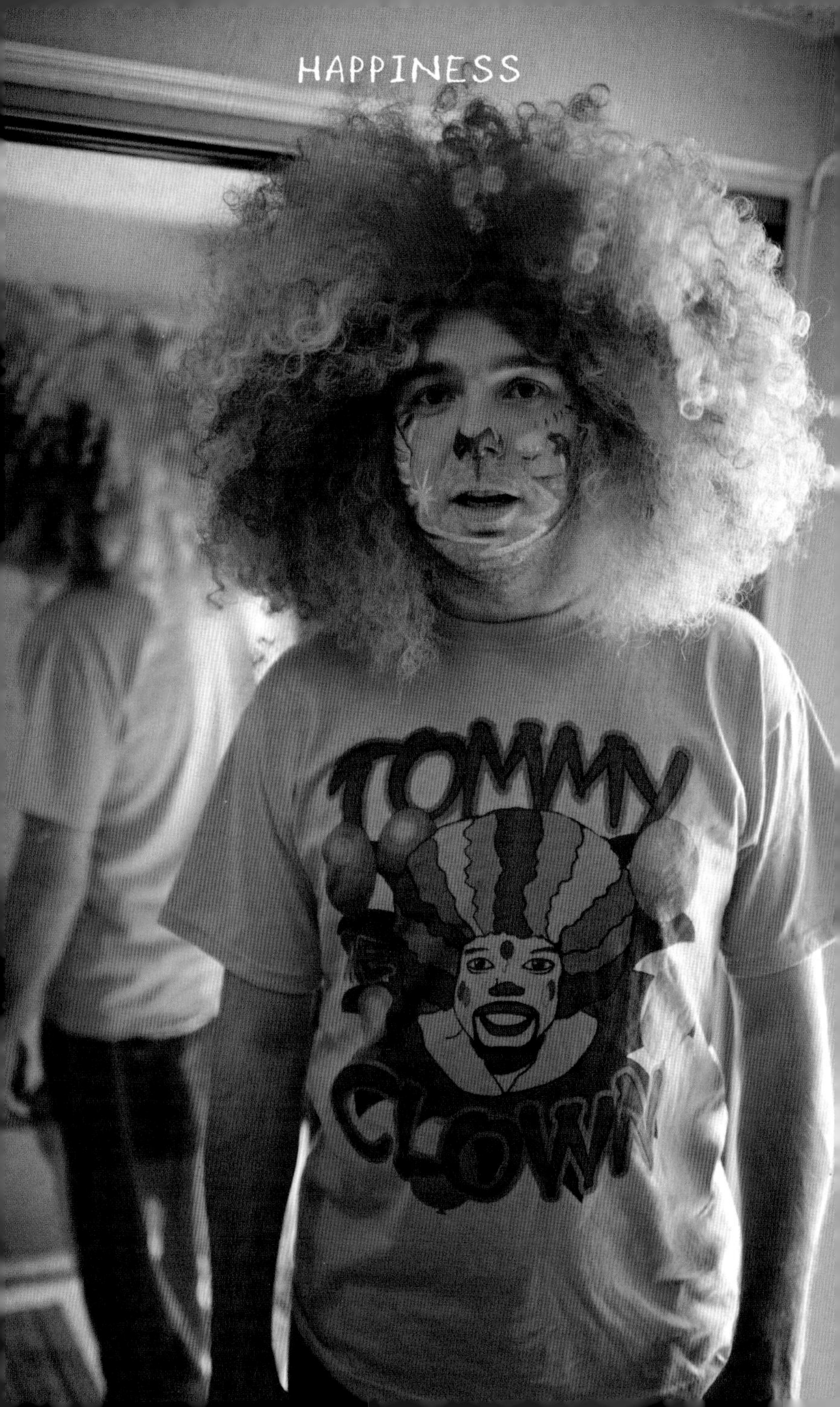

HAPPINESS

TOMMY

CAKED IN MAKE-UP.

Happiness

I JUST WANT you to know, before I start moaning, that I'd say I'm a fairly happy-go-lucky person. I don't want for much, and I find happiness in simple things like cutting my toenails. I was doing this in the garden a few weeks ago while Suzanne was messing about with some plants. When you have time to look over your feet, life must be good. It's like whistling – it's not something you do when you're in a bad mood. 'This is the life,' I thought, as I sipped on a cup of tea and took a bite of a Tunnock's Teacake before moving on to my other foot.

But now, as I write this, that nice moment seems long gone. It's Monday morning and I had a good start to the day. It was sunny, I'd had a fairly good night's sleep, I'd had crumpets and bacon for breakfast and a decent cup of tea. Some men were due to trim the tree outside our house, as it's been blocking out the light for ages. The council finally came round on Friday and put a big sign on the tree asking people not to park under it so they had space to do the work. I was just getting dressed when I heard a car door slam. I looked out the window and saw someone had parked under the tree. It was a woman with her hair pulled back in a bun. 'What's she doing?' I thought to myself. She couldn't possibly have missed the sign, as it's big and bright. I went to yell out of the window but couldn't open it properly because of the security bolts on it, so I only had an inch gap to shout through.

'Excuse me! There's a sign there!'

I looked up from the gap to see that she hadn't heard me. She now had her head in the boot of her car.

'Oi, you in the blue car!'

Still no reaction.

'Helllloooooo . . . Oi . . . WHAT THE . . . ARE YOU DEAF?!'

I felt like Bruce Willis in *The Sixth Sense*. She closed the boot and I saw she was wearing headphones. I bet she could hear but chose to ignore me. I sometimes wear headphones even though I'm not listening to anything just so I'm left alone. It's the next best thing to wearing a 'Do Not Disturb' sign.

I gave one last 'OOOOOOiiiiii!!!!!!', but it was pointless. If I was fully dressed I could have nipped out after her, but she was already walking at a pace so she'd be long gone by the time I got downstairs.

Things like this are what annoy me in life and get me down: not that the tree won't get trimmed but the fact that

the woman couldn't care less about anyone else. People say I'm miserable and grumpy, but I'm always considerate of others. I'd prefer to have a world of grumpy considerate people than happy selfish ones.

People who are grumpy are usually like that for a reason, but no one ever thinks to find out if they have a right to be grumpy. Look at Grumpy in *Snow White and the Seven Dwarfs*. He's got a reputation for being moody, but of course he's grumpy: half his colleagues are bleeding useless. If I had to work with Dopey, Sleepy and Sneezy I'd be well pissed off too, especially with Happy standing there acting like everything is fine. I don't know if anyone has ever done a study on each of the dwarfs' work rate, but I'd put money on Grumpy being the most productive out of that lot. I find I can get mundane jobs done pretty quickly when I'm in a mood. I often wash up pots if I've had an argument with Suzanne, and I do a thorough job in good time and then by the time I've finished I've calmed down. Actually, I wouldn't be surprised if there was a link between the rise in divorce rates and the introduction of the dishwasher.

Anyway, moments later the blokes came to sort the tree but said they couldn't do it as they needed the space where Bun Head had parked to put the shredding machine and would have to come back another time. Bloody great, innit?!

HAPPINESS THROUGH EXERCISE

This trip was all about looking at happiness and the various ways people try to achieve it. We started in Mexico on board the Chihuahua al Pacifico train on a six-hour journey from Los Mochis to Divisadero. It was a nice start to the trip, as the train wasn't too busy, they sold tea and snacks and went at a pace that didn't make you feel sick like on some of those high-speed bendy trains. I was heading to meet the ancient Rarámuri tribe, who believe their happiness comes from running mega-long distances. They've been known to run for days and are thought to be the healthiest and most serene people on earth.

I've never been one for running or doing any sort of exercise. Getting fit is one of those things I know I need to do but keep putting off. A bit like when my computer says it requires a software update, it never picks the right time to ask. I'm happy to get a sweat on walking, cleaning windows or doing my own removals, but running to nowhere seems like a waste of time and energy to me. A mate who does it for fun says he gets a buzz off the breathlessness at the end of it – he should take up smoking so he can get that feeling after climbing a flight of stairs instead of having to run six miles.

I thought about joining a gym a few years ago when Suzanne suggested it would be good for me, but my issue was the cost and the way they lock you into a contract for a minimum of six months. Suzanne couldn't understand why I was worried about leaving before I had even joined, but it's the same as people setting up pre-nups before getting married. You've always got to expect the worst, haven't you? That's why we pop a seat belt on when we get in a car.

On average the gyms were asking for £65 a month, which I wasn't willing to pay. For that price I'd want someone to do the workout for me. I eventually found a cheaper gym advertised in a local paper called Gym'll Fix It that was £34 a month and you only had to give a month's notice to cancel the contract. 'Bargain,' I thought.

The bloke who ran it was a big fella, but big-fat rather than big-muscly. He had the words 'Veni, Vidi, Vici' tattooed on his arm. Trying to be friendly I asked if they were the names of his kids. He snarled at me and told me it was Latin for 'I came, I saw, I conquered'. Those were probably the words that went round in his head each time he left an all-you-can-eat buffet. I've never understood why people have tattoos in Latin when most of the world can't read it. You may as well have a tattoo done in Morse code – it would be a lot less painful. The Latin tattoo didn't make him look suave or intelligent either, especially next to his Union Jack tattoo. Tattoos are like peanuts in the way that people can't just have one. I had an uncle who did all his own and was totally covered in them. Some of his looked like Latin phrases, but I don't think they were, it was just that he was dyslexic. He had all sorts scribbled on his arms, like they were Post-it notes.

Anyway, it was clear on my first visit why the cost was so low. They didn't have many fitness machines, so the only workout I got was the mad dash to get to one of the few that worked. It was a rough place and the machines they had were knackered. The one cycling machine that did work wasn't easy to operate, as someone had stolen the seat! In the end I must have only used the gym five times, and the last two visits I didn't work out at all, I just helped myself to toilet rolls and shampoo sachets from the changing rooms until my membership was up. What's Latin for 'I came, I saw, and I thought it was shite'? I should get that tattooed on my arm.

I was enjoying the train journey to Divisadero. It was a scenic ride cutting through countryside and over the Copper Canyon. As I was taking in the views, Ben the director talked about how he had done some running and could understand how the tribe get a lot from it. I explained I wasn't very sporty. Even at school sports day I never really got involved, and I was most active during the breaks, as we'd give each other Chinese burns and dead arms until we got dark red bruises that made our arms look like corned beef. I used to enjoy arm wrestling too. We played it so much that most lads had a big right arm like the fiddler crab which has one massive claw. The obsession with arm wrestling was probably at its peak in the late 80s and there was even a film all about it with Sylvester Stallone, *Over the Top*. It's mad to think they managed to make a film about such an insignificant sport. They might as well have tried to make a blockbuster about the game Swingball.

All the talk of arm wrestling led to me suggesting I take on one of the passengers on the train. A man in our carriage fancied the challenge and we agreed to play the best of three. Without going into too much detail, let's just say there was no need to play the third game, but he did anyway just to humiliate me. I should've known I didn't have a chance of winning, as these days I struggle separating shopping trolleys in Sainsbury's.

To build my confidence for the run I had ahead of me with the Rarámuri tribe, I wanted to take on another passenger I had come across who was a little smaller. I just had to get his mother's permission beforehand. He was eleven. His mum said it was fine if he was happy to play. He was tough for an eleven-year-old, though. Maybe this is why kids are running riot these days – parents are scared to chastise them as they're terrified of being put in a headlock by the little shits. But as tough as he was, I won. I decided there would be no best of three, as I wanted to quit while I was ahead. I left the carriage to some boos from the Mexican passengers. I think they thought I should've let him win, but I don't agree with that. I think it's healthy for kids to learn that you don't always win in life. Ben said it was the way I celebrated that might have upset a few people, which just goes to show that being happy can annoy people just as much as if you walk about with a grumpy face on. I had a cup of tea and some biscuits to build my energy back up before the big race.

KARL'S Facts

If you challenge someone exactly your equal in strength and technique to an arm wrestle, the person with the shorter arm has a very slight advantage.

We eventually got to the village. Ben told me that the local Rarámuri Indians are some of the best long-distance runners in the world, and that it was probably due to them needing to chase down their food. They would outrun the animal over days until it gave up from exhaustion and collapsed. There's no way I'd have the energy for that every time I wanted a meal – I'd end up having sloth with a side order of slugs every night. The Rarámuri still run long distances to this day and believe it to be a big part of what makes them happy.

I wouldn't say I was greeted with the happiest faces I'd ever seen. Saying that, maybe I shouldn't judge, as I don't put much effort into smiling for no reason either. We seem to live in a world where you have to walk around grinning like a loon. I can't understand all the fuss about the Mona Lisa painting, everyone wondering why she's not smiling, if she's depressed or heartbroken. No, she was just normal!

Emotions are always extreme these days: you either have to be crying with laughter or crying in pain. No wonder water levels are rising. It's not global warming, it's all the tears from crying.

I met a local man named Lorenzo. He handed me some clothes to run in. The top was made of a light white cotton which was quite cooling, so that made sense. I was given some material to wrap around my waist as a type of skirt, which would also be cooling for my legs. I was then given two strips of an old worn-out car tyre that had less grip than I have hair on me head. This was to be my footwear. I reckon using two slices of wafer-thin ham would have offered more protection than those things. Thin leather straps were used to keep the tyre shoes in place, and they wrapped around a couple of toes and then up around my ankle. I had a quick walk about and didn't have a good feeling about them, as the straps tightened whenever I put pressure on them. They were the sort of thing you could imagine Tarzan wearing to protect his feet, but then maybe that's why he swung everywhere – he couldn't stand the agony of walking. Ben told me this was the traditional way and that the footwear might help me cover more distance. I knew it wouldn't. The reason they wear these homemade trainers is because they haven't got a JD Sports nearby. But to be fair, I think a lot of this new aerodynamic clothing isn't called for. I used to do PE in my underpants if I forgot my kit and I didn't do too badly. I think runners need to slow down a bit anyway. Usain Bolt doing one hundred metres in 9.77 seconds is too fast. It's hardly worth buying a ticket to watch him, is it?

While Lorenzo was helping me adjust my straps he explained that this race wasn't about who could run the fastest but who could run for the longest. We headed over to the starting line, where I was given a stick.

'What's this for?' I asked.

'Hitting the ball,' he said.

It turned out that while running, the person in the lead had to hit a wooden ball with a stick. I didn't ask why, as I knew at no point would I be in the lead and I didn't need to worry about it.

There was a lot of hanging around, as we were still waiting for a few runners to arrive. Maybe they were trying to find the nearest Kwik Fit to get some new running shoes. When they said these running events go on for days, I don't think it's the race that takes up the time but getting everyone together. It was baking hot, and the idea of trying to run didn't fill me with glee, and the shoes were already cutting into my skin. Considering this run is supposed to bring happiness it wasn't starting off well. If my feet aren't comfy, I'm not happy. Never mind happiness being good for your soul, this wasn't good for my soles!

After forty minutes or so the other competitors finally arrived. Just going by their appearance my confidence was boosted. Ben hadn't exactly managed to pull together an elite team for the run. It looked like the Rolling Stones had turned up.

A goat on a rope was brought to the starting line. It was to be the prize for the person who ran for the longest time. And I guessed it wasn't going to be a pet. It would be someone's dinner. Now I had a reason to give the race my best shot. I practised hitting the ball with my stick. I whacked it as hard as I could. Suddenly everyone started running.

'What's going on?!' I shouted.

'I think you started the race!' said Ben, who wasn't happy, as the cameraman wasn't even filming. It was chaos. There was no false start called, the Rolling Stones were off and there was no stopping them, so I legged it as fast as I could to try and keep up. No wonder these races have never been televised. They wouldn't know what time to schedule it. It wasn't the gentle jog I expected it to be either. They left me in the dust so it wasn't long before they were totally out of sight. I only knew which way to go from white arrows that had been scratched into the ground. It was like the story of the tortoise and the hare, except the way I was already feeling I reckon a tortoise would have given me a run for my money. My feet were bleeding even though I hadn't even done one full lap. Bits of gravel were also getting into my car tyre shoes. You can have the comfiest shoes in the world, but if there's a little stone in there you can't think about anything else until it's out. I stopped and took the shoes off. Will the cameraman and Freddie the soundman came along on a quad bike and looked as confused about the whole thing as I was. Freddie said I could borrow his boots if I thought they would be comfier to run in. I wasn't in any doubt – if Lady Gaga was stood there offering a pair of her ridiculous shoes I would have chosen them over these car tyre flip-flops. Once the boots were on, off I went again. I was determined not to give up on this one. I ran as fast as I could, but I still couldn't see the other runners, as they were now behind me. They were about to bloody lap me! I was only aware of this when the wooden ball they were whacking went whizzing past my head. The pace was pretty unbelievable, especially in the heat. I decided to just keep going at my own stride.

I got to a point of the route that had a view over the canyon for as far as the eye could see. For me, just sitting there would have given me more happiness than this running lark. It was lovely and quiet. Peace and quiet is so underrated. Where I live, you only get a few minutes' peace before it's broken by the sound of a police siren. I'm thinking of writing to my local MP to see if they could introduce police lanes rather than bus lanes, as they'd definitely be used more. I heard the sound of a mountain goat and was reminded why I was running, so I got a move on.

After forty-five minutes I eventually finished a lap. A few of the villagers shouted things as I passed by, which I think were words of encouragement. One woman stood pointing at me and laughing her head off. I wasn't sure why until she pointed at my legs. I'd been so focused on the running that I hadn't noticed I'd lost my cloth skirt somewhere along the way. I must have looked a right sight running in Freddie's boots and just my boxer shorts. The good thing was that due to me not having any support down below, I could use the swinging of my bits as a sort of metronome to help me keep a pace, and I managed to do the next three laps without a problem. The others still lapped me twice, though. I really think they should get jobs as postmen or something so all their energy isn't wasted. They'd have your letters to you before the ink dried.

As I ran, it gave me time to think about what happiness is to me. It's simple things like walks with Suzanne, Magnum lollies, playing with the cat, and lemon muffins from the local café. But while I was thinking about these things my mind seemed to want to remind me of the things that annoy it, like Suzanne's mam nicking my chair when she visits and sitting there sucking on mints so loudly it sounds like someone is making a bloody cappuccino. My default setting is to have a moan. It gets on Suzanne's nerves, but she never engages with it most of the time; she just treats my rants like pissing-down rain that she knows will pass. But then I wondered if that's how we're programmed, as we learn more from mistakes. Maybe back when we were cavemen it was more important to always expect the bad stuff, as this would help us survive. If everyone was happy in the world I doubt a lot of things would get done. It's the squeaky wheel that gets the oil, isn't it? I presume I get my moaning off my dad. It's a full-time occupation for him. He called up the *Daily Star* newspaper the other day to complain about the supplement that came with the Saturday edition. The front cover had a big flash saying 'Free Supplement Inside' and he called to complain that it wasn't free at all cos the newspaper is more expensive on a Saturday. He knows nothing is going to change, but he enjoys getting it out of his system.

I was now on lap six. I'd been running for nearly six hours and it was starting to get dark, which made the run a bit difficult in the rocky areas, but at least the temperature was more bearable. I sat down at the canyon for a rest to take in the view one more time before it got too dark. It was a view I doubt I'd get sick of, as it looked different each time I passed in the changing light. I checked out the condition of my feet. They were as bumpy and rough as the canyon. I now had quite a few blisters on my heel and on my big toe. I can't help but mess with blisters when I have them. I sat and pushed the liquid around inside the bumps. They looked like little lava lamps. It's odd how the runners here get happiness from wrecking their feet when I usually get happiness from pampering them.

I got my breath back, popped the boots back on and set off running again. My back was aching. I often wonder if we should ever have stood upright. I read about a group of people somewhere in the world who walk on all fours and I bet they never have lower-back issues. The only problem is they need an extra pair of shoes for their hands, which left me wondering how they tie the laces on the last shoe.

KARL'S Facts

In medieval Europe, a painful and gruesome torture method involved goats licking the salt off the victim's feet.

As I got to the village Lorenzo was waiting to greet me. He told me the runners were on their twelfth lap and I was just about to finish my seventh. He said if I did one more lap he would let me have the goat, as I'd done really well. Apparently I was just shy of doing the length of the London marathon, which I was pretty happy with considering I'm unfit and the heat was unbearable. I still don't know if the last lap for the goat was Lorenzo's idea or if it was Ben's doing. It wouldn't surprise me if he'd rather pay for the goat so that he didn't have to hang around all night waiting for me to catch up with the others. Anyway, I wasn't going to argue with him about it. I was only doing the run for the goat so I could take it to a more remote part of the canyon in the morning and set it free. No doubt they will catch it again at some point, but I was happy knowing that it would at least roam free for a bit longer. That's the best I could do for it.

I went to my tent where I would be kipping for the night. I felt quite sick, either from exhaustion or from the two Twix and three Snickers I'd eaten while I was running. I also had a banging headache from dehydration and my joints ached too. What I would have given for a nice hot shower and a comfy bed. I nodded off wondering if I'd learned anything from this. All I'd say is, if the Rarámuri come knocking on your door asking you to sponsor them, just be careful how much you give per lap, otherwise you could end up having to remortgage your house.

HAPPINESS FROM PAIN

The next day my back, legs, bollocks and feet were in pain from the running and my arm still ached from the wrestling, but at least it helped me get in the mood for the next part of my trip. I was to attend a pain party. I can't say I was looking forward to it, not because it was a pain party but just because it was a party. Any party to me is a pain party. A man called Ricardo was hosting the event in his garden for friends and family. I got a taxi there and I mentioned the fact that I was going to a pain party to the driver.

KARL: Have you ever got any joy from pain?

TAXI DRIVER: From pain?!

KARL: I'm about to go to a party where people apparently put themselves through pain and they get happiness.

TAXI DRIVER: I think that's crazy. Pain hurts. If something hurts you it is because it is no good.

KARL: Exactly. I agree with you. That is what your nerves are for. What's the most pain you've ever experienced?

TAXI DRIVER: I had kidney stones.

KARL: Ya joking! I had kidney stones too.

TAXI DRIVER: It was four years ago. Painful, man. I couldn't walk, they give me a shot of morphine and that is the only way I could handle the pain. I was crying, crawling on the floor.

KARL: Yeah, it's horrible, innit. I thought I had it again recently, but it turned out it was just trapped wind.

I suppose that's the one good thing about pain: it brings people together if you've both been through a painful experience. It made me feel like I had a connection with Hector the taxi driver. Maybe that's what the pain party was all about.

When I arrived I met with Ricardo, a thirty-six-year-old man with a bald head, a smiley face and stretched earlobes. I don't see the point in having stretched earlobes. It would make more sense if people used the hole to put pound coins in. I've never got one on me and you need them these days to release shopping trolleys, but they don't use them for that, they just bung up the hole with an earplug. I've never seen an ear hole without a plug in it and I was wondering whether I should ask Ricardo if I could have a look, but I wasn't sure if that was a rude thing to ask, like asking an old woman to take her teeth out to see if her face collapses.

Ricardo explained that he and a few mates were going to be doing body suspension, which involved them sticking big hooks into their skin and then hanging themselves from a frame at the bottom of the garden. He first tried body suspension back in 2004 when a friend invited him to join in after he'd had a bad break-up with his girlfriend. He'd already had lots of piercings, so this seemed like a natural thing to do. The longer I chatted to him, the more I noticed the little modifications he had done to himself. He said his body could be seen as a piece of art, but I think it was more like browsing the pound shop where you see things and think, 'Why would anyone want that?!' He'd had implants, but not silicone implants to make him look muscly. These were made of Teflon to make him look . . . I dunno . . . like he'd injected Maltesers into his arm. If you gave Ricardo a Chinese burn it would be like popping bubblewrap. As well as the Teflon balls up his arm he'd had the letter 'R' inserted under his skin on the back of his hand. He said he likes modifying his body but isn't a fan of tattoos, which is just as well, as I reckon it would be pretty hard for a tattoo artist to try and draw anything on his lumpy arms.

KARL: What was the first thing you did to yourself?

RICARDO: It was my lip piercing in 1993. After that I got my nipples and my tongue done.

KARL: You haven't had anything done down below?

RICARDO: Yeah, of course.

KARL: What! You have?!

RICARDO: Something like this *(points to lumps on his arms)*.

KARL: That's ridiculous! It must look like a Picnic bar. Do you have Picnic chocolate bars over here? It's like you're destroying yourself in a way.

RICARDO: I'm destroying my body, but building my spirit.

KARL: What do you do?

RICARDO: I'm a qualified lawyer.

> KARL: You go to court looking like that?!
>
> RICARDO: Yes, I put my ear behind like this and just hide my arms with my clothes.
>
> KARL: If I was on jury duty and you came into the court-room I'd think you were the accused!

I asked Ricardo if I could see the big ear hole without the plug. It looked like a bit of limp defrosted calamari. I wish I hadn't asked. He said he used to have fifty or sixty piercings but now he only has twenty, which is still a lot of metal to be carrying around. When he has a shower I bet he uses WD40 instead of shower gel.

While we were talking I noticed a tiny screw coming out of his forehead. I asked him what it was and he said it's the remains of a piercing that he didn't like. The screw used to have a ball on the end but it kept getting caught up in his wife's hair when they were dancing and now he can't re-move the screw. It's mental. I can understand Frankenstein having bolts in his neck – he had to have them otherwise his bloody head would come off – but I struggle to understand why anyone else would want this.

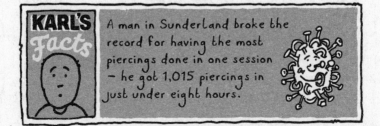

KARL'S *facts*

A man in Sunderland broke the record for having the most piercings done in one session – he got 1,015 piercings in just under eight hours.

Ricardo offered me some tacos and told me to be careful as they were hot. Which I suppose wasn't surprising at a pain party. I joked that I was expecting ice cream and razor blades for pudding. The thing is, that wasn't far from the truth – as I munched on a taco, Ricardo unscrewed a light-bulb from a garden light and asked me to stamp on it. Then he started to eat it.

KARL: You're just doing that for me though, aren't you? You wouldn't get home from a hard day at work and go, 'I'm starving and we're outta lightbulbs!'

RICARDO: I am trying to show you that if you suffer a little bit, you can find a higher view of the world. In the beginning I was scared; now I'm like, 'Okay, I can do this'. I don't know why I was afraid of doing this.

KARL: Because it's dangerous.

RICARDO: Yeah, it's dangerous but it doesn't mean that I shouldn't do it. Walking on the street with a lot of traffic is dangerous.

Maybe he misunderstands the saying 'a light lunch'. It was odd watching a thirty-six-year-old man scoffing down a light-bulb, but I'd be more interested to see how he reacted when it came out the other end. Let's see how much he really enjoys the pain then.

RICARDO: I don't drink alcohol, I don't smoke, I don't use drugs. This is like my drug and it really makes me happy

---

> because I know what I can do with my body and that makes me feel like a real person.

He was about to start doing some body suspensions. The hooks are specially made for the purpose. Mental! It amazes me that Woolworths had to close due to lack of custom and yet there's a business going strong that makes hooks for people to hang themselves with.

> KARL: So how does happiness come into this body suspension stuff? Does it make you happy?
>
> RICARDO: Yeah, very happy. When I'm under stress, body suspensions clear the stress. I have a thirteen-year-old son. When I first started doing this we were not living together and a friend of mine said let's do body suspensions. The pain of not living with my son was not so bad while the hook was in my skin.

He asked if I would like to have a go, as his brother-in-law was also trying it today for the first time. His brother-in-law didn't look the sort to be into this type of thing; he didn't have any piercings that I could see and no body implants. He just looked like an average young fella who wouldn't look out of place at a One Direction concert, so I asked Ricardo why he was getting involved.

> RICARDO: Because he saw me when I first started doing body suspensions. He knows this makes me happy so

he wants to try. He says he can see that I'm happy and he wants to be part of that happiness.

I suggested he should maybe start off smaller, maybe munch on a lightbulb first, but he was having none of it. A woman was massaging his back to loosen the muscles as it isn't good to tense up when you're about to have a hook inserted into your skin – a little tip there for anyone considering attempting this at home. (By the way, don't try this at home.) He sat down on a chair and one of Ricardo's friends made marks with a Sharpie pen where the hooks were going to be inserted. He seemed pretty relaxed, chewing gum and texting. In went the hooks and there was no scream or yelp or any kind of reaction. I think I reacted more to it than he did. Blood ran down his back as a further three hooks were inserted. Other people at the party didn't stop what they were doing as they'd all seen it before. Once the hooks were in place, he wandered over to the metal T-frame and stood on the chair so they could hook him up. Then he stepped off the chair and hung like a kitten being held by the scruff of its neck in its mother's jaw. He continued to chew his gum as a friend took a photograph on his phone. A few people who'd been busy chatting noticed he'd gone through with it and gave a few claps as if applauding a baby taking its first steps. He was now part of the club. A club I had no intention of joining. I can understand how it might clear your thoughts and stresses for the few minutes you are up there, but for me happiness comes when you sort your problems out properly and they go away permanently, rather than just temporarily like this. But if I did want to experience pain, it would be enough for me if I just stubbed my toe on the corner of the bed or ate some of the foil on a Kit Kat by accident, as that feels pretty bad if you have silver fillings. I don't need to go this extreme.

As soon as he was down off the hooks, Ricardo's other friends were queuing to be hung up like damp clothes on a washing line. Even the medic who was there for safety reasons wanted a go because he enjoyed pain! He's a bloody medic. Imagine telling him you were in agony only for him to say, 'Oh, you lucky sod.' Finally Ricardo went up there and was hung from his back and his legs. He had the biggest smile on his face. 'It's madness,' I said. I think if he'd been around when Jesus was put on the cross, he'd have been next in line to have a go.

I left the pain party none the wiser as to what it was all about, but knowing I was a lot happier being away from the sharp hooks and all that blood.

MAKING OTHER PEOPLE HAPPY

We left Mexico and headed for LA to meet a man called Tommy the clown, who gets his happiness from making others happy. I'm surprised clowns have ever brought happiness to anyone, but then to be honest I might not be the best one to judge, as I've never liked being told jokes either. I don't mind watching comedians telling jokes on the telly, as you don't have to react, but if someone tells me a joke to my face I feel under pressure to find it amusing. There's also the chance I might not even understand it. I suppose that's one good thing about jokes being passed around via text/email/Facebook/Twitter and the like: it takes that stress away and you can just reply with 'good one'. I never reply with LOL (laugh out loud) as most people seem to do these days. Or PMSL (piss myself laughing), LMAO (laugh my arse off) or ROFL (roll on floor laughing). I don't use these abbreviations, as I don't know the order that they should go in. Does laughing your arse off rank higher than pissing your pants? I've never had a reaction like that to any joke to be honest. I've ROFC (rolled on floor crying) with kidney stones, but I don't laugh that much. When I do, it's normally at things that you shouldn't laugh at. I laughed when I saw a baby fall out of a pram and its mother didn't notice as she was too busy on the phone. It was fine, she just picked it back up without stopping her call, but just picturing it can raise a smile. Suzanne says I shouldn't laugh at that, but then I've seen her chuckling at *You've Been Framed* which shows similar things every week, so what's the difference?

Last time I really, really laughed was Christmas 2011 watching *Bullseye* with Jim Bowen with me dad. It was a special charity episode and as they had the same shite prizes they gave away every week, they had to find a way of making them sound useful to the different charities. So when they popped the dart in red number four, Jim said something along the lines of, 'Well done, that's red number four. You've won the food blender, so that will be going to a special home where the patients need help chewing.' Me and me dad were crying. It just made me laugh, more so cos it wasn't supposed to be funny and cos Suzanne thought we shouldn't be laughing at it. That always makes something funnier.

Anyhow, the way Tommy the clown spreads happiness is through dance. He drives around the poorer areas of LA where he grew up blasting music out of his van. He'll pick a spot, park up, turn the music up and get out and dance with his crew of hip hop clowns. This generates a bit of a party atmosphere and attracts local kids who might be bored or a bit down in the dumps to come over and join in the dancing. After ten minutes or so, he's back in the van and off to another destination.

As we approached Tommy's place, I couldn't hear the sat nav in my hire car due to the loud music. I followed my ears and they took me to Tommy. There he was with his big multi-coloured Afro clown wig and bright clothes surrounded by about seven kids in their late teens dancing around his brightly coloured van. I asked Tommy how he came to be doing this.

TOMMY: Twenty years ago I did some time in jail, but I got out, got myself together and these girls at my church were doing the clown stuff and they showed me. They painted my face and said I'd probably be a good clown so I did a party for one of my co-workers and I stayed there three hours and said you know what, I'm going to come up with Tommy, the hip hop dancing clown, and I did, and it brings me joy and happiness to see other people smile. We are going to join forces with our energy and we are going to go through the neighbourhood and create an atmosphere that's unbelievable and we are gonna bring joy and happiness to the community today. You ready to do that?

I'm a bit of a fan of dancing and I agree that it can cheer you up. The only problem was I was still really aching from the running with the tribe a few days ago. If they had wanted me to do 80s robotic dancing that would have been fine, as my joints were really stiff, but this was a more energetic dance that involved fast, jerky movements and was called 'clowning'. They tried teaching me a few basic moves, but I think dancing should be improvised and you should just let your body do what it wants. If you have to think about what you're doing it takes the enjoyment out of it for me. Tommy said it was fine for me to do what I like as it's all about expressing yourself, and I think he's right. People at the pain party were covered in tattoos and they said it was a form of expression, but I didn't understand what they were expressing. There was a woman at the pain party with a tattoo of Johnny Depp on her knee, Spongebob Squarepants on her chest and Neil Morrissey from *Men Behaving Badly* on her back. That isn't expressing anything! She just looked like a page from a TV listings magazine. Though it turned out the tattoo wasn't Neil Morrissey, it was supposed to be Jim Morrison.

I danced to one track to show them the sort of thing I would do. They thought it was fine but said I'd have to get my face painted so that I fitted in with the rest of the crew. I liked the idea of this, as I was knackered from dancing to just one track and it meant I could rest before we went on the road. That's the problem these days – dance records are really long. Songs used to be only two minutes long, but now there are remixes that go on for nine minutes or more. I don't understand why some clubs won't let you in wearing trainers, as the workout you get just dancing to one song you'd be best wearing a tracksuit.

Rocco was one of the hip hop clowns. It was his job to paint my face.

ROCCO: So we going to paint you up, KP? I can't call you Karl no more, you have to be KP from now on. Question: what are some things that make you happy, keep you going in life?

KARL: Cake.

ROCCO: You like cake? What kind?

KARL: Lemon muffins.

ROCCO: Okay. You like the beach, the sun?

KARL: Yeah, yeah. So how did you get into this then, Rocco?

ROCCO: Well, I used to be a young knucklehead out gang-banging, doing crazy, acting silly.

KARL: Why? Just boredom?

ROCCO: Yeah, and then getting caught up in the neigh-bourhood it is too easy to just adapt to that if you're not keeping yourself busy and staying motivated. I had a life-changing experience where I almost got shot but luckily the gun jammed, so that was my opportunity to leave the fool-ishness behind and I took it. From then on I have been with Tommy and people look at me in a new light. I don't have to go outside and watch my back. Now people are actually happy to see me.

KARL: Well, what's the gun thing all about? How did that happen?

ROCCO: Just hanging out on a block, being from the gang, you know, some of our enemies just happened to be rolling through, looking for people from our gang. Pulled up on us and stuck a gauged shotgun out the window, and by the time I got up to run I heard a click but the gun had jammed, other-wise my whole back would be gone, I could've been dead.

KARL: Jesus!

ROCCO: Yeah, from that day on, it was like, this ain't the lifestyle. Got a second chance, though. I took it.

Sometimes we need something bad to happen for us to appreciate things more. I remember as a kid I nearly died eating a Mr Freeze ice pop, but my mam gave me the Heimlich manoeuvre and saved me from choking, and I felt amazing after. So, in a way, me and Rocco had something in common. Rocco went from someone pointing a gun at him and saying 'Freeze', and I nearly died eating a Mr Freeze. My dad always says I wasn't that close to dying and that I'm exaggerating but my mam remembers me collapsing on the floor and my lips going purple. My dad just carried on watching the telly and said I had purple lips from the blue raspberry ice pop!

Rocco did a good job of my face. A nice image of a cake on one cheek and a beach with bright blue sea on the other. Tommy gave me a bright T-shirt and pants and a big multi-coloured Afro to wear, and off we went.

We pulled up at a skate park and the music was turned up. When Tommy blew his whistle, that was the signal for us to get out and dance. I really went for it. As it was quite an aggressive type of dance I found it useful to think of the things that annoyed me in life, as that seemed to give me more energy. I pictured Suzanne's mam sucking loudly on her mints and sitting in my chair. It really helped, and I was like Popeye when he eats his spinach. I pictured myself waving my fists at Suzanne's mam and turned this into a dance move. Maybe this is how Michael Jackson came up with his moonwalk. Maybe he was acting out a time when he stepped in dogshit and tried to get it off his shoes.

A crowd was forming around us. It was like a scene from *Fame*. Even though we were blocking the road, the drivers didn't get angry, they just got out and danced with us or stood there clapping. I'm not sure if this would help me feel happier if I was down, though. Sometimes seeing really happy faces can be annoying if you're fed up. This was the reason I didn't take Happyface biscuits with me into the jungle in Peru when I was filming *An Idiot Abroad*. The idea of being hot and sticky and dehydrated in a sweaty tent and then having some biscuits with grinning faces on them would have driven me up the wall, so I ended up just taking some Ginger Crunch.

KARL'S Facts

Residents of a town in France were struck by the 'Dance Plague' in 1518. Over 400 people danced for a month and dropped dead from exhaustion.

We headed for another location and I was well up for it. I do think there's happiness to be found in dancing. We've been doing it for thousands of years, so there must be something in it. Every tribe I've visited around the world in the last three years always ended up dancing at some point during my stay. And when you think about it, babies do it naturally before they can even walk. Bees, beetles, birds and loads of other creatures do it too. Scientists have even discovered single-celled algae dancing about in ponds. It's part of life.

If there's music it's pretty hard to stop your body reacting, even if it's just a small shuffle or a finger tap. It's like putting a Rowntree's Fruit Pastille in your mouth without chewing it. It's impossible.

We stopped on the edge of the park and once again kids of all ages legged it over full of excitement as soon as they heard the music. I'm sure some of them must have thought we were the ice-cream man.

'DOES LAUGHING YOUR ARSE OFF (LMAO) rank higher than PISSING YOURSELF LAUGHING (PMSL)?'

TOMMY: Well, how do you feel? Did you have fun?

KARL: I enjoyed it, yeah. I wasn't really thinking about anyone else getting happy from what I was doing, though, but I had a good time.

TOMMY: Right, right. Well, this is your first time experiencing this type of wave and this type of movement. I got twenty years' experience, so I know I come to bring the joy. You get nervous when you pull up to a crowd of people. But you get out there and then it's fun, you look at them and they smile. They come and say, 'I wanna dance with you!' You just brought joy and happiness right there.

I know I said that I don't like people telling me jokes, but reading them is different, cos there's no pressure on you to laugh. This all reminded me of my favourite joke about dancing. I think it's a good one:

What sort of dance do they do in Arabia?
Sheik to sheik.
LOL!

CHANGING THE WAY YOU LOOK TO MAKE YOU HAPPY

Sometimes, people are unhappy because of the way they look. In LA it's not unusual to get that sorted by having some work done. I think it's down to the fact that they walk about with their body on show a lot more than we do. I feel like I'm being a bit flamboyant if I have my sleeves rolled up. I think I'm pretty average-looking; I don't stand out in a crowd and that's the way I like it. The best thing about me is probably my eyes, but then I suppose my eyes would think that, as it's them that are looking at them. I've got a pig nose. But I've found since going bald I don't need to look in the mirror as much as I used to. I only really see myself when I'm brushing my teeth and even then I just look at my teeth, which aren't that great either but better than some of the kids' I went to school with. They had teeth that could have been used as cogs. My wrinkly forehead isn't so great either. I have a head that resembles an elephant's knee because I've been frowning for most of my life. I think it's cos from a young age life has puzzled me. My mam said she can't remember me without a wrinkly head either, so much so that when it was fancy-dress day at school she suggested I went as a walnut.

Of all the things I've seen on this trip so far, beauty is probably something most people worry about or have worried about at some point in their life. People will go to great lengths to achieve the perfect look. The latest fad is smearing wormshit all over your face as they say it's full of anti-aging properties. It must be true, as a worm's face is as smooth as its arse and I can never tell which end is which. The wormshit isn't cheap either. You're looking at around £20 for a small tub of the stuff. But then I should think wormshit isn't easy to find, especially when you need to find enough to fill a tub.

I was in LA to meet a man called Justin who has had many operations over the years to try and perfect his body. People say he looks like a Ken doll (Barbie's fella). I met him by the side of a pool where he was topping up his tan.

KARL: So when did this start?

JUSTIN: I had my first nose job when I was eighteen years old and I've had five in total now.

KARL: Five nose jobs! How big was it?!

JUSTIN: It was pretty big, but it's been more tweaking over the years, little changes I wanted. What I wanted when I was eighteen wasn't the same as I wanted when I was thirty. My ideals of beauty changed. The standards, the trends . . . that all plays a part in what your optimal aesthetic is at the time. So I guess I've had 120 procedures, not all surgical. Some of them have been lasers, some have been non-invasive. But still, 120 procedures over fourteen years and about $154,000. A big investment.

There's not much he hasn't had done to his face, and the rest of his body. He's had solid silicone pec implants, biceps implants, triceps implants, shoulder implants – which to be fair did look pretty real, but I can't imagine it being very comfortable. I don't like lying down on pebbles on Brighton beach and I imagine this is how it feels for him wherever he lies. He said he's happy with the constant change, but I think if he did my job he wouldn't be so keen, as he'd have to keep updating his passport photo. If he took photos with a normal camera I reckon he'd look different before he'd had time to develop the film at the chemist.

KARL: I know I'm not perfect, but then I don't have to look at myself that often. Only when I'm brushing me teeth, and maybe a quick glance as I wash my face but that's it.

JUSTIN: I'd go crazy, Karl, I couldn't do that.

KARL: What, not look in a mirror?

JUSTIN: I've spent so much time and effort to make myself look a specific way, the validation that I get when I look at myself really gives me enjoyment. It makes me happy internally to see what I've created externally. It's neat for me to wake up in the morning and say, 'What do I want to take on next?' It is like a project for me, like a passion.

I showed Justin the lines on my head, and he said that he'd already noticed them and that I could get them removed by having Botox and putting filler through the creases, but the amount of times I frown I reckon they'd be back in no time. I'd be filling the lines on my head more than I fill my car with petrol. Plus, I think it's important to be able to have facial expressions. Suzanne knows what I'm thinking without me having to say anything due to the way my face moves. Sometimes I think my face knows how I feel about things before I do. I asked Justin to show me some facial expressions, but he couldn't.

The plan was for us to head over to a medical spa where Justin would be having a slight top-up done around his eyes, and to see what they would recommend to make me look better. We talked on the way about the other procedures that the place offers.

JUSTIN: I heard she does what they call ball ironing. It is like a resurfacing of your scrotum.

KARL: There's a call for that?!

JUSTIN: I guess. I'm sure people want to exfoliate all different parts of their bodies.

KARL: But getting rid of the wrinkledness in their bollocks?

JUSTIN: Yeah, I don't really think that is possible. Supposedly it burns off some of the top layers of the skin to reveal the fresh skin underneath.

KARL: Jesus!!

JUSTIN: So you'd have rejuvenated balls.

KARL: Who's worrying about that?

JUSTIN: Well, I guess you have people doing anal bleaching.

KARL: What . . . Anal bleaching?! I've not heard of that.

> JUSTIN: Maybe you should try that. They do like a chemical peel on it and it's the same idea, they are exfoliating off the skin.

I don't know what's going on in the world any more. I think we've really lost the plot. I mean, how many people are seeing your testicles and anus? I can sort of understand having work done on parts of your body that are on show if it means it gives you more confidence, but if you're showing off your balls and arse all the time I'd say you have too much confidence. The ball sack is supposed to be wrinkly; they're not bloody worry lines! I can't believe there's a machine that fixes this. I don't even own an iron. Balls don't need ironing! They're like a shellsuit, they're meant to be creased-looking. And anyway, I'm sat on them most of the time, so they'd only get creased again. As for getting your arse bleached, I don't know what to make of that. I couldn't tell you what mine looks like. If you showed me five photos of various anuses, I couldn't pick mine out from a line-up. I'd have more chance telling who's who in Jedward. I never understood why barbers used to show me the back of my head in a mirror after a quick trim, so I certainly wouldn't worry about the colour of my anus. I'd say if you're worrying about the colour of your anus, things must be good, as you can't have proper worries in your life.

KARL'S Facts

In recent years plastic surgeons have made a man look like a tiger, a woman look like her daughter and another woman look like a Barbie doll.

We got to the clinic and Justin handed me a leaflet listing all the procedures available. There was the 'ball ironing', otherwise known as a 'scrotal lift': $575! I wondered if they'd do a two-for-one offer. Nurse Jamie, who co-ran the place, came out to see us.

JAMIE: Welcome to Beauty Park. You are looking fabulous! So lean. You look good.

JUSTIN: I try! We're thinking about doing a bit of beautification. We want to get Karl fixed up for something.

KARL: Hiya. Yeah, I want to see if I get any happiness out of looking a bit better.

JAMIE: When you look good you feel good, I'm telling you.

We headed into one of the cubicles, where there was all sorts of machinery. I explained I wasn't planning on having anything done, as I'm not too fussed about my looks and how it's not what blokes do back in the UK.

JAMIE: I have a client from London and he says he can't even wear fitted shirts because all of his friends razz him for it, like you can't do any kind of male grooming at all. Why is it frowned upon so much there, do you think?

KARL: Erm, I don't think it is frowned upon. It is just that we have lines on our face. So you lot probably think it is frowned upon.

JAMIE: Haha. Right, let me tell you what I think. You have a little bit of redness in your skin, so I would maybe just tone that down a bit. This nasal labial fold is slightly deeper than the other one so I would just kind of soften it. These I don't like because I think they make us look sad. (*hands Karl a mirror*)

KARL: I don't even know what you are seeing there.

JAMIE: You don't see your oral commissure? You see here? They call them marionettes, like puppeteer lines. You see how you are losing a bit of tissue here and here?

KARL: Honest to God, I'm not messing about, I can't see what you mean, so should I bother sorting a problem that I don't see?

JAMIE: I mean, I think you're a handsome guy. You got the cake, let's just put some icing on it. Let's just make you look a little more rested. I am pretty subtle in what I do. I have been doing this for twenty-five years and my face still moves.

KARL: Have you had loads of work done?

JAMIE: Yeah, I've done stuff. I don't like anything frozen, I don't do, like, big lips, it's not what I'm known for. I don't mind my brow moving, but I don't like the lines to get etched.

KARL: Well, they're important, aren't they, the lines in your face? They're like the history of your life.

JAMIE: That is one way to look at it, but I never bought in to the idea that wrinkles make you look more distinguished. I just think they make you look older.

She used some bit of kit that vibrated and felt warm as she pushed it down on the creases on my face. I found it quite relaxing until I thought maybe this was the machine they use to do ball ironing, and now it was rubbing across my upper lip. I didn't ask, as I didn't want to know. After rolling my face out they moved on to another part of my head.

JAMIE: (*to her assistant*) You know what, let's do the eye lipo bone, Kelly.

KARL: Eye lipo?! I haven't got fat eyes!

JAMIE: A little eye lipo. Have you thought about doing that?

JUSTIN: What about using some of the eye lipo on his neck, under the chin. It would really help to tighten because it is a little full-on.

KARL: I ain't got a saggy neck!

JUSTIN: Just the beginnings of one, so nip it in the bud now.

I stopped listening to Justin. I don't think he likes to leave anything as nature intended. He'd iron out the lump on a camel's back and get a pelican to have its throat lifted. Jamie changed equipment and got back to work on my face. I had no idea what this one was doing, but she seemed to know how my face should look, so I let her get on with it. She was like an artist working on a canvas, working on an area and then stepping back and tilting her head before giving an approving smile.

JAMIE: And we should also try to soften these lines on your forehead. Do you want to do a tiny bit of filler here and maybe a little bit of laser here?

KARL: I know the lines on me forehead are bad. Can you fill that line there? That looks like the Nile or something going across my head.

JAMIE: I can do that.

BEN THE DIRECTOR: I'm worried you're getting a bit carried away.

KARL: I'm never going to come to a place like this again, so I might as well just get rid of that one there.

JUSTIN: I would say anything worth doing is worth overdoing. That is my motto.

BEN: Just so you understand, this would mean getting something injected into your face.

KARL: What is the stuff again?

JAMIE: It is hyaluronic acid, which is in your body already. I want to give you just a few more angles to your face because it is a bit round.

JUSTIN: That is what I said.

KARL: What is wrong with a round face?! Everybody is talking about my round head like it's a problem.

JUSTIN: Just needs a little more structure.

BEN: Karl, are you sure? Think now . . .

KARL: What do I have to be worried about? Thing is, I might be worried now, but no one can tell because you've got rid of some of me worry lines.

I know I have quite a round head. I have the jawline of a jelly baby. A lot of people have said I look quite Polish, as they tend to have round faces too. People have approached me before and I've thought they've wanted a photo with me cos they've seen me on the telly, but then they've asked for a quote to fit a new kitchen.

Two and a half hours later Jamie's work was done.

JAMIE: I am now happier.

KARL: Are you really? Shouldn't I be saying that, not you?

JAMIE: It's so subtle, you probably won't be able to tell because you couldn't see it before. But I can tell. Look in the mirror.

KARL: No, I can't tell the difference. You know what it is,

though, it's just that thing that you're saying I look better and that makes me feel better. It's not about what I can see because I don't have to look at it. That is all this is really, just having people saying, 'Oh, you look quite nice.'

JUSTIN: It's true. Getting validation from everybody that you look the best you can.

KARL: Validation. (*to Jamie*) Yeah, you're not just doing that though, are you, because this is your job. You actually think that looks better, don't you?

JAMIE: I do, honestly.

Afterwards I found out the real reason she was happier than when I first walked in. I'd had $2,500 of work done! I'd have thought I could have bought a new head for that!

ANGER THERAPY

We left LA and flew to Dallas to go to a place called the Anger Room, where for $25 people who aren't happy get five minutes to smash things up and help release their anger. Business is going well there, so well that they're opening up more of these Anger Rooms. The rate it's going, the high streets in Dallas will end up looking very similar to the London streets during the 2011 riots.

Releasing your anger to make you happier is an interesting idea. But while I do get angry from time to time, I never get the urge to damage things. I had mates who vandalised stuff for fun when I was a kid, but I never got involved, as I couldn't see how they got any satisfaction from breaking things. I think it's because I saw it as an unnecessary waste, and that annoys me. I really don't like waste. Just two days ago I ate six fish fingers as they were all frozen together and couldn't be separated. I cooked them and ate them all rather than throwing them away. Then there's the amount of junk mail that comes through my front door. It's unbelievable, and the waste of paper makes me angry. Three or four times a day leaflets are being shoved through my door. I'm convinced it's a government exercise initiative to get people off their arse and walking to their door and bending down three or four times a day. So yeah, no joy from demolition and waste. I'd say I get more enjoyment from fixing things that are broken.

I arrived at a scrapyard where the anger session would be taking place. Donna, who came up with the concept and owns the business, met me and took me to meet some of the other customers. A woman dressed in a boiler suit, hard hat and goggles was going hell for leather smashing something up with a sledgehammer as other customers watched. As I got closer, I could see it was a printer.

DONNA: She has a problem with printers.

KARL: Yeah, I can see that.

DONNA: She doesn't like office equipment, so we let her come out here and tear up office equipment. For people who don't like TVs, they can break TVs. If you don't like cars, you can break cars. If you don't like living-room things, you can break living-room things. Do you have something that you don't like?

KARL: Vandalism. So this doesn't really work for me, does it?

The woman who had been busy smashing the printer up was called Diana.

KARL: Looks like you've got a proper printer problem? It's normally just a paper jam, you know.

DIANA: Yeah, well, it's not so much about the equipment, per se. Printers never work and that does piss me off, but it's about taking all the things that are bothering you and channelling it into something that isn't gonna hurt you in real life, like screaming at your boss would get you fired, you know.

> So I save the anger, and then go for it here. It's a different way to kind of get it out.
>
> DONNA: Karl, do you have something that you don't like?

To give me ideas, Donna had lined up various bits of home electrical items that she had taken from junkyards or had donated to her. There was a TV, coffee machine, Wi-Fi router and DVD player. It seemed like such a waste, as most of these items worked, it's just that no one wanted them as they were old models. This is a big problem these days and it's made me buy fewer electrical items, as they are out of date within a year. I bought an Apple iPad and it was out of date sooner than a real apple would have been. We're forced into buying new things all the time, and then it's tricky to get rid of your stuff as everything is so cheap new that people don't want to buy second-hand. Charity shops won't even take stuff any more unless you have the box for it as evidence that it isn't stolen. Not that having a box proves it's not stolen; I might have nicked a job lot of them from Dixons. The charity shops also say they won't take electrical goods as they could be faulty and give the customer a shock, but if you visit charity shops often you'll know the shocks come not from the electrical appliances but the bloody prices they're selling the second-hand goods for.

I walked up and down trying to decide which one of the five items I should smash up. The problem was I wasn't that angry at the time, so I had to try and think about something that got me worked up, which kind of defeated the point of being there in the first place. I think this idea could work if people had a room in their house especially for smashing things up if a moment of rage came along, but with the Anger Room if you're livid about something and you call up to make an appointment and they say, 'Yes, sir, we can fit you in next Wednesday at 2.45 p.m. to smash up a toaster,' what use is that? Anger is like a fart: you need to release it when the pressure becomes too much and you can't wait.

If I was to smash something in anger I needed a reason. When Suzanne makes me a Sunday dinner she always has a go at me for messing it all up. She says she spent a while making it look nice on the plate but then I just go and mash it up. But I do it for a reason, as I prefer the taste when I can get a bit of everything in one mouthful. It's her choice to make it look nice, but for me it's all about the taste. I'd be happier if she just stuck it all in a blender and I had a Sunday dinner smoothie.

I asked another man what he was angry about to try and get some inspiration.

MAN: I would just say . . . life in general right now.

KARL: And what would you do if you didn't have this place to come and smash shit up? How would you get rid of that aggression?

MAN: I'd just bottle it up. There's nothing else you can do like this, really. Not without getting in trouble anyway.

WOMAN: This is a whole different level of therapy. It's so much better than sitting on a couch and listening to some-one blabbing about your problems. You just take everything you have internally and just bring it out and beat the shit out of stuff. And you walk away feeling lighter.

KARL: I moan a lot. I do moan. That's my release.

WOMAN: And do people listen to you when you complain?

KARL: No, but I don't think that's important. I'm almost not bothered by people hearing it, as long as I can release it.

Ben suggested I think about Suzanne's mam sucking on her mints, so that's what I did while I smashed up a forty-inch LCD widescreen TV with a sledgehammer. I really went for it for a good five minutes, but at the end when the TV was in bits, I honestly couldn't say I enjoyed it. I'd forgotten about Suzanne's mam sucking mints and was just amazed how little was inside the TV casing. It's like a bag of crisps – they used to be full but now you only get a measly handful.

KARL'S Facts
Experts on the Chinese version of the show 'Antiques Roadshow' smash artefacts that they judge to be fakes.

Coming here and realising I didn't enjoy smashing stuff up and hearing the way the other people were a bit pissed off with life confirmed to me that I'm a pretty happy person. It helps to be reminded of this. I think this is why people watch

HAPPINESS

HAPPINESS

DEATH

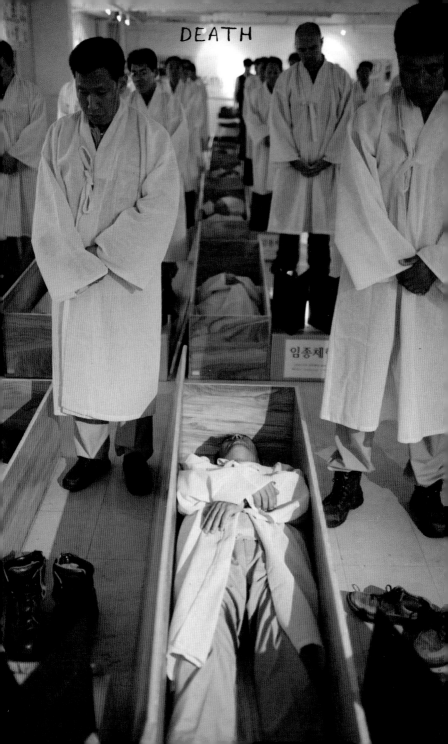

DEATH

BIN AND GONE . . .

the news. It's all bad news these days, but I'm sure we like it cos it makes us realise things aren't that bad. I know I moan a lot and am a bit of a pessimist, but I don't need to add to my negativity by smashing things up. I need a dose of positivity, which I get from fixing things, painting and improving stuff around the house. Maybe that's why I got into the face enhancement stuff with Jamie and Justin in LA, the idea of taking my wrinkly face and trying to make it look less shite.

Donna and the others asked me to move on to the car. It wasn't a bad-looking car, certainly in better condition than some I've seen on the road at home. They asked me to imagine that I'd just been cut up by someone and now the driver was flicking me the finger, but the problem was I wasn't seeing that. I saw it as a car that would be driven by a family man who's fairly easygoing, kids in the back, and I could imagine all the happy times they probably had in it. I got quite attached to my dad's cars when I was younger, and even though it was exciting if he bought a slightly newer model, there was something sad about seeing the old one go. If I was to smash this car up I needed something that really annoyed me. That's when I remembered the calls I'd been getting recently from some company that kept asking if I wanted my PPI back. I explained my irritant to the rest of the group.

DIANA: Yeah, they wait until you're at dinner, right when you're eating dinner with your family, that's when they're gonna call.

MAN: Well, that's the car they drive.

> **WOMAN**: Yeah, they drive that car.
>
> **KARL**: Right, I'm picturing it. They're sat outside my house in this car, they can see me eating dinner and now they're calling me.
>
> **WOMAN**: Yeah . . . this is it . . . payback time.

I was now getting in the zone and pretended I was on the phone to the PPI people.

> **KARL**: 'Why do you always call me at this time of night when you know I'm having my dinner?' 'Yeah, we're sat outside. We can see you. That's why we're calling you, just to annoy you.' 'What, you're sat outside now?' 'Yeah, we're sat outside. In the car.'
>
> **WOMAN**: Yeah. They wanna know if you want PPI.
>
> **KARL**: 'Right, I'm coming outside . . . Is that you sat in there? Why do you keep calling me?!!!'

I let loose as if the PPI man was sat in the car.

> **KARL**: 'Why do you keep bloody calling me, you dick! I'm trying to eat my dinner in there! It's going cold now . . . (*sledgehammer to the window*) Are you gonna keep calling now? (*hammer to the bonnet*) Dickhead! (*big slam to the roof*)
>
> **WOMAN**: Yeah! That's right, you defend yourself.

252

All the others piled in and finished the job even though they probably had no idea what PPI was. I had to sit down and rest, as I was exhausted from getting angry.

'I REALLY don't like waste Two days ago I ate SIX FISH FINGERS As they were FROZEN TOGETHER and couldn't BE SEPARATED.'

LIVING THE SIMPLE LIFE

To end my trip looking at happiness I went to meet a fifty-two-year-old man called Daniel Suelo, who gave up everything in 2000 to live a life without money. I couldn't see how living like this would be possible, never mind how it could make you happy. Money is the reason most things happen. It's why I'm sat writing this book. Even my dad, who is well into his seventies, still likes the idea of having more money, even though I doubt he'd want to change his life at this stage of it. He still gets me mam to do the lottery twice a week. I've told him he's wasting his time and that there's more chance of my mam getting run over on the way to buying a ticket than there is winning, but he just says, 'Well, as long as it's on the way back and not on the way, just in case it is the winning ticket.'

I like to have money, not to waste and buy things I don't need, but just so it's there for when I need it. When I was younger and was paid cash for my paper round and cleaning cars, I got a lot of happiness from changing pound coins into five-pound notes and seeing them grow in a white plastic tub I kept under my bed. It made me feel like I had worth and purpose.

Daniel normally lives in a cave in Utah, but I was going to meet him in Billings, Montana, where he had hitchhiked to in order to attend the Rainbow Gathering festival. He was planning to explain his way of living to other travellers who were keen to join him in his moneyless world. The idea was for me to experience Daniel's life for a full day and night to see if I could find happiness from living this way. So when Ben, the cameraman and the soundman all had breakfast that morning, I stayed in my hotel room with my stomach rumbling until it was time to go and meet him, as I wanted to see how I could feed myself without using money. Food is one of the best things in life for me. I get a lot of pleasure from feeding myself, so much so that I have done it at some point every day since I was born. I read recently that there are moths that don't have mouths. I'd hate that. I thought they'd be okay, though, as they are blind and can't see what they're missing, but then I read that they have a sense of smell, which must drive them up the wall when they smell cooked bacon, the nicest smell ever. They'd be like, 'Mmm, that smells good. I can't wait to tuck in . . . Oh, I can't as I've got no mouth.' Nature is cruel sometimes.

Daniel believes in experiencing inner peace without kidding yourself into being happy by surrounding yourself with materialistic stuff. I think he's right, but there was no way I could find inner peace that morning, as my inners were being pretty vocal letting me know I needed food. I'm sure Ben was trying to put me in a bad mood, as they all seemed to be having a really long breakfast that morning. Normally when we're filming we're lucky to get thirty minutes before we have to dash off to wherever we're going, so it was annoying that of all days they were in no hurry. Then I got more annoyed, as Ben said he'd like to film my thoughts on my day ahead as we drove to meet Daniel, which meant I'd have to wait a bit longer for food and drink. As every minute passed I got in more of a mood. I talked about how I couldn't see how the planet could operate if everybody lived the way Daniel did. 'He must be a scrounger or break the law to survive,' I said. If everyone just gave up, there would be no police, no rules, no councils. I think it's a nice idea that he believes we would all join together and help each other, but I doubt that would happen, not now the population is as big as it is. We'd soon run out of things if there was no order. I think the strong, tough people would group together and take over the fertile ground where food grew and would fight to keep it for themselves while the weak would starve. Which I suppose is what is happening now to a certain degree. There's people with a lot and people who have nothing, but at least everyone gets their bins emptied and has drains that work. Ben said the idea was that people would share.

BEN: It's just communism really but without a leader . . .

KARL: But someone would still have to do the grim jobs. It's all very well going, 'Let's live off the land, I'll grow the corn.' That bit is easy, and once you've put the seeds down you've got nowt to do for weeks. But what about the toilets that need cleaning? Who's going to do that? They'll say, 'Well, I'm not. I'm cleaning windows.' Who's going to volunteer when the drains are all backed up? We're not paying service charges any more so the council aren't sorting it. The shit is backed up, it's gurgling out of the grid and it's our responsibility! It's going on the road! You've got shit everywhere! Who's sorting that out?! They'd say, 'I'm not. I'm growing the corn' and I'd say, 'Stop growing corn, as it's making people shit more! Can someone make bread to bung people up while we sort the drainage out!' Yes, we'd probably all have more free time but we'd only spend it picking the shit out of our shoes with a stick. It wouldn't work! I wish I was back at the Anger Room.

Ben told me that when Dan first started this venture he kept his last $30 in his sock in case of emergencies, but then it stressed him out, as he didn't know when the right time was to use it and he got rid of the problem by leaving it in a phone booth. I said I couldn't do this, not only because I need money to live but because there are no bloody phone boxes any more.

KARL'S Facts

Reclaimed British telephone boxes are commonly used as novelty shower cubicles.

Ben then announced that before I met Dan, him and the rest of the crew were going to stop for lunch so that they could then just work on through the afternoon with no breaks. I thought he was joking, but he wasn't. 'I'm bloody starving, Ben. I've got the shakes here. You've had breakfast and now you're having lunch! Well, go and fill your fat face. And if you've got Bob Geldof's number, call him and tell him to send me a bloody food parcel.' It made no difference.

They went into a café to have burgers while I sat in the car getting more hungry and more irritated. It's pretty bad that I couldn't go half a day without eating something, but it's hard in America, as there are so many billboards advertising food. It's constantly in your face and I kept being reminded how starving I was. Ben promised they would be no more than thirty minutes. Thirty-five minutes later they came out and we set off to the park where we were to meet Daniel.

When we arrived, there was no sign of Daniel. We were supposed to meet at 1 p.m. And it was now 1.30 p.m. I had a headache and was in no mood for trying out this way of life. Ben pointed out that there was a water fountain. Daniel's rule is to 'only use what is freely given or discarded and what is already present and already running whether or not I existed', which meant I could use the water fountain. I'd just gulped down my first taste of the 'free life' when a thin man with glasses and grey longish hair wearing jeans, sandals and carrying a small rucksack came around the corner. It was Daniel.

KARL: How you doing?

DANIEL: Did we say two or one?

KARL: Ben told me it was meant to be one o'clock.

DANIEL: Oh, I'm sorry. I thought it was two. Well, good to see you.

KARL: I'm absolutely starving! I haven't eaten since last night because I wanted to try and experience your day properly, and you know the whole thing about finding happiness from living like this. But at the moment I'm not feeling it and I've got a headache coming on because I've not eaten.

DANIEL: Oh yeah? I have some food right here if you want it. I have some granola. I found it yesterday.

KARL: You found it? Where did you find granola?

DANIEL: It was in the health food store dumpster.

KARL: I suppose you can't get ill from old granola, can you?

DANIEL: No. It can go stale if it's quite old but this tastes pretty fresh.

KARL: I'd eat anything. I'm used to four meals a day and it's now close to two o'clock and I've had nothing.

DANIEL: Back at the camp I found some roadkill rabbit, freshly killed. I skinned it and cleaned it. We could cook it up if you like?

KARL: I think I'll start with the granola.

We sat on the grass under a tree and I ate the free granola until my shakes started to stop. When I was younger I used to eat free food from Hagenbach's bakery, as they put trays of unsold cakes out for people to take round the back. At the end of the day, me and a mate sat there scoffing them. On one occasion I got really bad stomach cramps after I'd eaten some cream donuts. The cream must have turned a bit. I never went back again after that.

Daniel explained why he's living the way he's living and how he gets happiness from it.

DANIEL: I gave up money thirteen years ago because I was tired of the rat race. I feel like the money system is a cancer on the earth. And also for spiritual reasons. It's about living in the present and taking what comes freely, which is the way nature works and our core religions teach that. Just doing things for people because we want to, and giving freely and receiving freely. That way I feel like things go into balance just as they are in nature because you don't see any two creatures consciously bartering with each other.

KARL: How was your life before this? Did you have a nice house or flat?

DANIEL: I was never really wealthy, but I had apartments that I rented and a car, a job, and I travelled a lot.

KARL: So what was it that happened thirteen years ago when you just thought, 'Right, that's it. I don't need money any more'?

DANIEL: It wasn't an instantaneous thing. I pretty much spent the 90s thinking about it and whittling down my possessions to live more simply. I was suffering severe clinical depression in the early 90s and I moved to Utah to get away from the rat race and simplify my life because I felt like my mind was filled with useless thoughts, and useless thoughts were an extension of useless possessions, like they go hand in hand.

KARL: What do you mean? Give me an example of a useless thought.

DANIEL: Like just worrying. Worrying in itself is a useless thought and it does no good. And when we have more stuff we worry more.

KARL: But you must still have worries, they're just different worries. I'm spending twenty-four hours with you and I'm worrying about later when I'm hungry again and I'm sick of granola and I want something else. And then what happens when the rain comes? How are we going to stay dry? Where are we going to sleep tonight?

DANIEL: Your suffering is not from anything in reality, it's in your mind, and those useless thoughts don't do any good. That's what both the Buddha and Jesus teach: live in the moment. The future will take care of itself.

The thing is, I think it would have been easy for Jesus to follow this lifestyle back when he was around. There weren't adverts in his face telling him he needs a new car, iPad, plasma TV, holiday. You can't go anywhere or do anything without being told what you need in your life and how much better it will be if you buy or do the thing they are selling. I rarely look at magazines, but when I do all that is in them is adverts. I thought I needed glasses one time, as my eyes were stinging after reading a feature, but it was because of all the smelly samples of aftershaves that are stuck to the pages to try and get you to buy them. And as for Buddha, the Dalai Lama isn't exactly living the basic life. I read somewhere he's got a bloody Twitter account.

I know what Daniel means about living in the moment, though. Too many people these days are thinking about the next thing they want to do before finishing the thing they are doing. Everybody wants to work their way up the ladder as fast as they can and find something better. Mike Baldwin ran the knicker factory in *Coronation Street* for my entire childhood. You don't get people sticking at jobs like that any more.

Once I got my energy back from eating the granola, we went out looking for more supplies. I wanted to see how easy it was to survive and how Daniel spends his day. As we walked, we talked about happiness.

DANIEL: I find that most of my unhappiness, if not all, is in my mind and it's an illusion. Even when I'm really hungry, my unhappiness isn't really from the hunger, it's from thinking about what I could have. My mind is not present, it's in the future or thinking of what I've had in the past. When my mind is completely present I feel intense peace and joy.

That sort of made sense to me. My mind is probably my worst enemy, but it's hard to ignore it. It's always there looking over things I'm doing. I'll try my best at fixing something or painting something, and at the end when I've finished my mind starts offering its opinions like some inner critic. It's never there to help sort the problem, it seems to just come along to diss my work at the end. But then it's the same mind that has pushed me to do things in life that have turned out well. It'll be interesting to see if when my mind reads all this back before sending it to the publisher it decides to delete this part as I'm slagging it off.

I told Daniel that even though I was now full from granola, my mind was still thinking about my next meal, so he said he'd take me on the hunt to show me how you can get by. We got to a takeaway pizza shop and he took me round the back where the big dumpsters were. He leaned into one and pulled out three twelve-inch boxes containing different types of pizza. Totally untouched. I was convinced he or Ben had put them there, but they swore that they hadn't.

KARL'S Facts

On average, Americans eat 90 acres of pizza every day which is equivalent to around 350 slices per second.

DANIEL: I think when people order pizzas and the delivery man arrives and they're not home they just throw them out. That happens all the time.

KARL: Was that a pineapple one? Can I have a piece of that?

DANIEL: Yeah.

KARL: When was the last time you were ill from eating something from a dumpster?

> DANIEL: The only time I've ever gotten ill from dumpsters is if I eat too many sweets or junk food.
>
> KARL: There's a good nine or ten pizzas in there. If you ever did want to go back to using money, you could take these out of the bin and sell them door to door. A pizza service where you don't even have to order.

Okay, the pizza was cold, but to be honest pizza that you pay for can sometimes turn up cold if the lad who delivers it is useless at finding your address. I think it almost tasted better as I knew it was free. We took a couple more and carried on walking. We then went round the back of some more shops and Daniel got into another dumpster and found some clothing. He found us both a fairly decent jacket to wear. I've still got mine as it fitted perfectly. It didn't stop there. We walked for a good three hours finding more on the way – a pair of jeans that were my size left on someone's garden wall, some chicken fillets, a Dutch apple pie and a near-new blanket and cushion in another bin close to the train station. Before I met Daniel I was expecting him to be begging and stealing, but he was more like a dung beetle, making use of other people's shit.

I told Daniel I liked how we never know what's going to be in a new dumpster and it's the expectation that makes it more exciting.

> DANIEL: It's like why we wrap presents for kids under a Christmas tree. They wouldn't be as fun if they weren't

wrapped up and we knew what they were. When I first started living this way, I felt this intense gratitude for everything because it was unexpected and free.

I tell you what, why Bear Grylls goes about eating dead beavers and cutting up a dead camel to use as a sleeping bag, I don't know. He should just take a wander round the back of Asda. I wasn't sure I would choose to live like this myself, but it was definitely reassuring to know that if things went tits up, I wouldn't die. And I doubt Suzanne would be up for living like this either. She thinks she's roughing it if a B&B we stay in hasn't got a hairdryer in the room. It wouldn't be for her.

KARL: What about a partner in your life? I've got a long-term girlfriend and she wouldn't want this, but I can't imagine life on me own. Would it make it easier to get through the days when you can't find some Dutch apple pie to cheer you up?

DANIEL: Yeah, I'll admit that's a hard one because this has been a solitary path. There aren't many who want to do it, and I'm gay on top of that, which makes it a little harder.

KARL: Yeah, I can't imagine you'd get that many gays doing this.

DANIEL: It's something that I would like if it came along, but if not that's okay. I feel like my principles are more important than a relationship.

KARL: Have you ever been close to saying enough is enough? I mean, you're in your fifties, can you see yourself wanting to do this when you're in your sixties?

DANIEL: I don't really worry about it. I guess I just feel like something will work out. Maybe that's irresponsible, but that's kind of how I feel.

Maybe he'll be okay. He seemed pretty healthy. I know my Auntie Nora wouldn't be able to survive like this now that she's older. She's only got about two teeth in her head, so she's never going to be able to work her way through stale pizza. Plus, the amount of tablets that are keeping her going she would have problems finding them on the street. She'd have to wander up and down the back of Harley Street to find what she needed. I thought she was showing an interest in computers recently, but it was just a Samsung Tablet that had piqued her interest. She thought it was a tablet that she hadn't tried yet.

KARL: Are your mam and dad still alive?

DANIEL: Yeah.

KARL: Do they ever come and stay? I picture you sort of rushing out to bins for three courses because you know you've got company coming.

DANIEL: My parents are both eighty-five, and that is one thing I'm a little concerned about, because I don't believe in nursing homes and I would want to take care of them if they need it.

KARL: So do you think you'll get much interest at the Rainbow Gathering, selling this as a way of living?

DANIEL: Well, this has been a solo thing for the past decade, and now other people tell me they want to do it and they want to join me, so I'm feeling like maybe it's time to do it as a community now. And it's a big jump in the dark. I have no idea if this is gonna work out. But that's also part of the exhilaration of it; I don't know if this is gonna work. It's like another big chance.

I'm not sure the idea of asking people to join him is such a good idea. I can imagine that people would join for the ride but not for the same reasons that Daniel is doing it. I can see people who are just lazy and don't want to work thinking it's an easy option and sponging off Daniel. It would be fine to begin with, like it is on *Big Brother* when everyone gets along, but then two weeks down the line everyone would be at each other's throats. And how do you ask someone to leave when you don't own the land you're on? Also, and I mean this in a nice way, Daniel doesn't seem like a natural leader, and I could imagine someone trying to take over and change the rules. In a way, I suppose that's how we've got to where we are now, though.

We covered around six miles, nibbling on some grass and berries from trees as we walked. Eventually we left the town and got into the more wooded area where Daniel had set up camp. For some reason I thought he'd have a decent tent. I thought he may have come across one round the back of a camping shop or found one that had been discarded, but it was just a plastic tarpaulin hanging between two trees. The rain that had been threatening for most of the day finally came. We got under the tarpaulin and moved bin bags of granola, roadkill and stale bread to make room. This is where we'd both be sleeping tonight. Suddenly, for the first time that day I started to think about the hotel room that was still there as an option. Sure, I could sleep under the tarpaulin for one night and it wouldn't kill me, but this programme was about me finding happiness. I could stay like many other presenters would and wake up saying how amazing it was to lie under the stars with nature then never do it again unless a camera was rolling. The thing was, I had a choice. I explained all this to Ben. As I talked about the bed in the hotel room, just the thought of it made me laugh. The decision had been made. I would actually enjoy the comfy bed more knowing that this was the other option.

BEN: You better tell Daniel what you're doing.

KARL: I feel well bad telling him this. I think he's gonna be a bit disappointed. It's cheeky, isn't it? I've just eaten a full bar of chocolate and now I'm saying, 'Nah, I'm not staying with you.' (to Daniel) Have you got a minute, Dan? I've given in.

DANIEL: Oh yeah? You're not gonna stay?

KARL: Are you disappointed?

DANIEL: You gotta do what you wanna do.

KARL: It's just that it's all about happiness and joy in life, and just now when I was talking to Ben and picturing the bed in the hotel . . . it fills me with joy.

DANIEL: Well, if it does, you gotta do what you gotta do.

KARL: Listen though, I know your rules are that you're allowed to accept help as long as you don't use money. Are you sure you don't want me to get you a room there for the night? You've given me a full day of your time, and you've fed me all day. It's the least I can do.

DANIEL: You have given me a full day of your time too.

KARL: Yeah, but think about it. Nice comfy bed, clean linen sheets . . . See, you're laughing, that is the reaction I had when I thought about it.

DANIEL: No, I'm happy out here tonight.

KARL: Why don't you just try it though?

DANIEL: I have tried it before. I've stayed in hotels, I know what it is like. No hotel can create this beauty I have here.

KARL: Well, if that is how you feel, you are clearly getting the same happiness as I am from the comfy bed.

DANIEL: Yeah, that's why I live this way. I could live the other way if I wanted to. I have a college degree and a good résumé and whatever. Of course my résumé has been blank for the past decade so I don't know how that would be, but I'm happy.

KARL: Well, I've got to do what I feel inside and I feel like the hotel is what I wanna do.

DANIEL: There is a part of me that likes the hotel thing, and part of me that likes this, and that part of me is stronger.

KARL: Fair enough. But you know it has been good. I've enjoyed it.

DANIEL: Me too, it's been really fun. And if by some chance you are in the hotel room and think, 'I wanna go camp,' you are welcome here.

KARL: Yeah, well . . . don't wait up.

When I did get back to the hotel the bed was even comfier than I imagined. I lay on it smiling to myself. On top of that I knew I was going home the next day. That always makes me happy. And Suzanne had got me a box of Tunnock's in.

'Laughter is the sun that drives winter from the human face.'
~ VICTOR HUGO

'LAUGHTER ISN'T ALWAYS GOOD.

A BABY LAUGHING in the DAYTIME is CUTE.

A BABY LAUGHING in its COT at 3AM in THE DARK is TERRIFYING.'

~ KARL PILKINGTON

DEATH

'HELLO, THIS IS Death Watch calling,' is how my mam and dad should start their phone calls. Every time they hear of a death they phone to tell me the news. It doesn't matter if it's someone famous or someone they knew but haven't seen for forty years, they still ring to tell me about it. My dad joined *Friends Reunited* just to keep tabs on old mates who have died. He actually calls it 'Friends Ignited' these days as that's how he finds out who's been recently cremated. They're not alone, though, as I think most people are obsessed with death. The moment it's announced on the news that anyone famous has died, someone somewhere will immediately update their Wikipedia page. I suppose we're obsessed with death because we're all in line for it. The world is just one big waiting room before death.

I'm quite good at accepting that fact. I never really think about how I'll go, not that it matters anyway, as long as it's not drawn out. It annoys me when I hear news stories about people who died while doing their hobby and you get friends of the deceased saying, 'Well, at least they died doing what they loved.' I don't understand that at all! I've said before that I love Happyface biscuits, but I wouldn't want to die choking on one. If anything, isn't it better to die doing something you don't like doing? For me, that would be taking the dry clothes off the clothes horse. It's such a boring job having to fold it all and make sure the socks are in pairs. Wouldn't it be good dying just as you start to do that, knowing you don't have to finish doing it and will never have to do it again?

About twenty years ago I worked at a tape duplication company where it was my job to stick labels on cassettes, pop them into cassette cases and then shrinkwrap them before boxing them up. It was a job I knew I didn't want to do forever. At the time I also had my foot in the door at a local radio station where I'd been asked to fill in for an old bloke who was ill. I did the overnight shift from 2 a.m. to 6 a.m. And I'd play music from the 60s and 70s and talk about whatever was in my head. I did this for two weeks, working at the tape company during the day and then working at the radio station through the night. It felt like there was no end to the work and it was depressing. The only thing that kept me going during those two weeks was the fact that I could see an end, and that's how I see life. A life without death would be like a day without sleep. I'm pretty sure people only enjoy things as they know at some point they will end.

I've read that certain species of lobster and jellyfish don't die of old age, they only ever die from being killed. Imagine how horrible that would be. The thought terrifies me. I think getting old is like getting to the end of a packet of Maltesers – it's not until I realise I've only got a couple left that I really enjoy them. Then I start to eat them slower, making them last by nibbling the chocolate off before sucking on the honeycomb. Weirdly, the last few always seem to taste better too. If it was an ever-lasting bag, I'd never get that moment. It's the same with life. I remember playing Pac-Man as a kid and I typed in a cheat code that meant I had endless lives to play with, and it was rubbish. I ended up feeling sorry for Pac-Man. His whole existence was spent running away from those ghosts that chased him around the maze. He only had a few moments of happiness when he gulped a power pill, but when that eventually wore off he was back to being chased again. I think the only time Pac-Man was stress-free and happy was when he died, and I'd taken that away from him.

CHOOSING YOUR OWN COFFIN

My trip looking at how other cultures deal with death started in Ghana. It's a place where they seem to have a healthier outlook on death than we do. Rather than it being a quiet, low-key affair, your death is the biggest, loudest event of your life, even though you don't get to witness it. The Ghanaians spend more money on celebrating someone's life at their funeral than they do on weddings or sending their kids to school. It almost seems like death is the meaning of life in Ghana. And it's in your face a lot more over there, so much so that just on the way from the airport to my hotel in the capital city of Accra I spotted three coffin shops. They aren't places that are trying to disguise what's inside with net curtains and plastic flowers like the funeral directors at home; instead they display their goods like a fishmonger – their wares are all on show. Another reason they reminded me of fishmongers was the fact that the first thing that caught my eye in one of the coffin shops was a six-foot fish and crab coffin. We parked up so I could get a closer look at all the different designs. Kane Kwei Carpentry, a workshop that specialises in coffinmaking, was situated between a hairdressers and a garage. There were no employees in dark suits whispering while sombre music played inside; instead there was sawing and banging coming from out the back as the workers were trying to meet their deadlines making the customised coffins. I think those brightly painted coffins would definitely help to lighten the mood of the situation. At home, death is an 'elephant in the room' topic that we avoid at all costs, whereas here the 'elephant in the room' would probably be the design of choice for a coffin if you're willing to pay the price, which isn't as much as you would expect given the craftsmanship that goes into making them. They start at around only $500. As well as the giant crab and fish, there was also a hammer, a camera, a Coke bottle, a shrimp, a shoe and one that looked like a chocolate éclair.

I met a man in front of the shop who had ordered a coffin. His dad had recently died and he'd come to see how they were getting on with it. It was in the design of a Lada car. They were still working on the front grille and head-lights. Glass for the windows would be fitted last.

KARL: Why a Lada?

CUSTOMER: Because he was a mechanic. He specialised in this car and had been repairing them for some time before he passed away, so we decided to bury him in the car.

KARL: Did he know before he died that this is what he'd be buried in?

CUSTOMER: Yeah, yeah, yeah. You tell your family what you want before you pass away, so when you are no more your family knows what to do.

KARL: I like it. Are you happy with it?

CUSTOMER: Yeah, I'm happy. I'm happy that the old man is also happy.

The attention to detail is what makes them so amazing. The Lada car was considered a bit of a joke when I was growing up. Every time you saw a Lada someone would have a joke to tell like, 'What do you call a Lada with a twin exhaust? A wheelbarrow.' The funny thing is, this Lada was probably better made than the real thing and would probably last for longer. The only real shame is that once it was finished, this remarkably detailed artwork would just get buried. It's mental that Damien Hirst makes art with chopped-up dead cows and sharks that should be pushing up daisies, and yet these masterpieces end up six feet under.

KARL: So what are you having when you die?

CUSTOMER: Me? I'm going to have a pen. A pen you use to write.

KARL: Like a big Bic. Why?

CUSTOMER: Because I'm a teacher.

KARL: You won't change your mind?

CUSTOMER: No, I will never change my mind.

KARL: I'd have thought you'd go for, like, a blackboard duster. Cos it's the shape of a coffin.

CUSTOMER: Yeah, but I prefer the pen.

I suppose it does make sense to get involved in picking your own coffin. It's the thing that you are last seen in by lots of people and you have to spend eternity lying in it, yet normally we have no say in the matter. I'm not sure what my mam and dad would want if they had to choose their coffins. My dad often says he's not bothered; he's always saying, 'Stick me in a bin bag for all I care.' He doesn't like the idea of money being wasted on the dead. If he was ever close to death and saw the light at the end of the tunnel like people who've had that experience claim to, his last words would probably be, 'Turn the bloody light out, I'm not made of money!'

For my mam I think I'd have a coffin designed in the shape of a skip. She keeps threatening to leave all her knick-knacks, ornaments and stuff behind for me. She knows I don't want any of it, so it would be good to chuck it all in with her like they did in Egyptian times, when they believed in popping things in the casket for the dead to take with them to the other side. I'm pretty sure there would be so much crap in there it would be considered more of a landfill than a funeral service. If the lid was ever lifted off again it would be like opening a massive Kinder egg full of useless surprises inside.

KARL'S Facts The ashes of the inventor of the Frisbee were moulded into several Frisbees that were given to family and friends.

279

I met Eric, whose family owns the coffin business. He runs the place with his army of highly skilled carpenters.

KARL: So if I am buying myself a coffin, what should I be thinking about?

ERIC: Normally what people think about is the profession of the person, what the person was doing when they were alive, and sometimes the family would say he would love to be buried in this kind of a coffin. Not because it is their job, but because they love it. What is your profession?

KARL: This . . . what I'm doing now. I sort of travel around. A suitcase would be an obvious choice.

ERIC: You travel around? We have something like an aeroplane for businessmen.

KARL: But I'm sick of planes, I'm always on them. I don't like the idea of being forever in eternity sat in a plane. I want something totally different. I want something that gives me a bit of joy.

ERIC: What do you normally carry in your briefcase?

KARL: Clothes, chocolate, crisps, treats, socks.

ERIC: Maybe something you really admire when you are tired and weak that refreshes your brain.

KARL: Should it come to you just like that? (*clicks fingers*) Should this be an easy decision?

ERIC: Normally when a family arrives here, they have in mind two or three things they have discussed among themselves. Knowing that the person was doing something, loved it and wanted it as a coffin.

KARL: Erm . . . it's a big deal, isn't it? I haven't thought about it. It's not been in me head. I like chocolate . . . do you have Twix in Ghana? Google 'Twix'. Have you got Google on your laptop?

Eric tried to get his modem to work but wasn't having any joy, so I nipped round to the garage next door and bought a few Twixes. I liked the idea of having a Twix coffin. We're all different in life and yet most of us are last seen in a box that only comes in a choice of three colours with either silver or bronze handles. That says nothing about us as people, does it?

KARL: Here you go. I don't know if it has ever been done, but I've got a girlfriend, right, and with a Twix you get two bars – I've already eaten one on the way back from the garage – but you get two chocolate bars. Would it be possible . . . I'm thinking two spaces, one coffin. So then I get buried and when she dies they dig it back up and put her in it as well. So only one cost.

ERIC: One coffin but it does two people? Yeah, sure.

I thought it was quite a nice idea being buried with Suzanne. She'd probably say she doesn't want to go out in a Twix, but she does like them. Whenever I buy myself one, she always tries to have some of it, even though when I asked if she wanted any chocolate before nipping to the shop she said no. So in a way, I'm sharing my final Twix with her in the afterlife. It was the best thing I could come up with on the spot, but I find that decisions that are made quickly are normally the best ones. I went with my gut feeling. But then I suppose my gut would always be thinking of food-based ideas.

Eric said he needed a couple of weeks but thought it was possible and would get to work on the designs straight away and email me photos of his progress.

A DIFFERENT KIND OF FUNERAL

Eric at the coffin shop said there were plenty of funerals every Saturday in Accra and that I would be welcome to join any I fancied as they believe the more people the merrier, even if you've never met the deceased.

I've never been to a funeral before. People have died who I once knew, but I never felt the need to pop along to their funeral as I've always thought it was best to remember them from the time when they were living. The idea of going along and paying your final respects isn't really something I believe in. You should give people respect when they're living as that's when I think it counts.

It wasn't hard to find out where a funeral was taking place, as there were posters pasted on top of layers of other posters on virtually every wall with the obituaries of local people informing anyone who was interested where and when the funeral would be taking place. The posters also included a short biography of the person and the names of family and friends they had left behind. If someone you vaguely know has died in Ghana you would know about it pretty soon, which is different to at home. I lived next door but one to someone who died and I only found out about it months later when a 'For Sale' sign went up outside their house. I reckon my mam and dad would love the idea of the obituary posters, as it would save them buying the local paper to search them. I speak to them more often during the winter, as that seems to be when most people pop their clogs. My dad treats the months of

December and January like the transfer window in football at the end of August where players make surprising moves to other clubs.

I was going along to a funeral of a woman called Madam Comfort Asaaba Cofie who had died a month earlier at the age of seventy-eight. In this part of the world, it's not unusual for a dead body to hang around for quite a while before it's buried. A family member of Comfort's explained that he had heard of a person who wasn't buried for a year, as his friends and family had to travel from afar to see the body before it was buried, and sometimes that isn't easy if they are low on funds.

Comfort was now lying in state in a small room off a courtyard waiting to be made up by 'The Iceman'. The Iceman, real name Roland, got his name as he often uses ice to keep the body cool to stop it decomposing. The Iceman wanted me to help him make Comfort look as good as possible before her friends and family came to say goodbye for the final time. Even though I haven't been to a funeral before, I have seen dead bodies. I saw a load of them when I visited the Body Worlds exhibition in Manchester. It was an exhibition put on by a man called Gunther von Hagens, who strips dead bodies of their skin so people can go and see real-life organs close up. He uses a method called plastination to suspend the bodies in positions that make them look like they are in the middle of playing certain sports to show you how the muscles look. I didn't find the exhibition strange, as the bodies were doing everyday things like playing football, playing basketball or just sitting round a table playing cards.

In fact, some of the dead bodies were doing things I hadn't even done, like playing badminton.

I entered the small building off the courtyard where Comfort was lying in state. I'd say she was lying in a right state. It was nothing like the Body Worlds exhibition. She wasn't playing cards or football. She was just lying in the corner. She didn't look good, but mostly because her skin was all grey. I thought it was because the skin was dying, but it turned out it was just dust from the road outside. Before I arrived, her ten children had been rolling her around in it, as that's what she had requested. She saw it as her last chance to play together as a family.

The room was warm with just a faint breeze coming in through the open doorway, which was covered by a single net curtain. I was speechless for a few moments and was taking in what was in front of me, listening to the sound of her ten children, neighbours and friends chatting outside and the flies buzzing around her.

Roland the Iceman explained that I was going to help apply make-up to Comfort and then stand her up in the corner of the room. Before we got to work, he put some cotton wool up her nose to stop any blood running out once she was propped up. He then super-glued her mouth shut. I felt odd being there. Comfort's family were fine with me doing part of the job, but it was weird for me. It was the first time I was meeting someone for a TV programme without them knowing about it. It wasn't long before Roland passed me some rubber gloves, handed me some cotton wool and some antibacterial solution and asked me to wipe down

Comfort's arms so they were free of the grey dust from the earlier family activity. Her skin was hard and tight, and it was like wiping down a leather sofa. I reckon Mr Sheen would have left a nicer finish. The Iceman then asked me to lift Comfort's legs and push them as far back as I could so he could find her waist. She was really stiff, but then she had been dead for over a month. I looked down over her as I pushed as hard as I could with all my weight.

THE ICEMAN: Push harder! Come closer, come closer!

KARL: Jesus, she's heavy. What are we trying to do?

THE ICEMAN: More, more, more, more, more.

KARL: More?! I'm pushing!

THE ICEMAN: More!

KARL: Right, that's as far as her legs are going to go.

THE ICEMAN: More!

KARL: It's not going to go any more!

THE ICEMAN: It's okay, thank you.

It was one of the weirdest things, if not the weirdest thing, I've ever done in my life. I was pretty impressed with how far her legs could go for a dead woman in her late seventies. I'm only forty and I can't bend over and touch my feet. She was in better bloody shape than I am. Earlier in the day, Richard the director had suggested I should have bought a suit for the occasion to show my respect, and yet there

I was sweating my arse off playing bloody Twister with a dead woman!

I then helped the Iceman put some make-up on Comfort. Rather than a small, fine brush, we used one that you'd use for slapping paint on a shed, as we had to pile it on to give her face a living person's colour. I wasn't impressed with my make-up applying skills and was worried she was going to end up looking like Eddie Izzard by the time I had finished. Roland the Iceman tried to make friendly chat, asking me what I had thought of Ghana so far. 'I've only been here about seven hours. I've met four people and one of them is dead,' I said.

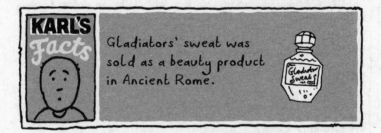

KARL'S *Facts*

Gladiators' sweat was sold as a beauty product in Ancient Rome.

It all seemed a bit rushed. It reminded me of the London Olympics – four years' notice and yet the paint on the stadium was still drying when the fireworks were going off during the opening ceremony. Comfort had been dead a month and now suddenly the pressure was on to get her ready for the spectators.

I left Roland to change Comfort's clothes, as I think that would have been too much for me to handle. It took him quite some time. I remember trying to put a coat on

Suzanne years ago after she had been to a work do and had her drink spiked and was in too much of a state to do it herself. It's a tough thing to do when the person is alive, so putting clothes on a dead body can't be easy. It's probably like trying to stick a pair of tights on a giraffe.

Once Comfort was clothed, Roland then wanted to stand her up in the corner of the room. I didn't ask why at the time, as I'd got sick of asking that same question during all of this madness. His friend Nana came to help. I grabbed Comfort by the arms.

THE ICEMAN: Let's go.

KARL: Okay, someone on the feet. Who is going to stop her sliding that way?

NANA: I'll stand there.

THE ICEMAN: Ready.

KARL: Yeah, here she goes. Come on.

THE ICEMAN: Like this . . . like this, like this!

KARL: Watch her head! Watch her head! Down, down, down! Okay . . . okay.

We hadn't moved her at all. She was a lot heavier than I'd thought she was going to be: literally a dead weight, and I didn't really know how to handle her. It's hard to describe the chaos, but just imagine the Chuckle Brothers trying to shift a mattress.

THE ICEMAN: Let's go again.

KARL: Okay, let's go. 1, 2, 3 . . . Keep hold, keep hold of her . . . Back towards the wall?

THE ICEMAN: Yes!

KARL: I can't move her that way. Oh, Jesus. I can't! I'm not doing anything here.

THE ICEMAN: Back, back, back!

KARL: I can't move her back! Do I move the feet, the leg?

THE ICEMAN: Back!

KARL: No, I can't. Alright, I've got her leg, she won't fall. I have her feet. Come forward, a bit more forward. Have you got hold of her? It doesn't look natural . . . it just doesn't look natural at all that. How does she stay up? It just looks shit.

I finally realised what he was trying to do. He wanted her to be stood in the corner in front of the table she used to sit at all day long selling vegetables to the passing public. The problem was, she was slumping. The Iceman tried using bricks and wooden poles to prop her up, but her knees couldn't hold her own weight, so he ended up sitting her in a chair behind the table. Once again, I had to leave the room to get some fresh air for ten minutes. I sat down. More and more people were outside now waiting to see Comfort. She was nowhere near ready. It's like how Nick Knowles gets stressed in those DIY programmes when he knows he's only got twenty minutes left before the owners of the house are due back home and he's still got to paint the skirting boards, but this was a whole different league.

Richard looked as shocked by the whole experience as I was. I suppose he was wondering if any of this could actually be shown on Sky One HD, the channel we were filming it all for. It's a channel that's known for light-hearted programmes like *Dogs with Jobs* and *Greggs: More Than Meats the Pie*. How was all this going to fit alongside that lot! It would be like scheduling *The Shining* on CBeebies.

After a ten-minute break I went back in. The Iceman had done a good job. He could probably give Gok Wan a run for his money the way he had given Comfort a makeover. In just the ten minutes that I was gone he had fixed her make-up, popped on a head scarf and decorated the table with a big barrel full of the vegetables she sold when she was alive. Her family and friends queued up to take it in turns to see her. They took photos and some people went over and tried to put money in her hand, just like they would have done if she was still alive and selling her goods on the street. Seeing this, I felt like I had more of an idea of what Comfort was like as a person, and it no longer seemed so strange being there. She had been brought to life just like the bodies at the Body Worlds exhibition.

The next day Comfort was to be buried. We were told to get there early so as not to miss anything. We arrived at 8 a.m. Comfort was still sitting in the corner. The coffin had been brought into the room. They had decided to go for a normal white coffin, not a traditional Ghanaian one like the ones we saw in the shop the day before. There were quite a few people milling about, and it was a bit like the atmosphere at a car boot sale when you get there early, with people preparing for the day ahead and trying to nab the best spot. I think the people that were there so early were mainly close family. A band was tuning up and checking microphones, and chairs were being unstacked and placed under a huge gazebo in the street.

We sat around for about three and a half hours as the last of Comfort's friends and various locals nipped in to pay their final respects. They didn't stay in there for long. I suppose visiting a dead person is less awkward than visiting an ill person in hospital, as you don't have to worry about leaving too soon and offending anyone. People were coming out smiling, looking at the photos they had taken on their phones. I was handed a little pamphlet with a few words on it about Comfort and her family alongside some photos of her kids, grandkids and great-grandkids as a memento, which I thought was a nice idea.

By 10 a.m. the Iceman had moved Comfort from the corner of the room and into her coffin. I went in to have one final look. He had redone the make-up and had also put a wig on her, which was strange. It's the one thing that I don't think humans have been able to crack. In the millions of years we've been around, a wig still looks like a wig to me. I thought it made her look like the little woman out of The Krankies, and on that thought, the lid was slid into place.

By now there were a few hundred people sitting in chairs in the street listening to live music and telling tales of Comfort's life. At 11.45 a.m. I was introduced to the Jama group, who were a bunch of fellas who chant and dance and make as much noise as possible while the coffin is carried to the cemetery. The idea is that the noise draws people out of their houses to see what all the fuss is about, and the more people out on the streets the bigger the celebration. The group gave me a bit of old piping and a stick to hit it with. I was practising a tune when I was told the procession had started. I turned to see the pallbearers carrying Comfort's white coffin towards us, but unlike funerals at home where the pace is slow, they were throwing it up in the air. 'No way will that wig still be on her head,' I thought. They went from tossing the coffin in the air to crawling along the ground with it balanced on their backs. It looked amazing. I'm guessing this way of doing things came about from boredom. I saw a bloke in America do a similar thing with a sign that said 'Pizza restaurant this way>>>>'. The problem with that was that the bloke was throwing it about so much I had no idea which way to go for the pizza. So I had a burger instead.

The Jama group jumped in at the front of the parade, and I worked hard at dancing and hitting my metal pipe in time with the chanting and singing. I felt like the Pied Piper of Hamelin. Even though I'd never been to a funeral before, I was well aware that this doesn't usually happen. There was a good feeling about the whole thing. There wasn't much crying, just people smiling and dancing. As we walked along, the crowd got bigger and started to stop traffic. Once we got to the main road we joined another funeral parade. They could really do with having a special funeral lane in the road like buses do at home.

KARL'S Facts

Magpies hold funerals for their dead. They lay grass on the corpse and stand by it for a few minutes before flying off.

We got to the cemetery after about thirty minutes. Some of the women who had dressed up and worn high heels were probably now regretting it, as they'd worn them down to flip-flops with all that dancing and walking. I found myself crying, not from being upset but due to the fact that I'd been dancing and sweating in the midday sun and the sweat had got into my eyes and was making them sting. The cemetery was massive and it was packed with gravestones. It looked like the car park of Westfield shopping centre on a Saturday – every spot seemed to be taken. We had to jump from one grave to another to get to the place where Comfort would be laid to rest. Even the pallbearers had to stop dancing and concentrate on their steps. Fifteen minutes later the coffin had been put in the ground, a few words had been said, the hole had been covered, and that was the end of my first ever funeral. It was an experience that I doubt I will ever forget.

Everyone made their way back home, a lot quieter than they had been on the journey there. Judging by the condition of most of the graves in the cemetery, I got the impression that once the person is buried people don't visit the grave very often. Probably because the following weekend the whole thing just happens all over again.

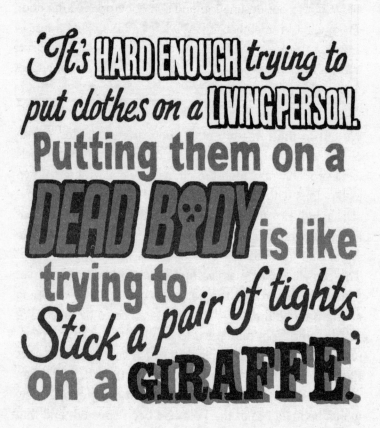

'It's HARD ENOUGH trying to put clothes on a LIVING PERSON. Putting them on a DEAD BODY is like trying to Stick a pair of tights on a GIRAFFE.'

LEARNING HOW TO MOURN

My emotions are quite limited. I'm either content and relaxed, or moaning. I'm not much of a crier. I didn't even cry much as a kid. When I was born and the midwife slapped me to make me cry, it probably took about three punches and a headlock to get me going. Even once when I trapped my fingers in the door of the car I didn't cry, I just sat quietly until we got to our destination and someone opened the door. From what I remember, it was when people made a fuss of me that the tears were triggered. I got into a fight outside the youth centre when I was about eleven. The fight ended, I was fine and I walked home. Twenty minutes later I got in the house and my mam noticed my head was a bit red from being punched and she started making a fuss asking what had happened, who had done it, and I started crying.

Since then I don't think I've had a proper cry. I can get upset when I'm watching a film, but I usually just get a bit of a lump in my throat. Two films do this to me every time – *The Elephant Man* and *Kes*. Nature programmes can also do this to me, but I'm more likely to cry over my phone battery dying than I am over the death of someone I don't know, like some people do. The first time I can remember people being happy to cry openly in public was when Princess Diana died. She seemed like a nice enough woman who did a lot of good for certain causes, and I felt sorry for her kids, but I didn't cry or get that upset. Don't get me wrong, it had some effect, as I can still remember finding out she was dead. I was in bed with Suzanne in our flat in Salford. The day before, I had put a bracket on the wall to hold a thirteen-inch portable telly so we could watch it in bed. I popped it on in the morning and the screen was filled with hundreds of people crying their eyes out. I called my mam and dad, who had obviously already heard the news. I was only surprised they hadn't called to tell me first. My dad said he wished he had got into selling flowers as a job, as the whole of Pall Mall looked like the Hanging Gardens of Babylon. The newspapers were full of stories blaming the journalists who were chasing her for photographs for her death, but my dad thought Interflora were responsible, as they knew how much money they would make from it. But while I remember what I was doing when it all happened, I also remember that I didn't cry. Didn't even come close.

To see if I could wake my emotions up, I travelled to Taipei in Taiwan, where staging a dramatic funeral for family or friends who have passed away is of the utmost importance. In order to create the right atmosphere, families hire professional mourners to come and cry and writhe around on the floor at funerals. I met with a professional mourner called Liu Jun-Lin, who has been crying professionally for nineteen years.

I asked her what it was all about.

LIU: At the beginning you feel very bad when someone is dead, but by the time the funeral comes it's already a long time so you need someone to lead you into the grieving mood.

We were supposed to be practising crying in her flat, but I was concerned about annoying the neighbours, as I know I wouldn't be happy having to listen to people wailing all day. So we went to a local park instead, just down the road and out of earshot. Since I've been back home, I've found out that there is a threat of the tradition of professional mourners being hired to attend funerals dying out due to a new noise pollution law. I can understand this, as I think noise is one of the worst pollutions that humans create. Air pollution is bad, but at least you can sleep through it. You can't with noise. But it's an important tradition to Liu, not just because it's her job but also because her mum and gran were professional mourners too. It means a lot to her to try and keep the tradition alive. I think if you want a tradition to last these days it has to involve food, as this is the thing we love the most. Easter, Christmas, Pancake Tuesday and Thanksgiving will never go away as it's an excuse to fill our fat faces.

KARL'S *Facts*

In the eighteenth century, an American businessman faked his own death, held a mock funeral, and shouted at his wife for not crying.

Liu gave me a type of white silk gown that was like the one she wears when she's working. The first part of the lesson involved learning to speak clearly while crying. The trick is not to scream or shout at the start, as then you have nowhere to build to, so it's best to start low and soft with more of a tremble to your voice. 'Make the noise come from the middle of the stomach,' Liu told me. I struggle to do things like this. When people have suggested I use core muscles to lift things, I have literally no idea what they mean. How do you go about selecting certain muscles? As long as some of them are doing the job, I'm not too concerned which ones are getting involved.

Liu gave me a demonstration of how it should be done. She started with a quiet weep, making a breathless sort of noise, and built to a bit of a wail. It reminded me of that song by the Irish band The Cranberries. I had a go at copying what she had done, but Liu said it sounded as though I was in pain rather than full of sadness. I wasn't messing around, I was really trying hard. So I kept at it and tried again and again and again. I'd say it's one of the most difficult things to fake if you're not really upset. I doubt I'd get very far if I entered *The X Factor*, as crying seems to be one of the requirements to get through. I just didn't have a memory in my head that could make me properly upset. I tried to think about the end of *Kes* when his pet bird gets killed (spoiler alert – perhaps I should have said that earlier), but it didn't work. I would need to get caught up in the whole story from the start for that to have an effect. I'm much more of a professional moaner than a professional mourner. I told Liu I thought it must be quite a difficult job to do if she is ever feeling in a particularly happy mood, but she said it comes naturally after seeing the sad faces of the grieving family.

The next stage was even more difficult, as I wasn't just required to cry sounds, I now also had to put my sadness into words.

> LIU: Try something like 'I am your daughter and I can't bear that you are gone'.
>
> KARL: (*sobbing*) I can't believe it! Oh, why did you have to go?
>
> LIU: More. Keep going.
>
> KARL: But I don't know what I would say. See, when I get upset I don't really cry, I tend to just swear.
>
> LIU: Well, you can't swear during a funeral service. A lot of people are there and everybody is crying, so you cannot swear.

The final stage was to crawl while sobbing and talking.

> LIU: (*crying and crawling*) I am your daughter, I am now in front of the altar at your funeral service!
>
> KARL: (*sobbing*) I am your son and I am here at the front of the church for ya!
>
> LIU: I can't bear the idea that you are gone!
>
> KARL: (*wailing*) I can't stand it! I can't be doing with this, I'm sick of it! I can't . . . I wasn't ready for this yet, where have you gone? Why did you have to go?
>
> LIU: Okay. Better.

We kept going. The more I did it, the more I got the hang of it. It does seem odd, though, to pay Liu for her skills. She charged about £380 for a session. I would save that money by just not telling a close member of the family the bad news until the day of the funeral. *Et voilà*, real tears on demand. Or maybe just take a shrieking baby along. But to be honest, I struggle to understand why having tears at a funeral is so important anyway. Just because you don't cry it doesn't mean you're not missing that person loads or that you didn't love them. Maybe some people are just more in control of their feelings. I can understand grief if someone is taken away at an early age, but if your gran dies at the age of eighty-three I don't think you should be bawling your eyes out, as she's had a good innings. My mam and dad are at an age now that every time they have their birthday they say they're trespassing, as they can't believe they're still around.

Richard the director suggested I should try to imagine Suzanne has died, as that would have more impact on my life. Liu played some music from her portable stereo to help me get in the mood. She asked me to talk as much as I could, just like she does when she does it for real. The service goes on for around twenty minutes, so you have to keep thinking of things to say without hesitation. I got down on my knees.

KARL: (*crying*) Ohhh, twenty years! And now you're gone. Twenty bloody years! We've been through so much. The first flat in Salford. (*sobbing*) You didn't really want to live there, but it's all I could give you. It's all I could afford. You wanted a holiday, after we moved in. I said, 'You're joking, aren't you? I'm bloody skint!' Wahhh! I had to get you a second-hand mattress because I couldn't afford a new one. I thought the mattress came with the bed when I bought it. (*wailing and crawling*) But it didn't. And I didn't know. And I had to get one off Alf the cobbler, because he was the only man I knew who had one in his van and he let me have it. I think I gave you most things that you wanted, though. (*sniff*) And I know I didn't always say the right things. Having a go at your haircuts. Saying you had a fat arse. But I was just being honest! (*wailing*) And now I'm being honest and I'm gonna miss you. Mind you, your fish pie, I never liked your fish pie. But you knew that. (*sob*) Your chicken Kievs were good. And the apple pie that you made. I'm gonna miss you. (*bowing to ground*) But I was sick of you watching *Grease*. And *When Harry Met Sally*. It's just that you'd seen it so many times. Why did you have to keep watching it?! And . . . erm . . . you never really asked for that much. You weren't too much of a pain. Just now and again. So y'know, you weren't a bad one. Right, is that enough?

Honestly, as I'm writing all this up on my laptop now, Suzanne is watching *Grease* for about the two-hundredth time.

Anyway, I really tried my best, but it just wasn't a natural thing to do. I felt really dizzy and had to have some Minstrels, as I felt weak from exhaustion. I felt like a One

Direction fan at one of their gigs and was close to needing attention from someone from the St John Ambulance crew. I was all cried out.

We finished up with the lesson and headed off to a memorial where Liu had been booked to cry. I wasn't going to get involved, as I thought I would end up making the family cry with laughter rather than sorrow and it was probably best left to the professional. We arrived at the funeral parlour and there was a small van parked outside with a tiny stage and a woman pole dancing on the back. I thought that was a bit of bad luck to have that going on outside the memorial, but it was actually part of the service! The vehicles are known as Electric Flower Carts and are booked as adult entertainment to attract more people to the service. After all, the more people who attend the funeral, the more honour is given to the deceased. The woman who was doing the pole dancing didn't look that happy to be there. No doubt the noise pollution rule wasn't helping her business either, and money must have been tight as her tights were full of holes and showed off her bruised arse and the fag burns on her legs. She danced round the pole looking bored, like she was waiting at a bus stop. Liu put on a clean silk gown and a big triangular hood over her head that totally covered her face. She looked like a PG Tips pyramid teabag. I suppose it's a good idea to cover your face when you're doing this job, as most people don't look too good when they're crying. I think the only person to ever pull it off as a good look was Sinéad O'Connor in her video for 'Nothing Compares 2 U'. She managed to make one single tear roll down her face without having red puffy eyes or snot hanging off her top lip.

The music started and Liu was on her knees crawling along the carpet into the memorial service. After all this trouble, there were only a handful of people in there. It was a service for a woman who had passed away three or four years ago. Considering that Liu was only a small woman, she could really create some noise, and I could well understand why it could be classed as noise pollution. It sounded like the sort of noise you would hear if someone fell down a lift shaft. It was enough to wake the dead. Maybe that was the idea.

CONFRONTING DEATH

I find that thinking about death helps me to sleep. I've tried counting sheep like everyone recommends, but what tends to happen is that my brain thinks it's seen the same sheep twice and that messes up my count, and when I think there's no more sheep to count, another three will come running along and startle me. Or just as I think I've finished counting, an elephant comes running in. By this point I'm wide awake. Yet if I think about death it calms me down. It's probably because suddenly any problems I have going round in my head and keeping me awake don't seem as important once I remind myself that none of it really matters. I think it's good to think about death, and I'm not alone in this. A company in South Korea is doing good business running a Well-Dying course. They visit big corporations and get employees thinking about their own mortality. They put the workers in caskets and end up reducing them to tears.

I was in South Korea to attend one of these Well-Dying courses to see what it was all about. I went along to the Daewoo shipbuilding factory, the second biggest in the world, where I was to join some of its employees who were taking time off from the usual daily grind to swap their overalls for a traditional hemp death robe and contemplate death for the rest of the afternoon (with a fifteen-minute break for tea and biscuits).

In one of the many anonymous meeting rooms, sixty or so workers sat up straight like soldiers taking instructions from the representative from the Well-Dying course. We were handed a few pieces of paper: one blank and another that featured an image of a gravestone. We were given thirty minutes to go off and write down on the gravestone how we would like to be remembered, and on the other piece of paper we had to write a farewell letter to our loved ones. The idea was that doing all this would help us appreciate what we have in life a bit more.

I got a bit stressed out, as I'm not good at things like this, especially when I have a time limit to do it in. Thirty minutes is nothing. I need that much time to write a message in a birthday card. I tried to think about how I wanted to be remembered. Even though I've thought a lot about death and the fact that I won't be around forever, I haven't really thought or worried about how I will be remembered. It would have been quick and easy just to write, 'As a kind person who tried my best and paid my way in life and was quite a good friend', but I think I was just thinking that as it's what I've heard other people say when someone has died. Deep down, I don't know what I thought. To be honest, I just wish people would remember me now while I'm still alive. A builder was supposed to come round to sort a wall out for me three weeks ago. We arranged the date and time yet he didn't show his face. He can forget me all he wants when I'm dead, but he made me waste a full afternoon that I'll never get back. The other thing is, at the end of the day not everyone is going to remember me the same way, so why worry about it? I'm pretty sure even Mother Teresa, who is known as one of the kindest women to ever have walked the earth, pissed her neighbours off with the sound of her flip-flops flapping about. As the saying goes: 'You can please some of the people some of the time, all of the people some of the time, some of the people all of the time, but you can never please all of the people all of the time.'

Richard the director tried to help me and said, 'Well, what about final words? That's a way of leaving an impression. What would you want to say with your final breath?' But I don't believe anyone really comes up with anything amazing when they are dying, I think it's all a myth. I'm struggling to come up with something to say now, never mind when I'm keeling over with a heart attack. What I'd be worried about is using my last breath to tell someone how much they did my head in only for the doctors to bring me back to life. I'd prefer to just slip off without anyone knowing, like I do when I'm leaving a party. It's a pain saying all the goodbyes. It's always awkward and I can't wait to get out of the door. I imagine that is what death is like. I told Richard I think I'd prefer my final few breaths to be used to whistle. I've got nothing I want to say, so I think I'd whistle the *Coronation Street* theme tune. It's on three or four times a week these days, so at least whoever heard my final whistle would always remember me when they heard it on the TV.

KARL'S *Facts*

The American inventor Thomas Edison's last breath was captured in a bottle.

I left the piece of paper with the gravestone on it blank. I think blackboards would make good gravestones, as people could then write up a memory of the person on it each time they visit. Good idea, that. Now I only had about fifteen minutes to write a farewell letter! Again, my brain couldn't think. The factory was a noisy place and not the ideal setting for writing a farewell letter. The representative asked us to imagine if we died today, what we would tell our family. What would we say about our job and our life? I think it would be more useful to write down PIN numbers and passwords for websites and accounts. Suzanne knows that I love her, why waste time and ink on that? Maybe it would be good to list all the rubbish things about me to make the fact that I'm dead not such a bad thing. Remind her of all the biscuits I'd eaten before she had a chance to have one, and how I never cleaned the toilet properly after I'd used it. In the end I wrote:

HELLO, WHOEVER IS READING THIS. CAN'T BELIEVE IT, BUT I'VE JUST FOUND OUT I'VE ONLY GOT THIRTY MINUTES LEFT TO LIVE. I TRIED CALLING ALL THREE OF YOU (SUZANNE, MAM, DAD), BUT NONE OF YOU ANSWERED YOUR PHONES. THANKS FOR EVERYTHING.

It was a rubbish attempt. Even my handwriting doesn't suit this sort of letter, as I never got into the idea of fancy joined-up writing. It's meant to be a faster way of writing, but I never knew where I was supposed to join the letters so it always took longer to do and I stuck with writing in capitals instead. It was never an issue when I was younger, whereas these days it means that you're SHOUTING. I'd be better off sending an email and then I can cc everyone I know on it to save Suzanne the job of telling everyone.

Richard asked me if I'd thought of how I was going to die and if I had any kind of instinct about it. 'Just stress, from trying to fill these forms out probably,' I said. I think an odd death would suit me. I read recently about a bloke whose life was ended after he was squashed by a cow that fell through the roof. As tragic as it is, I think I'd prefer that to a long drawn-out illness or a horrible plane crash with people around me screaming. If a cow landed on top of me I'm pretty sure I wouldn't have to worry about people re-membering me. And I reckon I'd come up with some pretty lively final words too.

We were then called into another room, which was candlelit. I was paired up with a young woman called Jahee. A man dressed a bit like the Grim Reaper walked us to one of thirty coffins that were lined up on the floor. One of the employees was chosen at random to read out his farewell letter in front of everyone. I didn't have a clue what he was saying as he was speaking Korean, but I could see that he and his co-workers were getting quite emotional, so I think he probably managed to write a really good letter.

We had to take it in turns to get inside the coffins. I let Jahee go first. She told me that the representative said that while in the coffin you should think about your life and what you have done with it, and the partner who is outside the coffin should take time to imagine what life will be like without the person in the coffin. She got inside and the lid was placed on top. Pan-pipe music was playing in the background. I couldn't get too upset about the idea of not having Jahee in my life, as I'd only just met her about an hour ago. Surely you need to have had some special moment together to get upset about someone dying? Look at James Bond: he meets a woman, sleeps with her and she ends up getting killed by the baddie in the space of twenty minutes, and he doesn't get upset. He'd be in Moscow with another woman before the first woman was even in the morgue. So if James Bond doesn't get upset, even after he'd slept with the woman, I'm not going to get upset about a woman I've just met in a shipbuilding factory.

The rep was talking at the front. I think she was saying nice things, as I could see that some people were getting a little bit teary-eyed, but I didn't have a clue what was being said as the only person who could translate for me was now pretending to be dead in a box. Fifteen minutes later, a man helped me remove the lid and Jahee got out, all blinky-eyed. I think she'd been having a quick kip. I suppose this might be why employees are happy to get involved with all this: it's a paid break in a way.

It was now my turn to get in. It was odd at first, being in a tight space in total darkness, but after a few minutes I did relax enough to focus on how my life had been so far and I found I didn't have any regrets or feel like I should try any harder than I already do. Me and Suzanne are good, and I speak to my mam and dad as much as I can. Life is alright. I then started to think about the other people in the coffins, wondering how many of them were lying there having doubts about their life. It made me think about whether this had ever backfired on the company. There must be quite a few employees who lay there and realise they're wasting their life doing a job they don't like and working for a company that sticks them in a coffin.

After having some time to think about the gravestone message, I now think I'd have 'I was what I was meant to be'. That seems to work.

LIVING WITH THE DEAD

One of the main problems I have with death is the amount of space that is taken up by graves. I think it's barmy how land is getting more and more expensive and the living are having to make do with smaller spaces to live in, yet there's acres and acres of land taken up by the dead. Not only do they take up space, but a lot of the time they are in the nicer areas too, so while you're living in a small flat by a noisy four-lane motorway, Granny Elsie, who's dead, has a nice quiet spot by the park. How is that right?! I've always thought a better space for the dead would be on those big roundabouts you get with a huge mound of grass in the middle. Nobody would want to live there, but it would be an ideal space for twenty or so graves. Not only would it be making good use of a space, family members of the dead would pass by it all the time and would frequently be reminded of the person who is lying there, under the round-about. Good idea, isn't it?

In Manila in the Philippines, the most densely populated city in the world and the next stop on my trip, the dead don't get to keep an area for themselves for long, as they have to share it with the living. I went along to the North Cemetery, where an estimated 6,000 people live. Due to the lack of adequate housing or welfare in Manila, these people have made a home for themselves living amongst the dead in the tombs and mausoleums. Arriving in the cemetery took me right back to the time I visited the Taj Mahal in India. I found it really annoying – it was an amazing building, but it didn't seem right that it was being used to store a dead body when just outside the grounds were millions of people who had nowhere to live. It was the complete opposite here, which I liked. The poor get a roof over their heads and the dead get someone to take care of their surroundings. Everyone was a winner.

The cemetery was a busy and bustling place. The atmosphere was more like a housing estate than a cemetery. Kids were riding around on bikes and playing basketball while the older residents were sat talking, playing cards or hanging out the washing as they watched a hearse drive past carrying a quiet soon-to-be neighbour.

I was at the cemetery to meet with a woman called Mercy who was going to tell me all about living in a place like this, but I wanted to take it all in on my own first, so I walked slowly to the plot where she lived. I passed loads of grand mausoleums and tombs, all different shapes and sizes, that made having a stroll a lot more interesting than walking down most streets people live on back at home where every house looks the same. I've moved house quite a lot, and whenever I'm looking for a different place to live I always want to know if it passes the Twix test. I ask myself: if I suddenly fancied a Twix, how much of a pain would it be to get one? This place would have passed with flying colours, as some of the mausoleums had been converted into shops selling chocolate, tins of beans, noodles and mobile phone cards, using the actual tombs themselves as counters. The shops are used by residents, as well as visitors to the graves. Richard the director said he wasn't sure people should be munching on crisps when other people are trying to remember the dead, but I don't think people should be munching on popcorn when you're trying to watch a film in the cinema and they still do.

It was obvious that the residents took pride in their homes. As I walked past each one some job was being done: the metal railings were being given a fresh coat of paint or the marble plaques on the tombs were being polished. I think getting a tomb to look after here is quite an achievement, like getting an allotment at home, so once you manage to get one you really take care of it. The place was certainly kept a lot better than the cemetery in Ghana where Comfort was buried. Some of the mausoleums were painted in bright pastel colours, which gave them a look of the multi-million-pound houses in Notting Hill and Camden in London, and they had basic kitchens fitted with ovens and fridges that were running off illegal electricity cables. There was no running water, but some residents took it from fire hydrants outside the cemetery, bottled it up and then sold it from pushcarts to the cemetery dwellers.

The larger mausoleums offered about the same amount of space as the first few London flats I lived in, but the exteriors of these buildings were a lot more impressive. And they come part-furnished, as the larger tombs are ideal as a base for a bed and the smaller tombs made of the highest-quality marble could be used as kitchen worktops. Even though it was a cemetery, if I was in the same position as these people I would much rather live here than the dark grey slums that would be their only other option.

Richard was surprised that I was so impressed by the set-up and couldn't understand how I would be happy sleeping on top of corpses, but the tombs were well and truly sealed, so no germs could cause any harm. In fact, I'd say there's probably more harmful dust and muck under our bed at home than there is here, as Suzanne can never be bothered cleaning under it. One tomb we were looking at had a body in there from four years ago, but we've had fish fingers that were older than that in the back of our freezer.

By the time I reached Mercy's place it no longer seemed strange at all. I wasn't seeing them as mausoleums any more, but as bungalows. Mercy was busy sweeping up outside. She explained that her grandmother was the first to move into the cemetery and the rest of the family has been living there ever since. She's thirty-eight years old now and doesn't know any different to this way of life. She had a smaller, more basic mausoleum than some of the ones with the fancier exteriors, but she said it was enough for her. The mausoleums are built more solidly and can take the bad weather a lot more than the shacks that some people live in outside the cemetery.

Like everyone else here seemed to do, Mercy used the tomb as the base for the bed and had a mattress on top. I asked if I could lay on it to see what it was like. It wasn't too bad, no worse than the cheap futon that me and Suzanne put up with for over a year. A futon is just a bread crate really. It would probably be more comfy if the bread was left on top. Mercy hung a piece of fabric up over the metal railings

on either side to give herself some privacy. Rather than photographs or paintings on the walls, there were permanent
plaques showing the names of some of the dead people who
were in the tomb. Again, Richard thought this was a bit
morbid, but I didn't see how it was any different to the blue
plaques you see outside houses at home that say things like
'So-and-so lived and died here'. I think it's spookier being
somewhere someone actually died than where their dead
body lies.

People have been living in the cemeteries since the 50s,
and even though it's illegal to live there, the authorities have
turned a blind eye, as kicking people out would mean they'd
just have to find somewhere to house them and that would
be another problem to sort. Plus, the residents help to keep
the place tidy. Mercy explained there was an unwritten rule
that if you live there you must pick up litter, dig up weeds
and help paint the tombs to keep them looking nice. She
asked if I would like to help her brother-in-law Manuel do
his job. I said yes before I found out what the job was, which
wasn't wise, as I had to help him do an exhumation and remove an old dead body from a grave. Manuel did this about
four times a week. It was a way of controlling the numbers
of dead bodies in the cemetery. When a body is laid to rest
it's agreed that it has a five-year lease. If the family want it to
stay there any longer they extend and renew the lease, and if
they don't it was Manuel's job to remove the body and make
room for newcomers.

I was handed a hammer and chisel, and off we went
looking at the dates on the tombs, like traffic wardens look-

ing for expired parking permits. We jumped from tomb to tomb like frogs on lily pads. There were loads of them. Big boxes were lined up like on *Deal or No Deal*, painted in pastel blues, pinks and greens. We found the one Manuel was looking for. It contained Mary. She was buried there in 2008 and her family had decided not to extend the lease, so it was time for her to come out.

We set to work chipping away at the cement. It wasn't too difficult, as there was a weak spot where the tomb had been broken and then resealed many times over the years. There was something quite sad about what we were doing, but no sadder than the fact that people have to live here and do this job to earn their keep. As we got closer to breaking the end off the tomb I was preparing myself for the worst. I was basing what I thought I might see on what I've seen in films, where cockroaches come running out of coffins like they did in that film *The Mummy* or a ghost comes rushing out like in *Raiders of the Lost Ark*.

Richard asked if I felt bad about disturbing the dead, but I think it's a daft saying. Out of everyone on the planet, if you're going to disturb someone I'd say disturb the dead. It doesn't bother them too much and I've never heard of a dead person complaining. I get bloody disturbed with the endless sales calls I get, door-to-door salesmen trying to flog me tea towels and flannels, and men wanting to come in to read my gas, water and electricity meters. How about not disturbing the living! Why is that allowed?!

KARL'S Facts

In Madagascar people dig up the bones of their loved ones and dance with them.

We had managed to chip all the way around the end of the tomb in about twenty minutes and now had to lift it off. As well as being ready for cockroaches, I was also ready for a bad smell. Surely there would be a smell? Just lifting the lid on the food-recycling bin in the kitchen can sometimes be a bit whiffy, and that's only got a few old bits of carrot and potato, so I was prepared for this to be rough. But we pulled back the end and there was nothing too terrible to see. No cockroaches and no bad smell. Manuel didn't mess about, and he pulled what was left of the rotten wooden coffin towards him like he was sliding a chicken out of the oven and shoved his bare hands inside and pulled out the bones. He started with the head, and that shocked me. Not because it was scary; I've never had an issue with skulls, as they tend to look quite happy with all their teeth on show. No, what shocked me was that it still had bloody hair on it. Mary had been dead for five years and she still had a better head of hair than me! I didn't expect that. The skeletons in *Jason and the Argonauts* didn't run about fighting with swords while sporting a nice mullet.

Before I had a chance to get a closer look at the skull, Manuel had put it in a bag. He was using one of those strong bags that are normally used to transport fruit and veg. Once the head was in, he grabbed another handful of Mary: this time it was her hip and backbones. It was like he was bagging up his weekly shop at a self-service checkout in Sainsbury's. Another thing that caught me off guard was seeing a bra. I don't know why, but I just found it odd. I didn't think women would be buried still wearing their bra. Suzanne hates wearing them and doesn't feel that relaxed until she's got it off, so I'm not sure I'd have her buried wearing one, especially if we're to believe that the deceased would be wearing that for bra for eternity. Plus, they're expensive things. Suzanne asked for some money to buy herself a couple of decent ones for her birthday once. I thought they would be about £4 each, turns out they're around £20. So why bury them? No wonder there are grave robbers when people are leaving £20 bras on the dead.

Once all the bones were out, Manuel buried the bag next to the tomb so if the family wanted to come and collect them, they could. I couldn't help but think they wouldn't.

FINDING A RESTING PLACE

After all my gripes about the amount of good land being taken up by dead bodies, I travelled to Sagada, which is a place famous for being resourceful with where they put their dead. In Sagada they don't waste any land on the dead, as they prefer to use it for more important things like agriculture. So instead they hang coffins on cliff faces, and have been doing this for over 2,000 years.

It wasn't easy to get there. It was an eventful fifteen-hour drive from Manila, which included having to change a popped tyre three times, driving in monsoon conditions along crumbling clifftop roads, avoiding rubble from landslides and pulling over five times to let the crew have a shit in bushes after they got food poisoning from a place we stopped at for food. We were only going there to see the hanging coffins, but during that journey there was a part of me that thought I might be joining them.

Once we had arrived I met with a local man called Esteban, who was busy putting the last few nails into a coffin he had been making for a friend called Kaga, who was the oldest man in the village at a hundred years old. I remember thinking at the time how they must be a close-knit community for Esteban to go to all the trouble of making a coffin for a local old resident who wasn't even dead yet, but to be honest if the choice is between making one or travelling ten hours on their mental dangerous roads to the nearest coffin shop, I think I'd have a go at making one too.

As I helped Esteban knock in the last few nails, I told him I don't think I'd like to live to be a hundred years old, as life would be so different by that time. I'm already feeling like I'm being left behind now, especially as my back aches all the time, so I'd be in a right state in another sixty years. I want death to catch me off guard, but if I was a hundred years old I doubt I'd even bother buying a bottle of long-life milk as I'd always be thinking every day was my last. People always say you should 'live every day as if it's your last', but I don't think you'd ever do anything if you followed that mantra. You wouldn't bother washing up, or getting more food in the house, and you'd never book a holiday. Better to say 'live every month as if it's your last' – that would be more sensible. My dad got annoyed recently when he had to buy a ten-year passport. He said he's not going to be around for another ten years so he couldn't see why he wasn't able to just buy a five-year one for half the price. Even though he's facing death head on, he's still thinking about saving a few quid. Esteban got me to write 'Kaga' on both sides of the white coffin in big block capitals and then we both coloured the name in, in a light-ocean-blue-coloured paint. It wasn't a great place to do a paint job, as loads of flies kept landing where we were working and getting stuck in the paint. Blue-bottles became 'light-ocean-bluebottles'. The paint hadn't even had time to dry properly before Esteban was keen to move it to the cliffs where it would be hung. He explained that the coffin would be put onto the cliff edge so that Kaga could see his final resting place, and then once he died the body would be taken up there separately.

KARL'S Facts

Tibetan Buddhists cut up and beat a dead body to a pulp and leave the remains for vultures to eat.

We set about carrying it, trying not to smudge the blue paint. It was heavy and the path was not easy to walk on. There was quite a steep drop down, and the ground was muddy and slippy from the heavy rain. Add to that the fact that we were lugging a coffin and it was also pretty dangerous. I'm sure it would have been a lot easier to construct the coffin at the spot where they wanted to hang it. We'd done the equivalent of buying a wardrobe from Ikea and putting it together in the car park before taking it home. The paint was getting badly smudged, and on more than one occasion we almost lost the coffin altogether over the edge. I was knackered. I had a headache coming on, either from dehydration or from the smell of the toxic light-ocean-blue paint.

We took a break at the halfway point. Esteban pointed out coffins in the distance that had been hung on the side of the cliff, but I couldn't see them, as the aged wood of the coffins had blended into the dark grey cliffs. I asked who would normally be carrying the coffin if I wasn't here, and Esteban said it would be the job of the family. I bet they couldn't believe their luck that they'd got out of doing this. And anyway, if Kaga is a hundred years old, his family are going to be in their sixties and I'm sure they'd really have struggled carrying this at that age.

KARL: So why do you do this?

ESTEBAN: They are going to put it there so that the dog cannot reach it.

KARL: What?! What dog?!

ESTEBAN: After daylight the dog will go and open the coffin. They're going to eat the body. That's why we have to place it where the dog cannot go.

KARL: This is a lot of messing around just because of a dog. Do you hear that, Richard? It's because of a dog.

RICHARD THE DIRECTOR: It's a cultural thing as well, isn't it?

KARL: No, it's mainly so a dog can't get at the body.

ESTEBAN: Yeah, the dog cannot enter that way because it is very high.

KARL: Could you not fit a lock?

ESTEBAN: The dogs here will go and open up the coffin.

KARL: Not if you put a lock on.

ESTEBAN: Yeah.

KARL: So do they?

ESTEBAN: (*laughing*) Yeah, yeah!

I wasn't sure if he was winding me up or not. This happens a lot on my travels. I suppose this is how history happens. It's just one man making shit up that people then pass on. I didn't know what to believe. Is there even a man called Kaga who's a hundred years old or am I just helping Esteban do a delivery job?!

As we set off again, the walk got tougher, not because of the rough pathway but due to the tourists. The place attracts a lot of them. As we walked through the crowd I felt like I was on some novelty fun run because they were all clapping and yelling. I soon realised they were cheering us on, though, and they were yelling because we had reached Echo Valley. Great, innit! It's meant to be a special resting place for the dead, but they've turned it into a tourist trap. I was surprised not to see a stall selling T-shirts with a picture of a coffin and the slogan 'DON'T LEAVE ME HANGIN''. I suppose this is another reason to keep traditions going.

We eventually got to the spot where there were around fifteen weather-beaten coffins hanging up on the rock face. Many had been there for years, including one with Esteban's grandfather, who was put up there in 1969. An old chair also dangled by the coffins. Esteban told me it was there as a place to sit the dead body before getting it into the coffin. Again, I wasn't sure if he was winding me up or if this was really what it was for. I felt like I was playing *Call My Bluff* every time he opened his mouth.

One of Esteban's mates climbed up and inserted two metal rods into the rock face that would hold the coffin in place. Then the fun began as we tried to get the coffin up there. It was total chaos. I've seen ants shift stuff as a team with more coordination. I can't explain how much of a pain it was to get it up there. Esteban stayed on the ground as I made my way up a shaky home-made ladder, trying to keep hold of one end of a twenty-stone coffin while I was twenty-five feet up a cliff with a bunch of people I couldn't communicate with. It would have been easier to fly the pallbearers in from Ghana and get them to just throw the coffin up to me. And the paint was still tacky!

'Surely six feet high would be enough to keep it away from dogs if that's what this is all about?' I shouted down to Esteban.

KARL: Esteban, how do they get the . . . you know, when Kaga dies, how do they get him up here then?

ESTEBAN: Kaga?

KARL: Yeah, you know, the old man we're carrying this for, when he dies.

ESTEBAN: I do not know. I do not know when he dies.

KARL: No, no, I know, but when he does, how do you get him up here?

ESTEBAN: Just like that.

KARL: Like this?! What, six fellas and a load of old rope?

ESTEBAN: Yeah.

KARL: And you said you do this just so dogs can't get at them?

> ESTEBAN: No . . . Yes . . . that is why they put the dead very high. For safe keeping, but also for the spirit being nearer to God.

Even though Esteban's explanation seemed more like a reason for this type of tradition to exist, I'd prefer it if we were doing it because the bloke in the village couldn't keep his dog tied up, as I doubt being another thirty feet closer to the gods in the sky is going to make much difference to anything, is it? People are dying every second, so no matter how close to heaven you are, there is always going to be a queue. Doing this would just mean you'd be maybe three or four spaces ahead than you would have been. And what's the rush to get to heaven if it does exist anyway? You're going to be there forever, so if there's one journey that you don't have to rush, it's that one. I imagine heaven to be a bit like an airport – a big echoey space with thousands of people all pushing and shoving to get to the head of the queue where people with false smiles check your ID before you can go through the Pearly Gates. Heaven can't be all it's cracked up to be, as it's bound to be chock-a-block. I imagine years ago it would have been harder to get into heaven and they wouldn't let the evil people in. There were loads more evil people back in the day with the likes of Henry VIII beheading his wives and that King Herod getting up to evil tricks, so I bet heaven was really nice and quiet, whereas these days those people have excuses for everything. If someone has committed murder, they just say it wasn't their fault as they've got brain abnormalities and then they'd be let into

heaven. It would be really busy. Especially with everyone doing so much charity work these days. By the time I get there
(if I get there), it'll be Davina McCall and Lenny Henry and
the bloke who used to be Doctor Who, as they all do work
for Comic Relief. It'll be like *Celebrity Big Brother* up there,
except I won't just be stuck with them for six weeks, it'll be
for eternity.

Once the coffin was in place, some thin wire was used
to tie it to the rods and down I went. I stood back and
looked at it, tilting my head like I'd popped up a shelf and
was checking it was level. It looked good. I was impressed
that I'd helped get it up there, as I normally struggle at
home just hanging curtains. Even the smudges to the paint
couldn't really be seen from the ground. It suddenly oc-
curred to me that my giant Twix coffin that was being made
for me in Ghana would look good up on the side of a cliff.
Surely if a brand knew you were planning on using one of
their products as a coffin and it was going to be hung on
the side of a cliff face forever like a big advert, they'd be
keen to cover the costs of your funeral. Or, even better, pay
you some money to enjoy spending while you're alive too.

Since being back home I've looked online to see if what
Esteban said about why they hang the coffins on the side
of the cliff was true, and it was for both of the reasons he
said – to keep the bodies away from wild animals and to
be closer to heaven. I also found out that not everyone can
have a hanging coffin. You have to be married and have
grandchildren to get one. I'm guessing this is the case as the
grandchildren would be the only ones fit enough to carry the

coffin up there. Unless some daft TV presenter was willing to get involved.

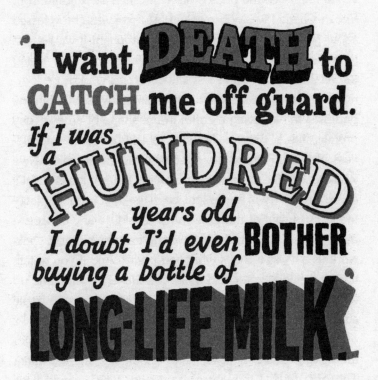

'I want DEATH to CATCH me off guard. If I was a HUNDRED years old I doubt I'd even BOTHER buying a bottle of LONG-LIFE MILK.'

REMEMBERING THE DEAD

When I received the photos of my finished Twix coffin from Eric in Ghana I was gobsmacked. At first I wasn't too fussed about getting it sent back home, as I thought it would cost too much money and be too much of a faff, but after seeing the final thing I couldn't just leave it in his workshop. It arrived in England and looked just as amazing as it had in the photos. I think having a coffin in the shape of an everyday product like a Twix really helps to take away the morbidness of it all. Richard the director was concerned that we wouldn't be able to show the coffin on TV as it looks like it's an advert for Twix and might be classed as product placement, but I said at the time that it could be any chocolate bar. I picked Twix as it's one of my favourites, but it could work as a Twirl if that's what you prefer. And if you're tall, thin and single, you could make it a Flake. I even came up with the idea that if a whole family got killed in some tragic accident a KFC Family Bucket could work really well.

Eric had managed to use all the right colours and got the design exactly right to make it look like the real thing. The only thing I thought was missing, which would have been a nice detail, was to have the Use By date as the date I died. I really liked the idea that if I was buried in this, at some point in the future the equivalent of Tony Robinson's *Time Team* would dig me up and be puzzled by what a Twix was.

The only problem with the Twix (other chocolate bars are available) was the size. As I requested, Eric had made it a coffin for two so that both me and Suzanne could lay to rest in it, but this meant it was huge, and I haven't got the room for it at home. It's the size of a single bed, and as much as Suzanne was impressed with it and kind of into the idea of us lying together for eternity, she didn't want a coffin in the house. So it's currently in a storage unit until I work out what's best to do with it.

After visiting the Twix in the lock-up we headed off to the seafront in Hastings, where I wanted to try out an idea I'd had for a good way of remembering loved ones who have passed away without having to take up valuable land with coffins. It was memorial benches that gave me the idea. I've always been a big fan of them, and you see a lot of them in seaside towns. Benches paid for by the family of the dead that have a small plaque or message etched into the wood like 'Albert died at the age of seventy-six and had many a happy day walking down Bournemouth seafront'. What I like about this idea is that no matter how useless someone is when they are alive, they can do something good once they're dead, rather than just taking up valuable space. Years ago you had to get up early to find a seat on the seafront, but thanks to all the people dying and leaving behind benches there are now loads of places to sit. But as I've said before, with everything in life when you sort one problem out there's always another to solve. And with this it's rubbish. People mob the beaches during the summer and on bank holidays, and in no time the bins are over-flowing and the litter ends up all over the place. So I came up with the great invention of the memorial bin. Just like with the benches, the death of someone can help the living even though they are no longer around. To me it makes more sense putting money into keeping the country tidy than spending it on a gravestone that is just taking up space and won't be visited for very long. At least with this idea the family can have a weekend by the sea, get some fresh air and take some time to remember the person by the memorial bin. Some people might say they wouldn't want to hang around a bin to remember their loved ones, but what's so nice about being by a grave where there is a body slowly rotting away six feet from where you're standing?

KARL'S *Facts*

A faithful and heartbroken German Shepherd dog in Argentina has visited the grave of his owner every day for the last six years.

Hastings council thought my memorial bin was a good idea and they allowed me to install a new bin on the seafront, where it still stands today. I bought a nice new bin and had a brass plaque fitted to it, dedicated to a woman I never met. Not while she was alive anyway. The plaque read 'In Memory of Madam Comfort Asaaba Cofie 1934–2013' and had a picture of Comfort from her obituary poster.

As I sat in one of the shelters on the seafront on a sunny August morning, I watched as people stopped to read the plaque. Some people just looked puzzled, while others chatted about it with each other. I watched as an old man walked by the bin with his daughter, pushing his wife along in a wheelchair.

'I'm not sure I want to be remembered on the side of a bin,' he said to his daughter.

'Yeah, but you'd be keeping the place tidy. You'd like that. You always complain about litter.'

'Mmmm, I guess so,' he said. I think he'd bought the idea. I hope it catches on.

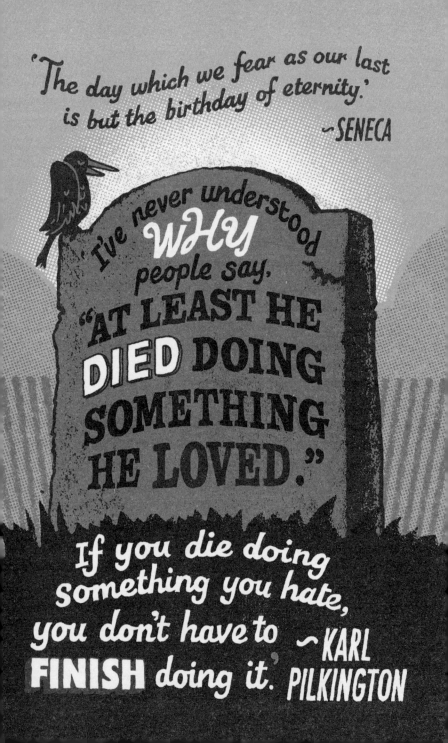

THANKS TO: Michael Timney (Main Camera on Marriage, Kids and Death); Will Churchill (Main Camera on Vocation & Money and Happiness); Freddie Claire (Sound Recordist and Photographer); Richard Yee (Executive Producer/Director on Marriage, Kids and Death); Krishnendu Majumdar (Executive Producer); Celia Taylor (Executive Producer for Sky1 HD); Ben Green (Series Producer/Director on Vocation & Money and Happiness); Kevin Forde (Producer on Marriage and Happiness); Vicky Bennetts (Producer on Kids); Daniel Dewsbury (Producer on Vocation & Money and Death); Lynda Featherstone (Editor on Kids and Death); Andy Linton (Editor on Marriage, Vocation & Money and Happiness); Carmelina Palumbo (Production Executive); Jenny Hargreaves (Production Manager); Hannah James (Production Coordinator); Jessica Winteringham (Assistant Producer); Mel Bezalel (Assistant Producer).

The ORIGINAL travel diaries of KARL PILKINGTON
RICKY GERVAIS AND STEPHEN MERCHANT SENT
AN IDIOT ABROAD
THE TRAVEL DIARIES OF
KARL PILKINGTON
THE HILARIOUS NUMBER ONE BESTSELLER
KARL PILKINGTON
HIS HILARIOUS NEW BESTSELLER
THE FURTHER ADVENTURES OF AN IDIOT ABROAD
'Brilliant' THE TIMES
'Stupidly funny' SUNDAY MIRROR
Available in paperback and ebook.
CANONGATE
www.canongate.tv

CANON█GATE.tv

CHANNELLING GREAT CONTENT

 WATCH   INTERVIEWS, TRAILERS, ANIMATIONS, READINGS, GIGS

 LISTEN   AUDIO BOOKS, PODCASTS, MUSIC, PLAYLISTS

 READ   CHAPTERS, EXCERPTS, SNEAK PEEKS, RECOMMENDATIONS

 DISCOVER   BLOGS, EVENTS, NEWS, CREATIVE PARTNERS

 SHOP   LIMITED EDITIONS, BUNDLES, SECRET SALES